Clari

Selected
Crônicas

Translated by
GIOVANNI PONTIERO

A NEW DIRECTIONS BOOK

Translated from *A Descoberta do Mundo* copyright © Editora Nova Fronteiro 1984
Translation copyright © 1992 by Giovanni Pontiero
Published by arrangement with Carcanet Press Limited, Manchester, and Agencia Literaria Carmen Balcells, Barcelona

Publisher's Note: The contents of *Selected Crônicas* are taken from the larger U.K. edition, *Discovering the World,* published in 1992 by Carcanet Press. The introduction by Giovanni Pontiero in this volume has also been excerpted from the longer version in the Carcanet edition.

Translator's Note: I should like to express my indebtedness and gratitude to Michael Schmidt and Robyn Marsack and their colleagues at Carcanet Press; to the National Book Institute and the VITAE Foundation in Brazil for their financial support; to Eudinyr Fraga and Otto Lara Resende who painstakingly answered all my queries about the Brazilian personalities and locations mentioned throughout the chronicles; to Nancy Stalhammer, Gordon Kinder and Neil Ferguson who carefully read the manuscript and offered many useful suggestions towards improving my translation; and finally to Stephanie Goodfellow who prepared several drafts of the manuscript on the word processor with admirable skill and patience.
—Giovanni Pontiero, Manchester, 1991

Manufactured in the United States of America
New Directions Books are printed on acid-free paper.
First published as New Directions Paperbook 834 in 1996
Published simultaneously in Canada by Penguin Books Canada Limited

Library of Congress Cataloging-in-Publication Data

Lispector, Clarice.
    [Descoberta do mundo. English. Selections]
    Selected cronicas / Clarice Lispector ; translated by Giovanni Pontiero.
        p.   cm.
ISBN 978-0-8112-1340-0 (alk. paper)
    I. Pontiero, Giovanni. II. Title.
PQ9697.L585D4713   1996
869.4—dc20   96-23768
                                                    CIP

10 9 8 7 6

Celebrating 60 years of publishing for James Laughlin
by New Directions Publishing Corporation
80 Eighth Avenue, New York 10011

CONTENTS

Preface by Giovanni Pontiero   vii

1967
Torture and Glory, *September 2*   1
Undying Love, *September 9*   3
Searching, *September 16*   7
Dies Irae, *October 14*   7
Yes, *October 21*   9
In Favour of Fear, *November 11*   9
The Quiet Woman from Minas, *November 25*   12
The Clairvoyant, *November 25*   12
God's Sweet Ways, *December 16*   13
The Case of the Gold Fountain Pen, *December 23*   16

1968
Gentle as a Fawn, *January 27*   18
The White Dress, *March 9*   21
The Remnants of Carnival, *March 16*   21
State of Grace (Extract), *April 6*   24
Pointless Scandal, *April 27*   27
Return to Nature (Extract), *May 4*   29
As You Sleep, *May 18*   30
A Bourgeois Ideal, *June 8*   31
Belonging, *June 15*   32
An Experience, *June 22*   34
Discovering the World, *July 6*   34
Ritual (Extract), *July 27*   36
A Challenge for the Psychoanalysts, *August 3*   38
The Sweater, *August 3*   38
How to Treat One's Possessions, *August 3*   39
A Remarkable Love Story, *August 10*   40
Excess and Privation, *September 14*   42
Memory of a Small Boy, *September 28*   42
Terror, *October 5*   44
I Know What Spring Is Like, *October 5*   45
'Wanted,' *October 19*   46
Bravado, *October 26*   46
A Knowing Sensibility, *November 2*   49
The Dream, *November 9*   49
Rebellion, *November 9*   50

Eat Up, Eat Up, *November 16*   50
The Birth of Pleasure (Extract), *November 23*   51
If It Were Me, *November 30*   51
A Dialogue, *November 30*   52
My Christmas, *December 21*   53
Annunciation, *December 21*   54
Learning to Live, *December 28*   54

1 9 6 9
Miraculous Leaves, *January 11*   56
Almost, *January 18*   57
Sea-Bathing, *January 25*   59
Anguished Protection, *February 1*   61
Earth's Sweetness, *February 1*   62
So Sensitive, *March 1*   63
A Happy Man, *March 29*   64
Lightning Interview with Pablo Neruda (II), *April 19*   64
Charlatans, *April 26*   67
Enigma, *April 26*   68
Social Column, *May 3*   68
Rebellion, *May 10*   72
Silken Threads, *May 17*   72
Non-Acceptance, *May 17*   73
Perilous Night, *June 7*   73
Unwelcome Compassion, *June 7*   74
Sharing Bread, *June 21*   74
Supernatural Life, *June 28*   77
The Egg and the Chicken (I), *July 5*   77
The Egg and the Chicken (II), *July 12*   81
The Egg and the Chicken (III), *July 19*   84
Five Stories on a Single Theme, *July 26*   86
The Princess (I), *August 3*   88
The Princess (II), *August 9*   91
The Princess (III), *August 16*   94
The Princess (IV), *August 23*   97
The Princess (V), *August 30*   100
Racing Against the Typewriter, *September 20*   103
The Learned Man, *September 20*   103
The Haunted Room, *September 20*   104
Pen Drawing of a Little Boy, *October 18*   107
Impasse, *October 25*   110
Brainstorm, *November 22*   111
Hateful Charity, *December 6*   114
The Immortal Man, *December 13*   117

Freedom, *December 13* 117
Cruelty, *December 13* 117
Interrogation, *December 13* 118
The Expedients of a Primitive Being, *December 20* 118

1 9 7 0
A Mischievous Little Girl (I), *January 3* 118
A Mischievous Little Girl (II), *January 10* 121
A Mischievous Little Girl (III), *January 17* 124
A Mischievous Little Girl (IV), *January 24* 126
A Mischievous Little Girl (V), *February 7* 128
The Party, *March 7* 131
Keeping an Eye on the World, *March 4* 132
A Variation on the Distracted Man, *March 14* 134
Gentle Weeping, *March 14* 134
The Italian Woman, *April 4* 135
An Untranslated Epigraph, *April 25* 138
Old-Fashioned Tastes, *April 25* 138
Swimming Against the Tide, *April 25* 139
The Making of a Novel, *May 2* 139
Writing, *May 2* 141
Inspiration, *May 9* 141
Idle Conversation, *May 16* 143
Fear of Eternity, *June 6* 143
Creating Brasilia, *June 20* 145
Irresistible Incarnation, *July 4* 149
Saturday, *July 11* 151
A Hundred Years' Pardon, *July 25* 152
Self-Inflicted Sorrow, *August 15* 154
The Advantages of Being Foolish, *September 12* 154
Forgiving God, *September 19* 156
Sunday, *September 26* 159
Posterity Will Judge Us, *September 26* 159
Your Secret, *September 26* 160
Ten Years Old, *September 26* 160
The Little Monster, *October 10* 161
Flying the Flag, *October 10* 161
Spring in Switzerland, *October 10* 161
Only an Insect, *October 31* 162
Taking What Was Mine, *October 31* 163
One Final Clarification, *November 14* 163
Spain, *November 28* 165
Because They Were Not Distracted, *December 12* 167
World Purely Physical, *December 12* 168

1 9 7 1

Animals (I), *March 13* 169
Animals (II), *March 20* 172
Family Outing, *April 24* 175
Mother's Day, A Pious Invention, *May 8* 176
Words from the Typewriter, *May 29* 177
A Ride on a Camel, the Sphinx, & a Belly-Dancer, *June 12* ... 179
Love, *September 11* 180
To Remember What Never Existed, *November 6* ... 182
One of the Chosen, *November 13* 182
London's Bridges, *November 20* 185
The Old Lady, *November 27* 187

1 9 7 2

Correct Assumptions, *January 15* 188
Mistaken Assumptions, *January 15* 189
Marriage in Progress, *January 15* 189
Living Jelly, *January 29* 190
In Pursuit of Pleasure, *February 5* 191
Summer Ball, *March 4* 191
Shady Dealings, *March 4* 191
The Gratuitous Act, *April 8* 192
To Good to Be True, *April 15* 194
Refuge, *April 22* 194
A Flower Bewitched and Too Bright by Far, *May 6* ... 195
Without Any Warning, *May 20* 196
Fear of the Unknown (Extract), *June 3* 197
The Gift, *July 8* 197
To Eat, *July 8* 198
Final Surrender, *July 8* 199
Playing with Mercury, *September 30* 199
The Sloth, *October 21* 200
Buying a Pig in a Poke, *November 25* 203
What Is Anguish?, *November 25* 204
The Obedient (I), *December 2* 204
The Obedient (II), *December 9* 207

1 9 7 3

What Love Can Lead To, *January 20* 210
Enlistment, *Janaury 20* 210
Submission to the Process, *January 20* 211
More than Simple Word-Play, *May 26* 211
A Mere Speck of Dust, *December 29* 211

PREFACE

CLARICE LISPECTOR is widely recognized as the most original and innovative Brazilian woman writer of this century. In 1984, seven years after she died of cancer, Lispector's son edited the so-called *crônicas* or chronicles which she published in the Saturday edition of the *Jornal do Brasil* [The Brazilian News] from August 1967 until December 1973. Arranged in chronological order, the book (A *Descoberta do Mundo*)* is a miscellaneous collection of aphorisms, diary entries, reminiscences, travel notes, interviews, serialized stories, essays, loosely defined as 'chronicles': a genre peculiar to Brazil which allows poets and writers to address a wider readership on a vast range of topics and themes. The general tone is one of greater freedom and intimacy than one finds in comparable articles or weekly columns in the European or U.S. press.

Lispector confessed she did not find it easy to adapt to the genre. She inquired: Is the chronicle a story? a conversation? the revelation of one's inner thoughts? She questioned the wisdom of tackling a genre which to some extent was alien to her introspective nature. Summing up her disquiet, she commented: 'I am apprehensive. Writing too much and too often can contaminate the word' or as Fernando Pessoa, a Portuguese poet whom she admired, once said: 'Speaking is the easiest way of becoming unknown'. She was afraid of becoming too personal, and the need to be topical and conform to the conditions and constraints of a weekly column worried her. As she acquired more confidence, she freely adapted the genre to suit her own purpose.

Varied and unpredictable, the chronicles allow us to piece together the life and career of this singular personality. The

---

* Publisher's note: New Directions' *Selected Crônicas* presents about two-thirds of the chronicles contained in A *Descoberta do Mundo*, and were selected from the complete U.K. edition of *Discovering the World* (Carcanet Press Ltd., 1992). This introduction by translator Giovanni Pontiero has likewise been adapted.

chronicles register contrasting moods, one moment whimsical, the next grave and questioning, but whatever the theme, disarmingly frank.

The autobiographical details in some of the chronicles offer a reliable account of her origins and background, and help to clarify a number of misconceptions. Her parents emigrated from the Ukraine to Alagoas in north-eastern Brazil when she was barely two months old. They subsequently moved on to Recife in Pernambuco, where her father found employment in agriculture, then commerce. The family had little money and her mother was in poor health. The youngest of three sisters, Lispector had a happy childhood, notwithstanding the difficulties her parents experienced in adjusting to their new environment. Precocious and imaginative, she soon discovered the world of books and by the age of seven she was already writing stories. She recalled: 'I thought a book was like a tree, an animal, something that grows. I had no idea there was an author standing in the wings.' She submitted her stories to the local *Diário de Pernambuco* [The Pernambucan Daily News] which ran a children's page, but they were rejected. For, even as a child, Lispector was much less interested in plot than in sensation, perception or intuition.

When she was twelve, the family moved to Rio which was then the capital. The year was 1937 and it coincided with the dictatorship of Getúlio Vargas and the formation of Brazil's New State. On completing her schooling, Lispector decided to study law. While still at the university she also began writing for *A Noite* [The Evening News]. This introduced her to the world of journalism and she covered a wide range of features with the exception of crime reports and the social column. Meanwhile, her interest in law began to wane but she persevered and completed the course. She soon abandoned any idea of practising law, however, and as she was to observe wryly: 'My law studies taught me nothing, not even how to protect the copyright of my own books.' In 1943 she married a fellow-student, Maury Gurgel Valente, who was soon to enter the diplomatic service, and in the following year she published her first novel *Perto do Coração selvagem* [Near to the Wild Heart]. Lispector was seventeen and unknown, but the unusual form and extraordinary language of this brutally honest account of marriage and betrayal attracted the attention of several important literary critics. Sérgio Milliet and Antônio Cândido recognized at once that a promising new writer had made her début. Their reviews spoke of a 'sudden break' with established criteria and of a radically different concept of fiction, which opened up new possibilities. Her début was timely.

Marriage to a diplomat meant foreign postings: Naples, Berne, Torquay, and Washington; the birth of two sons, Pedro (in Berne in 1949) and Paulo (in Washington in 1953), meant additional responsibilities. For some sixteen years Lispector was to be separated from her beloved Brazil, apart from brief return visits which only intensified her sense of exile and homesickness. She detested the social obligations required of a diplomat's wife. Writing became increasingly important for her spiritual survival. She longed for greater privacy in order to be able to meditate and write her books. Writing became synonymous with solitude and a more profound form of existence, and only her work and children kept her sane during those years in alien surroundings. In 1959, she finally separated from her husband and returned to Rio with her children. She was now free to concentrate on her chosen career. Her output was steady, and by the time she died of cancer in the winter of 1977, she had produced nine novels, eight collections of short stories, four tales for children and a Portuguese translation of Oscar Wilde's *The Picture of Dorian Gray*.

Despite her Ukrainian ancestry, Lispector identified completely with Brazil and most of all with north-eastern Brazil. Memories of her childhood, especially in Recife, evoked the authentic Brazil where traditions and folklore had been preserved. A slight speech defect made her sound like a foreigner, but she was adamant that she had forged her soul and innermost thoughts with the Portuguese language, 'a difficult language', which she was to transform and even re-invent by means of conceptual refinements, subtle nuances and bold experiments with syntax.

Brazil's other great writer of this century, João Guimarães Rosa, once told her: 'Clarice, I don't read you just for the literature, but in order to learn about life.' Most readers would agree. Her dramatic insights can surprise and shock, amuse and distress. Such is the intensity and vehemence of her prose that it unleashes everything which is gentle and violent in this world of ours. And as she herself confided: 'Everything affects me . . . I see too much, hear too much, everything demands too much of me.'

The intimate revelations of the *crônicas* take us through the various stages of womanhood from innocence to awakening perceptions of good and evil. The transition from adolescence to maturity is one of solemn rites, at once delicate and vulnerable. The lurking fear of 'ambush', both physical and emotional, is central to many of the narratives. Lispector walked the perilous path of life in fear and trepidation, yet she was curious and determined to unravel the mystery of existence. She dubbed herself 'an audacious coward' (*uma ousada encabulada*) and confronted life on those terms.

In all her work there is relentless self-questioning. Aware that she was speaking on behalf of all mankind, she was wont to say: 'I am so mysterious that I do not understand myself.' She saw the human condition as flawed, fragmentary and incomplete; the darker side of our nature as being compounded of fear, revulsion, cruelty and hatred. But once having recognized the inherent contradictions, she set about trying to reconcile freedom with restraint, humility with pride, solitude with the need to communicate. Strength had to be drawn from weakness, human reversals transformed into salvation.

In a television interview in February 1977, she confessed: 'When I am not writing, I am dead.' She believed that writing could turn a human being into a divinity. And when the words flowed in harmony with thought and feeling, she experienced something akin to ecstasy. She staunchly defended her individual freedom as a writer and insisted: 'If there exists such a thing as *expression*, then let it emanate from what I am.' Appropriately enough, the last item in this collection leaves us with the question which was to haunt her all her life: 'Could it be that the person who sees most, feels and suffers most?' That was the price she paid for the rare insights she so memorably expressed.

GIOVANNI PONTIERO
Manchester, May 1991

Selected Crônicas

She was fat, short and freckled and her hair was much too frizzy. Her bust had become enormous while all the rest of us were flat-chested. And as if this were not bad enough, she would fill the top pockets of her blouse with toffees. But she had what any little girl who adored stories would like to have: a father who owned a bookshop.

She did not appear to benefit much from this good fortune; the rest of us even less so. Instead of giving us a little book for our birthday, she would hand us a postcard from her father's shop. And what is more, with a view of Recife and its bridges, the city where we ourselves lived. On the back she would write words like *happy birthday* and *greetings* in fancy lettering.

But there was such a cruel streak in her nature. Making loud noises as she sucked her toffees, she found ways and means of being vindictive. How this little girl must have hated us, we who were unforgivably pretty, slender and tall, with long, smooth hair. She practised her sadism on me with calm ferocity. I was so anxious to borrow books that I did not even notice the humiliations to which she subjected me: I kept on begging her to lend me the books she never bothered to read. Until that glorious day for her when she began to subject me to Chinese torture. She casually informed me that she possessed a copy of *As reinações de Narizinho* [The Adventures of Little Snotty].

It was a big book, dear God, a book one could live with, eat and sleep with. And well beyond my means. She told me to call at her house the next day and she would lend me the book. Waiting for the following day to come, I became transformed into the very promise of happiness: I was not living, but swimming slowly in tranquil waters.

Next day I went to her house, running all the way. She lived in a house, not in a first-floor apartment like me. She did not ask me in. Looking me straight in the eye, she told me she had loaned the book to another girl and to come back the day after to collect it. Dumbfounded, I slowly walked away, but hope soon returned and I began skipping again, a strange habit of mine, as I went through the streets of Recife. This time I did not

1

stumble once: the promise of that book guided me: the next day would soon be here, the following days were to be my whole life and I went skipping through the streets as usual without stumbling even once.

Fine, but there was more to come. The secret plan of the book-seller's daughter was calculated and diabolical. Next day I was back on her doorstep with a smile, my heart pounding with excitement. Only to hear the calm reply: the book had still not been returned and I was to return the following day. Little did I suspect that, for the rest of my life, this drama of waiting until the following day would recur time and time again while my heart went on pounding.

And so it continued. For how long? I could not say. She knew there could be no definite time before the hatred drained from that thick body of hers. I had already become aware that I was her chosen victim. Sometimes I can sense such things. Yet even though perceiving them, I often resign myself, as if the person who wishes to cause me suffering needs to see me suffer.

For how long? I went to her house every day without fail. Sometimes she would say: I had the book here yesterday but you didn't come so I loaned it to another girl. And, unusual for me, I began to feel dark circles forming round my startled eyes.

Until finally one day, as I was standing at her door, listening humbly and in silence to her excuses, the girl's mother appeared. She was obviously puzzled by the strange appearance of this girl who turned up day after day. She questioned both of us. There was silent confusion, interrupted by words which explained little or nothing. The girl's mother became more and more exasperated. Until the truth finally dawned on her. She turned to her daughter and exclaimed with great surprise: But that book has never left the house and you have shown no interest in reading it! This discovery was bad enough but not nearly as bad as discovering the kind of daughter she had. She looked at us in horror: this perverse daughter whom she scarcely recognized and the little girl standing at the door, weary and exposed to the wind-blown streets of Recife. Then, pulling herself together, she spoke firmly to her daughter without raising her voice: You will lend *The Adventures of Narizinho* to this child at once. And to me she said the one thing I had never dared hope to hear: 'And you must keep the book for as long as you like. Is that clear?' Those words meant more to me than being given the book: for as long as you like is all that anyone, young or old, could possibly wish for.

How can I describe what followed? I was in a daze as I took the book. No, no, I did not go skipping off as usual. I went off, walking very slowly. I know that I was clutching the book in both hands, pressing it to my bosom. How long it took me to reach home is of no consequence. My breast was warm, my mood troubled and pensive.

On arriving home I did not start to read. I pretended not to have the book, so as to postpone the pleasure of discovering I had it. I opened the book some hours later and read some lines, I closed it once more, went wandering through the house, ate some bread and butter to pass the time, pretended I could not remember where I had put the book, found it again, opened it for several moments. I invented the most absurd strategies to postpone that clandestine thing called happiness. I felt proud yet insecure. I was a vulnerable queen.

Sometimes I would sit in the hammock, swinging back and forth in ecstasy, the book lying open on my lap yet never touching it. I was no longer a little girl with a book: I was a woman with her lover.

UNDYING LOVE

I still feel a little uncomfortable in my new role which cannot be strictly described as that of a columnist. And besides being a novice in the art of writing chronicles, I am also a novice when it comes to writing in order to earn money. I have had some experience as a professional journalist without ever signing my contributions. By signing my name I automatically become more personal. And I somehow feel as if I were selling my soul. I mentioned this to a friend who agreed: writing is rather like selling one's soul. It is true. Even when you are not doing it for money, you divulge a great deal about yourself. But a friend of mine who is a doctor disagreed: she argued that she puts body and soul into her work, although she still expects to be paid

3

because she also has to earn a living. So with the greatest pleasure I sell you part of my soul when I converse with you every Saturday.

But my lack of experience in writing a weekly column gets me into a frightful muddle when it comes to choosing suitable topics. I was mulling over this problem when I happened to be visiting a friend. The telephone rang and the caller was a mutual acquaintance. I also had a word with him and naturally mentioned that I was writing a weekly column. I then asked him: 'Which topics are likely to interest readers? Let's say to interest the women who read my column?' Before he could answer, my friend called out from the far end of her large sitting-room: 'Men, of course.' We laughed, but her answer is worth considering. I am somewhat ashamed to have to admit that women are mostly interested in men.

But there is really nothing to be ashamed of, because no one can oblige us to prefer topics of wider interest. We need not feel embarrassed, for if we were to ask the most famous electronics engineer in the world what interests men most of all, the immediate and only truthful answer would have to be: women. From time to time we need to be reminded of this obvious fact however humiliating it may be. You might well ask me: 'But if we are talking about people, surely our children are our greatest interest?' The relationship is quite different. Children are, as the saying goes, our flesh and blood, and the word interest is inappropriate. Children are something special. So much so that any child in this world could be our own flesh and blood. No, believe me, I am not indulging in fiction. I was once told about a little girl who was semi-paralytic. She would fly into a temper and take her revenge by breaking crockery. My blood ran cold. A daughter afflicted with cholera.

As for men, they are so appealing. Just as well. Are men a source of inspiration? Yes. Do they offer a challenge? Yes. Are they our enemies? Yes. Do they make stimulating rivals? Yes. Are men our equals and yet at the same time entirely different? Yes. Are men attractive? Yes. Are they amusing? Yes. Are men like little boys? Yes. Are men also fathers? Yes. Do we quarrel with men? We do. Can we get by without men to quarrel with? No. Are we interesting because men need interesting women? We are. Are our most important conversations with men? Yes.

4

Can men be boring? They can. Do we enjoy being bored by men? We do.

I could go on with this interminable list until my editor tells me to stop. But I do not believe any one else would ask me to stop. For I am sure that I have touched on a sore point. And being a sore point, it hurts, the way men hurt us. And the way women hurt men.

With my mania for taxis, I started interviewing all the taxi-drivers. One night, the driver was a young Spaniard with a tiny moustache and sad expression. Chatting about this and that, he asked me if I had any children. I asked him the same question whereupon he told me that he was not married and had no intention of ever marrying. Then he told me his story. Fourteen years ago he had fallen in love with a young girl in his native Spain. She lived in a small village with few doctors or medical facilities. The girl suddenly became ill. No one could diagnose what was wrong and within three days she was dead. Aware that she was dying, she had told him: 'I shall die in your arms.' And beseeching God's help, she passed away in her lover's arms. The taxi-driver could neither eat nor sleep for almost three years. In that small village everyone knew of his tragic love affair and tried to help him. They took him to parties where the girls, instead of waiting to be asked, took the initiative and invited the men to dance with them.

But it was hopeless. Everywhere he went he was reminded of Clarita – that was the dead girl's name – and it gave me a shock because her name was very similar to mine and I began to feel myself dead and loved. The young man finally decided to leave Spain without even telling his parents. He knew that there were only two countries at the time prepared to receive immigrants without sponsorship: Brazil and Venezuela. He chose Brazil where he soon made his fortune. First he set up a shoe factory and eventually sold it; then he opened a snack-bar and finally sold that as well. Nothing seemed to matter. He exchanged his car for a cab and became a taxi-driver. He lives in a house in Jacarepaguá 'where there are beautiful waterfalls with fresh water'. Yet during the last fourteen years he has not met any woman he could ever really love. Everything leaves him cold and indifferent. The Spaniard discreetly confided nevertheless that his constant longing for Clarita does not prevent him from

5

having affairs with other women. But as for falling in love – never again.

So there! But then my story took an unexpected and alarming twist.

I had almost reached my destination when the taxi-driver started telling me once more about his house in Jacarepaguá and those waterfalls with *fresh water*, as if they could possibly have been with salt water. Almost inadvertently, I said: 'How I'd love to spend a few days resting in such a place.'

That was my mistake. At the risk of crashing into some building or other, he turned round sharply and asked me in an insinuating voice: 'Are you serious? Feel free at any time!' Thrown into panic by this sudden change of climate, I could hear myself quickly replying in a shrill voice that I could not possibly accept his invitation because I was about to have an operation and would be convalescing for several months. In future I shall only conduct interviews with elderly taxi-drivers. This little episode nevertheless proves that the Spaniard is an honest fellow: he does not allow his intense longing for Clarita to interfere with his everyday life.

The finale of my story is bound to disappoint those readers of a romantic disposition. Lots of people would prefer adolescent love to *haunt* them for the rest of their lives. It would make a better story. But I cannot tell a lie just to please my readers. Besides, I feel it is only right that the young Spaniard should not be haunted by the past. Incapable of ever falling in love again, surely he has already suffered enough.

I forgot to mention that he also talked about fraud and embezzlement in the business world – the journey took ages and the traffic was impossible. But his revelations fell on deaf ears. All that interested me was his tale of *undying love*. Some of the things he revealed about shady dealings in the business world are now coming back to me. Perhaps if I concentrate, I shall remember the details and be able to tell you next Saturday. But I doubt whether you would find them interesting.

SEARCHING

A cat did so much wailing during the night that I have rarely felt such compassion for the living. It sounded like grief, and in human and animal terms that is what it was. But could it have been sorrow, or was it 'searching', that is to say 'searching for'? For everything alive is searching for something or someone.

DIES IRAE

I wake up in a rage. I am thoroughly dissatisfied with this world. Most people are dead without realizing it or they live like charlatans. And instead of giving, love makes demands. Those who show us affection expect us at least to satisfy some of their needs. Telling lies brings remorse. And not to lie is a gift the world does not deserve. And I am not even capable of smashing crockery like the semi-paralysed little girl when she took her revenge. I am not semi-paralysed. Although something deep down tells me that we are all semi-paralysed. And we die without so much as an explanation. And worst of all – we live without so much as an explanation. And having maids, whom we might as well call servants, is an offence to humanity. And to be obliged to be what is described as presentable irritates me. Why can I not go around in rags like those men I sometimes see in the street with beards down to their chests and a bible in one hand, these gods who have transformed insanity into a means of understanding? And just because I have done a little writing, why do people assume I must go on being a writer? I warned my children that I had woken up in a rage and advised them to ignore me. But I am in no mood to ignore anything. I should like to do something once and for all to burst this straining tendon which sustains my heart. And what about those who give up? I know a woman who gave up. And she seems quite contented: her way of coping with life is to keep herself occupied. But no occupation satisfies her. And nothing I have ever done satisfies me. Anything I did with love ended up in pieces. I did not even know how to love, not even how to love. And now they have set aside a Day for Illiterates.

I only read the headline but refused to read the text. I refuse to read the text of the world's affairs, the headlines are enough to make my blood boil. There is always some commemoration or other, some war being fought every five minutes. A whole world of semi-paralysed human beings. And everyone waiting in vain for a miracle. And those who are not waiting for a miracle are in an even worse state and ought to start smashing crockery. And the churches are full of those who fear God's wrath. And of those who plead for mercy which is the opposite of wrath.

No, no, I do not feel sorry for those who die of hunger. What I feel is rage. And I can see no harm in stealing to eat. – I have just been interrupted by a telephone call from a girl called Teresa who was delighted that I actually remembered her. I remember: she was a stranger who used to come and visit me in the hospital where I was a patient for almost three months after getting burned in a fire. She would sit down at my bedside, saying little or nothing. And then suddenly depart. And now she was telephoning me to express her frank opinion: that I should not write columns or any such thing for the newspapers. That she was not alone in hoping that I would give up my weekly column however well paid. That lots of people were buying my books in the hope of finding the same topics I dealt with in the newspaper. I kept saying yes because I would have liked it to be yes, and partly to show Teresa that I am not semi-paralysed and can still say yes.

Yes, dear God. To be able to say yes. Yet at that very moment something strange happened. I was writing in the morning when the sky suddenly became so dark that I had to switch on the light. Then the telephone rang once more: a call from a friend in a state of terror who wanted to know if the sky was dark here too. Yes, as dark as night and at ten o'clock in the morning. It is the wrath of God. And if this darkness should turn to rain, may the great flood return but without Noah's Ark. For we have failed to make a world fit to live in and afflicted with paralysis we do not know how to live. For if the flood should not come back, Sodom and Gomorrah will return and that would solve the problem. Why allow two of each species to enter the Ark? At least human couples have produced nothing except children, but not the other non-existent life which made me wake up in a rage.

Teresa, when you visited me in hospital, you saw me bandaged up and immobilised. Today you would find me even more immobilised. Today I am paralysed and mute. And if I try to speak, all that comes out is a mournful growl. So it is not only rage? No, there is sadness as well.

YES

I said to a friend:
– Life has always asked too much of me.
She replied:
– But don't forget that you also ask too much of life.
That is true.

IN FAVOUR OF FEAR

I am convinced that at some time during the Stone Age I was definitely ill-treated by some man who loved me. Ever since then I have been haunted by a secret terror.

It so happened that one warm evening I was having polite conversation with a man of some breeding. He was dressed in a dark suit, with well-manicured hands. I was sitting there eating some guavas and feeling *completely relaxed*, as Sérgio Porto would say, when suddenly the man asked me: 'Shall we go for a walk?'

No. I am going to be blunt. What he really said was: 'Shall we take a *little stroll*?'

Why he should say *little stroll* I never did discover. Because suddenly, from a height of thousands of centuries, the first stone of an avalanche came tumbling down: it was my heart. Who could it have been? Who could have taken me for that *little stroll* in the Stone Age from which I never returned because I ended up staying there?

I do not know what element of terror exists in the monstrous delicacy of that expression *a little stroll*.

Once my first heart came rolling down and I had wickedly

9

devoured those guavas, I felt foolish but terrified at the prospect of some improbable danger.

I can now say improbable, reassured as I am by civilized customs, by a strict police force, and my own ability to escape as fast as the most slippery of eels. Yet I should dearly love to know what I would have said in the Stone Age when, looking like a female ape they shook me from my leafy arbour. Such nostalgia! I really must spend some time in the countryside.

Having swallowed my tiny guavas, I turned pale without the colour draining altogether from my face: my fear was much too vertical in time to leave any traces on the surface. Besides, it was not fear. It was terror. It was my entire future disintegrating. This man, who was my equal, murdered me for love. For this is what they call love and they are right.

A little stroll? Those are the words the wolf used when he spoke to Little Red Riding Hood, who got wise only after the event. 'Just in case of lurking danger, beneath the leaves I'll build my nest' – where had I heard these lines before? I cannot remember, but the people of Pernambuco know what they are talking about.

May the Man forgive me if he should recognize himself in this tale of fear. Let him take comfort from the fact that I was to blame. I should have accepted his invitation without suspicion, as well as the roses he sent beforehand: such kindness, the night was warm, his car waiting outside. And he should know that – in the simplistic division the centuries imposed on me between good and evil – I know that he was A GOOD MAN, LIVED IN A CAVE, ONLY HAS FIVE WIVES, DOES NOT BEAT ANY OF THEM, ALL FIVE WIVES LIVE CONTENTEDLY.

And I beg of him to try and understand – I appeal to his good humour – for I know that an indecisive man like him uses the expression *a little stroll* quite naturally while for me those words conveyed the terrible threat of sweetness. I must thank him for this expression. Never having heard those words before, they left me deeply shocked.

Being polite, I explained to the Man that I could not take *a little stroll*. The centuries have prepared me and now I am as refined as any woman even if I choose to take the precaution of building my nest beneath the leaves to avoid any danger.

The Man did not insist, although it would not be true to say he was pleased. We confronted each other for less than a fraction of a second — after thousands of years we have come to understand each other much better, and now it takes less than a fraction of a second — we confronted each other and that no, however mumbled, echoed loudly against the walls of the cavern which have always been more favourable to the desires of Man.

After the Man's sudden retreat, here I am, safe but still shaken. Have I escaped a *little stroll* which might easily have cost me my life? Nowadays it is all too common to lose one's life by chance.

Once the Man had gone, I realized that I was overjoyed and a completely new person. Oh, not because of his invitation. For thousands of years we women have continually been invited to go for a walk, we are used to it and happy to accept without being pushed. I was happy and transformed — but out of fear.

Because I am in favour of fear.

For certain fears — if they are not demeaning and have indestructible roots — have given me my most incomprehensible reality. The illogical nature of my fears fascinates me, gives me an aura which can be disconcerting. I can barely conceal beneath this modest smile my extraordinary gift for succumbing to fear.

But in the case of this particular fear, I keep asking myself what could possibly have happened to me in the Stone Age? It was clearly something unnatural, otherwise I should not have been left with this tendency to look sideways, or have become so discreetly invisible, cunningly assuming the colour of the shadows and greenery, always keeping well into the side when walking along pavements and adopting a brisk pace. It had to be unnatural, otherwise it would never have frightened me, given my nature and circumstances. Or could it have been that even in that age when people lived in caves — where I continue to retire in secrecy — could it have been that even then I invented this *neurosis* about the motives behind that *little stroll*?

The answer is yes, but there is nothing wrong with having an oblique heart, it is a lighthouse, a compass, wisdom, sharp instinct, experience of death, the power to divine a disquieting but blissful lack of adjustment, because I am discovering that my own maladjustment stems from my origins. For everyone knows that mosquitoes are a sign of heavy rain, that to cut my hair under a new moon will give it greater strength, to mention

11

a name I dare not utter will cause delays and great misfortune, and tying the devil with red string to the leg of a piece of furniture has at least tied up my demons. And I know in my heart – which has never dared expose itself in the centre, and for centuries has kept well to the left under the cover of shadows – I know full well that Man is such a stranger, even unto himself, that innocence alone makes him natural.

No, this oblique heart of mine is right, even if the facts soon prove me wrong. *A Little Stroll* brings certain death, and the victim's startled face remains with glassy eyes staring up at that complacent moon.

THE QUIET WOMAN FROM MINAS

Aninha is a quiet woman from Minas who works here at our house. And when she speaks, which is very rarely, her voice sounds muffled. I have never had a maid called Aparecida, yet every time I am about to call Aninha, the only name that comes to mind is Aparecida. Aninha moves through the house like a silent apparition. One morning she was tidying up a corner of the sitting-room as I sat sewing in the opposite corner. Suddenly – no, not suddenly, nothing is sudden with her, but rather like a long, drawn-out silence – I could hear her voice asking me, as if reluctant to break the silence: 'Does Madam write books?' Taken aback, I said yes. Without interrupting her work or raising her voice, she asked me if I could lend her one of my books. I felt embarrassed but decided to speak frankly. I told her I did not think she would enjoy my books because they are rather complicated. Whereupon, still tidying up and with her voice sounding even more muffled, she replied: 'I like complicated things. I can't stomach *sugared water*.'

THE CLAIRVOYANT

Jandira is the cook. But as strong as a horse. So strong that she is clairvoyant. One of my sisters was paying me a visit. Jandira came into the room, looked at her seriously and unexpectedly announced: 'This trip Madam is hoping to make will happen, Madam is going through a very happy period in her life right now.' And with these words she bustled out of the room. My sister looked at me in astonishment. Somewhat embarrassed, I made a weak gesture with my hands as if to say there was nothing I could do, while at the same time explaining: 'It so happens she is clairvoyant.' My sister calmly replied: 'I see. Well, never mind, every woman gets the servants she deserves.'

GOD'S SWEET WAYS

You have probably already forgotten about my maid Aninha, that quiet little woman from Minas who wanted to read one of my books, no matter how complicated, because she could not stomach 'sugared water'. And you will almost certainly have forgotten that for some strange reason I used to call her Aparecida, whereupon she suggested: 'Perhaps it's because I just appeared from nowhere.' What I may have forgotten to mention is that you really had to like her in order to accept her as a person.

You may have forgotten her. I could never forget her. Neither her muffled voice, nor those false front teeth which she would wear to please me although she did not really need them. Not that they could be seen because she scarcely moved her lips and even her smile seemed to turn inwards. I also forgot to mention that Aninha was downright ugly.

One morning she went out shopping and did not come back for ages. When she finally reappeared she was smiling inanely to herself, as if she were toothless and all gums. The money I had given her to do the shopping was crumpled up in her right hand and the shopping bag was hanging from her left wrist.

There was something different about her appearance. But it was difficult to tell what it could be. She seemed even sweeter than usual. And a little more 'conspicuous', as if she had made some progress. This change in her appearance made us ask suspiciously: 'What about the shopping?' She replied: 'I had no money.' Taken aback we showed her the money in her hand. Gazing at it, all she could say was: 'Oh!' Something else about her strange behaviour made us look inside the shopping bag. It was full of milk bottle tops and other stoppers, along with scraps of dirty paper.

Then she said: 'I must lie down for I have the most awful pain right here' – and as if she were a tiny child she pointed to the crown of her head. She was not complaining, simply telling us. She stayed in bed for hours without saying a word. Having assured me that she did not like 'childish' books, Aninha now looked as innocent as any child. If we tried to question her, she would simply answer that she could not get up.

Before I knew what was happening, our clairvoyant cook, Jandira, had already called an ambulance, having decided that Aninha was quite mad. I went to see for myself. She lay there silent and mad. And I never saw such a sweet expression.

I explained to the cook that she should have asked for the emergency service run by the local Psychiatric Unit. Feeling rather stunned, I automatically rang the Pinel Institute myself. I also felt a curious sweetness inside me, which I cannot explain. Well, perhaps I can. That sweetness was my great love for Aninha.

In the meantime, the ambulance had arrived from the hospital. Sitting up in bed, she allowed the doctor to examine her. He could find nothing clinically wrong with her. Then he began to question Aninha: Why had she collected all those milk-bottle tops and scraps of paper? She replied in a quiet voice: to decorate my room. He asked her several other questions. Ugly, mad and gentle, Aninha patiently gave all the right answers as if she had prepared them beforehand. I told the doctor I had already called an ambulance from a Psychiatric Unit. He assured me: 'Just as well. This is a psychiatric case if ever there was one.'

We waited for the other ambulance to arrive, sitting there in bewilderment, silent and pensive. The ambulance arrived. The psychiatrist lost no time in making his diagnosis. The wards were full and she would have to be treated as an out-patient. But Aninha had no one to look after her. So I telephoned a doctor friend who contacted a colleague at the Pinel Institute where they agreed to admit her until my friend could examine her for himself. 'Are you a writer?' – asked the doctor, who turned out to be a distinguished academic, I began mumbling: 'I...' when he interrupted: 'It's just that your face is familiar and your friend mentioned your first name on the telephone.' In such a situation

I could scarcely remember my own name, but unperturbed he went on to say, all friendly and gushing and showing greater interest in me than in poor Aninha: 'Well I never, how delightful to meet you in person.' Sounding foolish and insincere, all I could think of to say was: 'I'm pleased to meet you, too.'

Then Aninha was carted off, that sweet, gentle creature from Minas, wearing her dazzling false teeth, more or less aware of what was happening. Only part of her was conscious: that part which can cause us pain. In short, my doctor friend examined her and diagnosed her condition as being extremely serious. She was admitted at once.

I spent that night in my sitting-room, smoking one cigarette after another until first light. The entire house seemed to be impregnated with an unnerving sweetness which only Aninha could have left behind.

Dear Aninha, how I miss you and the clumsy way you moved around the house. I shall write to your mother in Minas and tell her to come and fetch you. Who knows what will become of you? The one thing I do know is that you will go on being sweet and mad for the rest of your life, with the odd moment of lucidity. Of course you can use milk-bottle tops to decorate a room. And why not rescue crumpled bits of paper for the same purpose? She could not stomach 'sugared water' and the water she had to drink was anything but sugared. This world is anything but sugared. That was something I discovered as I sat up that night, aggressively smoking one cigarette after another. Oh, the aggression with which I smoked! At times I was overcome with rage, followed by fear, then resignation. God's sweetness can be very depressing. Can it be good for one to be as sweet as this?

Someone had given Aninha a red patterned skirt which was much too long for her. When she had a day off work, she would wear this skirt with a brown blouse. That was another sweet thing about Aninha. She had no taste whatsoever.

– You ought to get yourself a boyfriend, Aninha.

– I had one.

How come? What man could ever have fallen in love with her, for God's sake? There is the answer: he did it for God's sake.

THE CASE OF THE GOLD FOUNTAIN-PEN

I am going to call this *the case of the gold fountain-pen*. To tell the truth, there is no mystery. But nothing could please me more than to write something with at least a title reminiscent of Agatha Christie.

Some friends thought it would be a nice idea to make me a present of a gold fountain-pen. I had always written with a ballpoint pen or used a typewriter. But now that I possessed a gold pen, why not use it? It looks elegant and is of excellent quality. But then I came up against a problem I could not ignore. This was my problem: are the words written with a gold pen also made of gold? Would I be obliged to write more elaborate sentences because my implement was so much more precious? And would I end up writing in a completely different style? And if my style were to change, surely that would have the effect of changing me as well. But in what way? For the better? And there was another problem: what would happen if I were to find, like King Midas, that everything I wrote with my gold pen turned out to have the brilliance and unyielding hardness of gold?

As I said before, I did not pay too much attention to these little problems; thinking is not something I consider dangerous. And I can think without allowing it to upset me.

There was, however, a more serious problem to come. I had only been given one gold pen and I have two little boys. But I am racing ahead. Let me start at the beginning.

When my younger son saw the gold pen, his whole expression changed at once. After carefully examining the pen, he did not utter a word. But desire was written all over his face. The desire to possess something beautiful. His eyes shone in silence. I understood. He wanted the gold pen. It was quite obvious.

So I took the initiative: 'I know what you're thinking. You're wondering how you can get your hands on my pen.' He said nothing, torn between desire and remorse. He overcame his guilt and suggested without much enthusiasm: 'You could have your name engraved on the pen before using it.' I told him: 'If I were to do that, then you would have to use a pen with someone else's name engraved on it.' Silence. Deep reflection. Then he replied despondently: 'That's true, but if I use it right away, someone might steal it from me or I could lose it.' He was right. So we

16

both started to think hard. My efforts paid off. I came up with an idea. 'Listen, I'll give you the pen when you finish high school. By then you will be grown-up, no one will try to steal it from you, and you yourself will know how to look after your things.' 'I suppose so.' But he was still feeling remorseful, as if he were depriving me of a pen which rightfully belonged to me. Little did he know how much I enjoy seeing people take things away from me.

By the following day, any traces of guilt had vanished.

I could not find a pencil to write down a message and decided to use the gold pen. Just then my son walked into the room and caught me in the act. 'No, that's not fair!' he complained resentfully. 'Why not?' I asked. 'Surely you don't mind me using the pen now and then!' 'But you'll spoil the nib. Look, you've scratched it already!' He was right: one day the pen would be his and I should have taken more care. So I showed him where I intended to keep it and promised I would not use the pen any more.

But I have two little sons. And I could not understand why the older boy had shown no interest. This saddened me. I would have preferred to see them quarrel over the gold pen rather than have one of them show no interest whatsoever.

I waited until we were alone. I then told him the whole story and concluded by saying: 'If you had asked me first, I should have given the pen to you.' 'But I didn't even know you had a gold pen.' 'Then you should have known, you go around with your head in the clouds and pay no attention to other people's conversations.' Silence. I asked helpfully: 'But had you known that I had been given a gold pen, would you have wanted it?' 'No.' 'Why not?' 'Because gold pens cost a lot of money.' 'So you don't think you should be given anything that costs a lot of money?' 'You've had other things which cost a lot and I never asked you for them.' 'Whyever not?' 'Because they belonged to you.' 'That wouldn't have bothered me.'

We remained there in silence, not knowing what to say to each other.

Finally he decided to settle the matter once and for all and told me: 'I couldn't care less. So long as the pen writes, any old pen does me.'

No one could disagree, but I was far from satisfied. There was something about this conversation which was not quite right. I should have preferred to have been...well, who knows...how can I put it...I did not feel the least bit pleased, his answers upset me and I can say no more.

Suddenly, I discovered what was wrong. The gold pen did not really matter. What did matter was that one son had wanted it and the other did not. I pursued the conversation: 'Come here, tell me why you don't ask me for things.'

His reply was swift and bruising: 'I'm always asking for things and you always say no.'

The cruelty of this accusation left me dismayed. Besides, it simply was not true. That made his accusation all the more serious. The child had been bearing so deep a grudge that he had transformed it into this terrible lie.

'What are these things you asked for which I wouldn't give you?' 'When I was little, I asked for one of those round things you blow up to float in the water.' 'And didn't I buy you one?' 'No, you didn't.' 'Would you still like one?' 'No, I don't need it any more.' 'I'm sorry I didn't buy you one.' He took pity on me: 'You don't even remember. You wouldn't buy me one because you said they were dangerous, that the thing would start floating on the waves and carry me out to sea, and that I was far too little and couldn't swim.' 'Now I remember.' But the sadness had still lingered.

The fountain pen had taken us far. I thought it wise to call a halt. So we said no more. Sometimes there is little to be gained by probing things too deeply.

GENTLE AS A FAWN

Her name was Eremita. She was nineteen years old. A trusting face, some pimples. Where was the attraction? Yet there was something attractive about that body which was neither ugly nor beautiful, in that face where a sweetness craving greater sweetnesses brought a sign of life.

Beauty is perhaps the wrong word. There probably was no beauty there although certain indefinable traits attracted like water. There was certainly living substance; nails, flesh, teeth, a

18

mixture of resilience and weakness, constituting a vague presence which could suddenly materialize in the form of a questioning head ready to do one's bidding the moment you uttered the name: Eremita. Her brown eyes were indescribable and bore no relation to the rest of her face. As independent as if they had been planted in the flesh of an arm from where they could watch us – open and moist. Her whole being was of a sweetness close to tears.

Sometimes she would reply with the rudeness typical of maids. She explained that she had always been like that, even as a child. Yet it had nothing to do with her character. There was nothing hard about her, there was no suggestion of any perceptible law. 'I was afraid,' she would say quite naturally. 'Boy, was I hungry!' she would exclaim, and for some strange reason there was never any more to be said. 'He has a lot of respect for me,' she would say, referring to her boyfriend and, despite the cliché, anyone listening to her entered a delicate world of animals and birds, where all creatures respected each other. 'I feel so ashamed,' she would say, and then smile, enshrouded in her own shadows. If she hungered after bread – which she would quickly devour as if someone might snatch it away from her – it was thunder she feared, and having to speak which made her embarrassed. She was kind and honest. 'God forbid,' she would mutter, distracted.

For she had moments of distraction. Her face took on a smooth mask of impassive sadness. A sadness more ancient than her nature. Her eyes became vacant; one might even say a little cold. Anyone near her suffered without being able to help. All one could do was to wait.

For this strange infanta had succumbed to something. No one would dare to touch her at such a moment. One could only wait, solemnly watching over her with bated breath. All one could do was to hope that the danger might pass. Until with an unhurried gesture, almost like a sigh, she would awaken like a newborn fawn struggling to its feet. She had returned from her repose in sadness.

She was returning, perhaps no richer, but certainly more reassured after having drunk from who knows what fountain. But a fountain which must have been ancient and pure. Yes, she had hidden depths. Although nothing could be discovered simply by exploring those depths – profundity itself had to be explored, just as one discovers shadows in darkness. It is possible that if someone were to travel further, to cover leagues in the dark, they might find some trail, guided perhaps by the fluttering of wings, by an animal's tracks. Then – all of a sudden – the forest.

So that was her mystery: she had discovered a short cut into the forest. That was almost certainly where she vanished in her moments of distraction. Only to return, her eyes filled with sweetness and ignorance. Her eyes brimming with tears. An ignorance so vast that it could absorb all the wisdom of this world.

That was Eremita. Had she surfaced with everything she found in the forest, she would have gone up in flames. But what she had seen – the roots she had bitten into, the thorns which had drawn blood, the water in which she had bathed her feet, the golden darkness which had enfolded her in its light – none of this she could describe: it had been seen at a glance, and in great haste. So the mystery remained intact.

When she emerged, she was a housemaid once more. Who was constantly being summoned from the darkness of that short-cut to more servile tasks – to wash clothes, to mop the floor, to serve this one and that one.

But was she really serving? For anyone looking closely would have noticed that she washed clothes in the sun; that she mopped the floor – drenched by the rain; that she hung the sheets – out in the wind. She took care to serve from a much greater distance, and to serve other gods. Always with that integrity she had brought from the forest. Without thinking: simply a body, quietly going about her chores, her face radiating a gentle hope which can neither be given nor taken away.

The only trace of the danger she had faced was her furtive way of eating bread. In everything else she remained serene. Even when she stole money which had been left lying on the table or slipped the odd parcel of food to her boyfriend. For she had also mastered the art of petty theft during her excursions into the forest.

THE WHITE DRESS

I woke up in the middle of the night longing to possess a white dress. Made of the finest chiffon. My longing was intense and clear. I believe it was my perpetual innocence. I know that some people find me dangerous. They have even told me so to my face. But I am also innocent. The desire to dress in white has always been the thing that saved me. I know, and perhaps only I and a few others know, that if there is something dangerous about me, there is also something pure. And that purity is only dangerous for those who have danger inside them. The purity I speak of is transparent: one even accepts the bad things. And it has the same effect as that white chiffon dress. Perhaps I will never possess it, yet it is as if I possessed it already, because one learns to live with what is so sadly lacking. I also long for a black dress which will make me look fairer and accentuate my purity. Is this really purity? The primitive is pure. Spontaneity is pure. Is evil pure? I am not sure. What I do know for certain is that sometimes the root of evil is of an impossible purity.

I woke up in the middle of the night with such intense longing for a white chiffon dress, that I got up and looked in my wardrobe. I found one white dress in thick material with a round neckline. Is thickness purity? One thing I do know: love, however violent, is pure.

And that is how I have come to discover that I am not pure.

THE REMNANTS OF CARNIVAL

No, not of this latest carnival. Yet for some strange reason the last few days have taken me back to my childhood and those Ash Wednesdays in deserted streets where the debris of streamers and confetti was being blown around. Now and then, some old woman heading for church with a veil over her head, could be seen crossing the road which always looked so empty after carnival. Until the following year. And as the festivities approached, how can I describe my excitement? As if the world, like some great bud, were about to blossom into a huge red rose. As if the streets and squares of Recife were finally coming into

21

their own. As if human voices were chanting at long last my secret capacity for pleasure. Carnival was mine, all mine.

But in reality I took little part in carnival. I had never been to a children's ball, I had never worn a costume and mask. In recompense, I was allowed to stay up until eleven at night and to stand at the entrance on the ground floor of the two-storey building in which we lived, avidly watching others enjoying themselves. I was given two precious gifts which I used sparingly so that they would last for three days: one was an ether spray, the other a bag of confetti. Oh, how difficult to write about such moments. To this day I can remember how my heart would sink upon realizing that, even without taking part in the festivities, I was so excited that any little thing was enough to make me a happy little girl.

And those carnival masks? They frightened me but that fear was inevitable and necessary because it confirmed my deep suspicion that the human face is not unlike a mask. Standing there in the doorway, if a masquerader happened to speak to me, I would suddenly enter into vital contact with my inner world which consisted not only of dwarfs and enchanted princes, but of human beings with their own mystery. So even that fear of masqueraders was something I needed.

No one at home offered to make me a fancy dress. With so much worry because of my mother's illness, my sisters were too busy to think about carnival and the children's ball. But I persuaded one of my sisters to put my depressingly straight hair into curlers so that I might have the satisfaction of seeing my hair in curls, at least for carnival. During those three days my sister also gave in to my earnest pleas to be allowed to wear make-up like teenage girls, for I could scarcely wait to be rid of my vulnerable childhood. Wearing lipstick and rouge, I felt pretty and feminine and I was no longer a child.

But there was one carnival that was different from the others. So miraculous that I could scarcely believe my good fortune, for I had become accustomed to asking for so little. A friend's mother had decided to make her a costume and the theme was to be a rose. She had bought endless sheets of pink crepe-paper, presumably hoping to create the impression of layers and layers of rose-petals. I watched in amazement as the costume gradually took shape. The finished product bore no resemblance to rose-petals but I honestly believed it was one of the loveliest costumes I had ever seen.

Then the unexpected happened: there were still sheets of crepe-paper left over, lots of them. Perhaps in answer to my silent prayer, or sensing my envy and despair, or simply out of kindness, my friend's mother offered to make me a rose costume, too, with the remnants of the crepe-paper. So for the first time in my life, I was to have what I had always wanted. During those three days of carnival I would pretend to be someone else.

Even the preparations made me dizzy with excitement. I had never been kept so busy as my friend and I made careful plans. Beneath our costumes we would wear underslips so that if it started to rain and our costumes disintegrated, at least we would be respectable. The very thought of a sudden downpour of rain leaving two eight-year-old girls standing there in the street, dressed in nothing but flimsy underslips, caused us acute embarrassment before carnival had even started. But God would come to our assistance! There would be no rain! When I remembered that I only possessed a costume because enough crepe-paper had been left over, I swallowed my pride (which had always been ferocious) with some resentment, and humbly accepted what fate had charitably given me.

Yet why did that year's carnival, the only carnival when I possessed a costume, have to be so sad? Early on Sunday morning, I was already in my curlers so that my hair would be nicely set by the afternoon. The minutes dragged on, I was becoming so impatient. At last, at long last! Three o'clock in the afternoon. Taking care not to tear the paper, I dressed up as a rose.

Many worse things have happened to me and I have shrugged them off. But this particular set-back haunts me to this day. Why does the game of fate seem so irrational? So implacable and cruel? No sooner was I dressed in my crepe-paper costume with my hair still in curlers and waiting to have my face made up with lipstick and rouge, than my mother's condition suddenly deteriorated. The house was in a panic and I was sent in haste to a near-by chemist to buy medicine. I ran all the way dressed as a rose – my face bereft of make-up and so unmistakably that of a child. Bewildered and in a daze, I kept on running among streamers, confetti and the cries of carnival. The happiness of those revellers terrified me.

Hours later, when things had calmed down at home, my sister combed my hair and made up my face. But something had died inside me. As in those tales I used to read about fairies who bewitched people and then broke the spell, I felt my spell had been broken: I was no longer a rose and had turned back into a little girl. I went down on to the street and as I stood there I was no longer a flower, but a pensive clown with scarlet lips. In my desire to experience ecstasy I would start to feel happy, only to remember with remorse that my mother was seriously ill and once again something died inside me.

Salvation only came hours later. And how I clung to it, so great was my need to be saved. A handsome, twelve-year-old boy, who in my eyes seemed much older, came up to me and with a gesture of affection, daring, mischief and sensuality, covered my hair, no longer curly, with confetti. For a second we stood there, staring at each other, smiling in silence. And so this little eight-year-old woman was able to convince herself for the rest of the evening that someone had finally acknowledged her. I had become a rose after all.

STATE OF GRACE (EXTRACT)

Anyone who has experienced a state of grace will know what I am talking about. I am not referring to inspiration, which is a special grace that comes to those who struggle with art.

The state of grace to which I refer cannot be used for anything. It would appear to come just to let us know it really exists. When in this state, the tranquil happiness which radiates from people and things is enhanced by a lucidity which can only be described as light because in a state of grace everything is so very, very bright. It is the lucidity of those who are no longer surmising: they simply know. Just that: they know. Do not ask me what they know, for I can only reply in the same childish manner: they simply know.

And there is a physical bliss which cannot be compared to anything. The body is transformed into a gift. And one feels it is a gift because one is experiencing at source the unmistakable good fortune of material existence.

In a state of grace, one sometimes perceives the deep beauty, hitherto unattainable, of another person. And everything acquires a kind of halo which is not imaginary: it comes from the splendour of the almost mathematical light emanating from people and things. One starts to feel that everything in existence – whether people or things – breathes and exhales the subtle light of energy. The world's truth is impalpable.

It bears no relation to what I vaguely imagine the state of grace of saints to be. For that is a state of grace I myself have never experienced and cannot even envisage. No, this is simply the state of grace of an ordinary person who suddenly becomes totally real since he is ordinary, human, and recognizable.

The discoveries made in this state of grace cannot be described or conveyed. So when I find myself in a state of grace, I sit quietly without uttering a word. As if awaiting an annunciation. But unheralded by those angels who presumably precede the state of grace of the saints. As if the angel of life were coming to announce the world.

Then the angel slowly withdraws. Not in a state of trance – for there is no trance – the angel slowly withdraws, sighing, as if already familiar with the world as it is. The angel's sigh is also one of longing. For having tried to acquire a body and a soul and a place on earth, the angel desires these things more and more. It is useless to desire: things only come when desired spontaneously.

I cannot explain it, but I find that animals are more often in an existential state of grace than human beings. Except that animals do not know, while human beings can perceive these things. Human beings come up against obstacles which do not affect the lives of animals, such as reasoning, logic and understanding. While animals enjoy the splendour of that which is direct and proceeds directly.

God knows what He is doing: I do not believe the state of grace should be bestowed on us too often. Otherwise we might pass forever on to *the other side* of life, which is also real but no one would understand us any more. We should lose our common language.

It is also a good thing that grace should not come as often as I should like. For I might get used to happiness (I forgot to mention that one feels extremely happy when in a state of grace).

To get used to happiness could be dangerous. We could become more selfish because happy people are selfish. They are less sensitive to human suffering and we might not feel obliged to try and help those in need – simply because we possess the essence and compensation of life when we are in a state of grace.

No, even if the choice were mine, I should not want to be in a state of grace too often. It would be like becoming addicted to some vice. I should become a contemplative like those who smoke opium. And were that state of grace to occur too often, I feel certain I should abuse it: I should start expecting to live in a permanent state of grace. And this would result in an unforgivable flight from destiny, which is simply human, made up of conflict and suffering, of uncertainties and minor joys.

It is better if the state of grace is short-lived. Should it last too long, as I well know, familiar as I am with my almost childish ambitions, I should end up trying to penetrate the enigmas of Nature. And that would be enough to banish all grace. For grace is a gift which makes no demands, but it would disappear if we were to start demanding answers. We must never forget that the state of grace is only a tiny aperture which allows us to glimpse a sort of tranquil Paradise, but it is not an entrance, nor does it give us the right to eat the fruits of the orchards.

One emerges from a state of grace with clear skin and open, thoughtful eyes. And, even without a trace of happiness, it is as if one's whole body were bathed in a gentle smile. And one comes away a better person than when one entered. To have known grace is to have experienced something which appears to redeem the human condition while accentuating the strict limitations of that condition. After experiencing grace, the human condition is revealed in all its wretched poverty, thereby teaching us to love more, to forgive more, and show greater faith. One begins to have a certain confidence in suffering and its ways, which can so often become unbearable.

Some days are so arid and empty that I would give years of my life in exchange for a few minutes' grace.

P.S. – I am united, body and soul, with the students of Brazil in their tragic plight.

I know I am in danger of scandalizing both my female and male readers. And for some curious reason, more likely my male than female readers.

Let me start at the beginning. And the beginning is rather shocking. So be prepared. I decided to interview the proprietress of a hostel for women of dubious reputation.

There now, I have confessed. There is no need to feel nervous, I assure you. My motives were and remain quite harmless. I am innocent.

I am not allowed to say how I discovered the address and telephone number of this woman whom I shall refer to as 'Madame X'. I have no intention of naming her and getting her into trouble with the police, that is if they even bother about such establishments. Once in possession of the number, I telephoned her.

At the outset of our conversation, I sensed a note of mistrust on the part of Madame X: she was not quite sure what I wanted, and God alone knows what she thought I wanted. But soon she was saying to me: 'Well, of course, dearie.' I explained that I was anxious to arrange a meeting and asked if we could have a drink together, wherever she preferred. She suggested I should go to the hostel. But Dearie preferred not to. Nor can I imagine why she chose to meet me in front of the Jaci Pharmacy in José de Alencar Square. She could not have chosen a worse spot: men pass in droves and no need to ask what they must have thought on seeing a woman standing there on her own.

Why did I want to interview Madame X? Well, as an adolescent I was bewildered and confused and there was one silent but nagging question bothering me: 'What is the world like? And why this world?' Later, I was to learn lots of things. But that question from my adolescence continued to bother me, silent and persistent.

So what did I learn on Earth in order to open these narrow eyes of mine just a little? I recognized that the problem of prostitution is one of a social order. But there is also a deeper problem: the fact that lots of men prefer to pay, precisely in order to humiliate women and be humiliated in turn. This rejection of love is a sad reality. Men pay in order to avoid love. There are even married men who like to maintain a home in order to transform their wives into possessions for which they have paid.

Now then, I telephoned Madame X in the morning before setting out to meet her. But she explained she had an appointment to see her doctor. I asked her what was wrong. She had what every Madame running a hostel for women was bound to have: a weak heart. I said I would telephone her later. What a business trying to get through. Her number was constantly engaged. God knows why, and so do we. Her hostel is very *private and secluded*, as she was careful to point out, so any *meetings* had to be arranged by telephone. I finally managed to get through and Madame X announced: 'I feel much worse and I really must lie down. Ring me again at four o'clock.' I thought to myself: I wonder if the old girl is going to die on me before I get to meet her.

No, no, this was no easy assignment. When we first made contact by telephone, I had a violent headache and it only passed after I realized it had been brought on by the thought that I was committing a sin. That same night I had a nightmare in which Madame X confided she was suffering from leprosy. I was terrified of touching her and woke up in a panic. Why then did I insist on seeing her? Because I had to find some irrefutable reply.

I waited for one hour and a half in front of the Jaci Pharmacy. No sign of Madame X. I went back home and telephoned. She assured me she had waited half an hour for me. I lost all interest. Weeks passed, and I had almost forgotten all about her. But I am one of those people who do not give up easily. I telephoned her again. And once more, she arranged to meet me in front of the Jaci Pharmacy. This time she asked me to be there at ten because she would be *very busy* in the afternoon.

I did not have long to wait. At that hour in the morning, the only passers-by are women carrying their shopping. She arrived wearing the outfit she had described to me. And how elegant she looked. Certainly much more elegant than me who has no need to be elegant.

She explained at once that her hostel was a family business. The widowed brother-in-law who looked after her affairs also had other business interests. I asked her if the hostel made money. She replied in the negative. Liar! We retired to a nearby café which was just opening and I ordered the same thing as Madame: grape juice.

How insipid, dear God. Madame X has a daughter who studies ballet. Lost for conversation, we began discussing the horrors of fire. She told me she had experienced several fires but had always managed to throw the blazing mattress out of the window before it could do much damage.

The amusing thing is that she took a liking to me. She suggested: 'Now that we've got to know each other, telephone me when you have a spare moment so we can have a little chat.' I thought to myself: Not on your life, I am not interested.

She told me: 'Men, poor things! They need a place where they can feel safe. Thank goodness that Red Light district has disappeared. It was awful. Really awful.'

What more is there to tell? Nothing. She was in no hurry to leave nor was I. But I was the first to make a move. And she let me pay for the drinks. I lost any appetite for lunch that day.

What had I expected in the end? Had the question which nagged me in adolescence died? Is the world insipid? Or is it me? Or is it Madame X who is insipid? Probably all three of us. I felt that my day had been ruined.

When I told a friend of mine about the interview, his only comment was to calmly suggest: That's where the writer comes in. But I am not a writer. I am a person who is curious about the world. But who stopped being curious, at least on that day. I did not even feel hungry.

Full of indignation, Madame X also told me that the *girls* who take up this kind of work can think of nothing except getting rich. Who can blame them?

And here ends the interview which turned out to be a fiasco. But we all have our little fiascos.

RETURN TO NATURE (EXTRACT)

In Rio there was a place with an open hearth. And when she saw that it was not only cold but raining in the trees, she could not believe she had been given so much. The world awakening with something she did not even realize she needed, as if she were suffering from hunger. It was raining, raining. The flames wink at her and her man. He takes care of the things she takes for granted. He pokes the fire in the hearth as if it were his duty from birth. While she – who is ever restless and busying herself trying out this and that – never so much as remembers to poke the fire. That is not her job. After all, what does she have a man for? If he is a man, then let him carry out his mission. All she is prepared to do is to coax him: 'That piece of wood,' she tells him, 'still hasn't caught fire.' And before she can finish saying what she has to say, the man has seen the piece of wood for himself and is already poking at it. Not because she ordered him to, for she is the man's wife and he would lose his authority if she were to start giving him orders. His other hand, which is free, is within reach. She knows but does not take it. His hand is there for the taking if she so desires and that is all she asks.

Ah, to think all this will end! For it cannot last by itself. No, no, she is not referring to the fire, she is referring to what she feels. What she feels never lasts, what she feels always comes to an end, perhaps never to return. So she savours this moment, consumes its fire, and the sweet fire burns, burns and glows. Then she who knows that everything must end, reaches out and, as she takes the man's free hand in hers, she sweetly burns, burns and glows.

AS YOU SLEEP

There is something different about tonight. It is three o'clock in the morning. I am having one of my bouts of insomnia. I made myself some coffee since sleep seemed unlikely. I put in too much sugar and the coffee tasted horrid. I can hear the waves beating against the shore. Tonight is different because as you sleep I am talking to you. I break off, go out on to the terrace, look down on to the street, the long, narrow strip of beach and the sea. It is dark. So dark. I think of my favourite people: they are all asleep or out enjoying themselves. Some of them might even be drinking whisky. My coffee tastes even sweeter and becomes quite undrinkable. The night turns darker. I am sinking into painless melancholy. It is not so bad. Only to be expected. Tomorrow I might experience some happiness, not exactly ecstasy, just happiness. And that is not so bad either. True, but I am scarcely enjoying my pact with humdrum existence.

30

How does an untidy person become tidy? My papers are in disorder, my drawers need sorting out. (I must have a secretary because I am suffering from nervous exhaustion, according to my doctor.) This would not matter so much in my opinion if I had some inner order. But people who are over-preoccupied with external order are precisely those who are suffering from inner disorder and need some counter-balance to give them some reassurance. I need reassurance and this could be achieved if my drawers were to be put into some kind of order. Well, merely thinking of tidying out those drawers made me feel weary and lazy. The laziness that comes at weekends. I hope my laziness will strike a chord in some of my male and female readers so that they will not feel too superior. Frankly, when it comes to tidiness, what I should like is for someone to take it upon themselves to provide me with some semblance of order. My absurd idea of luxury would be for some sort of governess-cum-secretary to take care of my external life, even to the extent of going to certain parties and receptions on my behalf. Naturally, this person would have to adore me – but with the utmost discretion, because naked worship is more than I can bear. It is inhibiting and kills any spontaneity. It deprives us of our right to have those faults, innate or acquired, which we jealously hold on to for support, because it is not only our virtues which serve as crutches.

What else could this governess-cum-secretary do for me? She should not look at me too often so as not to embarrass me. She should speak to me quite naturally but also know when to be silent and leave me in peace. She should decide what to prepare for lunch and dinner – then meals would be a constant and pleasant surprise. And, of course, she would keep my papers in order. She would also understand my moments of sadness but be sufficiently discreet not to show that she had understood. And naturally, I would expect her to reply on my behalf to publishers with tact and diplomacy. As for my children, I myself would take care of them. But she could act as a surrogate mother whenever I want to work or go to the cinema. A surrogate mother has the advantage of not embarrassing children with too much affection. As children grow up, their mother has to become smaller. Alas, mothers tend to go on being enormous. If my sons ever read this, they will be amused. When mothers of Russian descent start to kiss their children, instead of being content with one kiss they want to give them forty. I tried to explain this to one of my sons but he told me I was just looking for an excuse to justify all those kisses.

BELONGING

A friend of mine who is a doctor has assured me that right from the cradle, children sense their surroundings, and want things. Right from the cradle the human being has started to exist.

I am certain that right from the cradle my first desire was to belong. For reasons of no importance here, I must have somehow felt that I did not belong to anything or anyone. That my birth was superfluous.

If I first experienced this human hunger in the cradle, it continues to accompany me throughout life, as if predestined. So that I feel pangs of envy and desire whenever I see a nun: for she belongs to God.

Precisely because of this deep longing to give myself to something or someone, I have become rather aloof: I am afraid of revealing how much I need and how poor I am. Yes, poor. Very poor. All I possess is a body and a soul. And I need something more. Perhaps I started writing so early in life because, at least by writing, I belonged to myself to some extent. Which is a pale imitation.

Over the years, especially of late, I have lost the knack of being like other people. I no longer know how it is done. And a whole new kind of 'solitude through not belonging' has started to smother me like ivy on a wall.

If I have always wanted to belong, why then have I never joined any club or association? Because that is not what I mean by belonging. What I want and cannot achieve, is to be able to give the best of myself to whomever or whatever I might belong. Even my moments of happiness can be so solitary at times. And solitary moments of happiness can be so moving. It is like holding a gift in your hands, beautifully wrapped, but with no one

32

to whom you can say: Here, this is for you, open it! Not wishing
to find myself in moving situations and somewhat inhibited and
reluctant to strike a tragic note, I rarely parcel up my feelings in
gift wrapping.

Belonging does not simply come from being weak and needing
to unite oneself to something or someone stronger. An intense
desire to belong often comes from my own inner strength – I
wish to belong so that my strength will not be useless and may
serve to strengthen some other person or thing.

But I do get some satisfaction out of life: for example, I belong
to my country and, like millions of others, I belong to Brazil in
the sense that I am Brazilian. And I, who in all sincerity have
never desired or could desire fame – I am far too much the indi-
vidualist to tolerate any invasion of my privacy – I, who do not
seek fame, nevertheless enjoy being associated with Brazilian
literature. No, no, not out of pride or ambition. I am happy to
be associated with Brazilian literature for reasons which have
nothing to do with literature, for I am not even what might be
called a bluestocking or intellectual. I am happy simply 'to par-
ticipate'.

I can almost visualize myself in the cradle, I can almost
recreate inside me that vague yet pressing need to belong. For
reasons which not even my father or mother could control, I was
born and remain: simply born.

Yet my birth was planned in such a pleasing way. My mother
was in poor health and there was a well-known superstition
which claimed that a woman could be cured of illness if she
gave birth to a son. So I was deliberately conceived: with love
and hope. Only I failed to cure my mother. And to this day I
carry this burden of guilt: my parents conceived me for a specific
mission and I failed them. As if they had been relying on me to
defend the trenches in time of war and I had deserted my post.
I know my parents forgave me my useless birth and forgot that
I had frustrated their great hopes. But I have not forgiven myself
or forgotten. I wanted to work a miracle: to be born and cure my
mother. Then I should truly have belonged to my father and
mother. I could not even confide my *solitude of not belonging*
because, as a deserter, I kept the secret of my escape which
shame forbade me to reveal.

Life has allowed me to belong now and then, as if to give me the measure of what I am losing by not belonging. And then I discovered that: *to belong is to live.* I experienced it with the thirst of someone in the desert who avidly drinks the last drops of water from a flask. And then my thirst returns and I find myself walking that same desert.

AN EXPERIENCE

Perhaps this is one of the most important experiences known to man and beast. The need to seek someone's help and receive it, out of sheer generosity and understanding. Perhaps it is worth being born in order to make a silent plea and be heard. I have pleaded for help. And received it.

I then felt like a dangerous tiger with an arrow stuck in its flesh, a tiger circling the terrified onlookers to discover who had inflicted this terrible pain. Until someone sensed that a wounded beast is no more dangerous than a child. Bravely approaching the tiger, the stranger carefully removed the arrow.

And the tiger? Certain things defy words of gratitude from humans and animals. So I, the tiger, slowly circled several times in front of my Good Samaritan, paused, and licked my paws, before withdrawing in silence, since words are unimportant.

DISCOVERING THE WORLD

What I wish to narrate is as delicate as life itself. And I should like to draw on the delicate side of my nature as well as that peasant streak which is my salvation.

In my childhood and subsequent adolescence I was precocious in many things. In absorbing atmosphere, for example, or in sensing someone's intimate aura. Yet in other important matters I was far from being precocious and incredibly backward. And I am still ignorant about so many things. What am I to do? There appears to be something childish in my nature which refuses to grow up.

Even beyond the age of thirteen, for example, I was still unaware of what Americans call *the facts of life.* The expression refers to that deep sexual relationship between a man and a woman which produces children. Or could it be that I had some vague perception of these facts which I deliberately suppressed in order to hide my embarrassment and go on being innocent and attractive to little boys? Being attractive at the age of eleven meant scrubbing my face until it shone. Then I felt prepared. Could my ignorance have been some foolish and senseless attempt to remain ingenuous in order to go on thinking about little boys without feeling guilty? Most likely. For I have always known about things without even being aware that I know them.

My friends at school knew about everything and even exchanged anecdotes about the things they knew. Completely bewildered, I would pretend that I understood rather than have them despising me for being so ignorant.

Yet for all my ignorance of the facts, I instinctively went on flirting with any boy who took my fancy. Instinct had outstripped my intelligence.

Until I became thirteen and felt sufficiently grown-up to discover facts which might shock me. I told a close friend about my guilty secret: I knew nothing about the things the other girls discussed, and had only pretended to understand. She was flabbergasted. My pretence had been so convincing. But I finally persuaded her I was telling the truth and she decided without further ado to unravel life's mysteries. Unfortunately she was also in her early teens and incapable of explaining things without causing me acute embarrassment. I stood there, paralysed, staring at her, my innocence mortally wounded, my emotions in turmoil, and overcome with bewilderment, fright and indignation. Mentally, I babbled to myself: But why? For what reason? The shock was so great – and traumatic for several weeks – that there and then on the street-corner I swore I would never marry.

Although some months later, I had forgotten my oath and resumed my little flirtations.

And as time passed, I was no longer shocked at the way men and women make love. I even came to find it quite perfect. And extremely delicate. By then I had already become a tall girl, pensive by nature and rebellious. Yet for all my wildness, I was still very shy.

Before coming to terms with the ritual of life, I experienced

35

much suffering which I might have been spared if some responsible adult had taken the trouble to tell me about love. That person would have known how to cope with my ingenuous nature without offending my sensibilities, without obliging me to be born anew in order to accept life and its mysteries.

For the greatest surprise of all was to find that, after discovering everything, the mystery remained intact. I know flowers grow from a plant yet I go on being surprised by nature's secret paths. And if I feel somewhat embarrassed to this day by the facts of life, it is not because I find them shameful, but simply out of feminine discretion.

For I am convinced that life is beautiful.

RITUAL (EXTRACT)

Beyond lies the sea, the most mysterious of non-human existences. While the woman stands here on the shore, the most mysterious of living creatures. The day mankind questioned its own nature, it became the most enigmatic of living creatures. The woman and the sea.

Their mysteries could only come together if the one were to surrender to the other: the surrender of two incomprehensible worlds enacted with the confidence of two understandings surrendering to each other.

She is capable of looking at the sea. Her vision is only restricted by the line on the horizon, that is to say, by her human incapacity to see beyond the Earth's curve.

It is six o'clock in the morning. There is nothing to be seen on the shore except a stray dog, a black dog which stops in its tracks. Why is a dog so free? Because the dog is that living mystery which does not question itself. The woman hesitates before entering the sea.

Her body consoles itself with its own smallness in relation to the sea's vastness, because the body's smallness helps to keep it warm. This same smallness also turns the human body into something poor but free with its share of that freedom enjoyed by the dog on the sands. This body will enter the infinite chill that roars without ire in the evening silence. Unwittingly, the

36

woman is testing her courage. The shore is deserted at this early hour so there are no other bathers to show her how entering the sea can be transformed into a frivolous game of life. She is alone. The salt-water is not alone because it is salt and fathomless, and that is an achievement. At this moment she is less familiar with herself than with the sea. Her courage is that of someone who, without knowing herself, nevertheless proceeds. It is fatal not to know oneself, and not to know oneself requires courage.

She starts to enter the sea. The salt-water is so cold it chills her legs as if part of the ritual. But a fatal happiness – happiness is fatal – has already possessed her although it never occurs to her to smile. On the contrary, she looks quite solemn. The powerful smell from those tossing waves rouses her from the slumbering depths of millennial dreams. She now becomes watchful, just as the hunter is unconsciously watchful. The woman has become impenetrable, light, and sharp, as she forces her way into the cold sea, liquid yet resistant, before allowing her to enter, just as in loving where resistance is often an act of pleading.

This slow passage increases her inner courage. And suddenly she allows herself to be immersed by the first wave. The salt and iodine, completely liquid, momentarily blind her, the water drenching her – as she stands there in terror and already fertile.

The cold becomes intense. Advancing, she penetrates the sea. She has found her courage. The familiar ritual is under way. She lowers her head into the gleaming waters and re-emerges, her hair dripping salt-water which causes her eyes to smart. Slowly she splashes the water with one hand. Her hair soon dries in the sun, the salt making it brittle. Cupping her hands to form a shell, she drinks the water in great, refreshing gulps, a time-honoured ritual which she performs with the arrogance of those who never offer explanations, not even to themselves.

This was what she needed: to feel the sea inside her like a man's dense sperm. Now she is truly equal to herself. Her nourished throat becomes parched with salt, her eyes redden as the salt dries in the sun, the gentle waves come beating against her and then retreat, her body acting as a solid shield.

She plunges in once more, swallows more water, now less avid and intense, for her thirst has been slaked. She is the lover who knows she will possess everything anew. The sun comes out further and causes her to shiver even as it dries her. She takes another plunge, ever less avid and intense. Now she knows what she wants. She wants to remain standing still in the water. And that is precisely what she does. As if beating against the side of a ship, the waves come beating against her, retract and return. There is no transmission. The woman needs no communication.

She then walks through the sea, heading for the shore. She is not walking over the waters – that she would never do, thousands of years after those waters have already been walked over – but no one can rob her of this: to be able to walk through the sea. Sometimes the waves put up resistance, pushing her back with force, whereupon the woman, like a ship's figurehead, presses on, a little more determined and severe.

Now she is treading the sands. Aware that she is gleaming with water, salt and sun. Even if she were to forget within minutes, all this will be hers forever. And she knows in some obscure way that her dripping hair belongs to someone who has been shipwrecked. Because she knows – she knows she has survived danger. A danger as ancient as man himself.

A CHALLENGE FOR THE PSYCHOANALYSTS

I dreamed that a fish was taking its clothes off and remained naked.

THE SWEATER

Someone gave me a sweater. That seems simple enough. But it is not.

The sweater was sent to me by a girl I did not know. I discovered through a mutual friend that she is a designer of considerable talent. She lives in São Paulo. On a visit to Rio, she had lunch with him. She arrived wearing a very pretty sweater and my friend, thinking it would look good on me, ordered one in exactly the same pattern. The girl happens to be one of my readers – or am I mistaken? And when she discovered who the present was for, she insisted on buying it for me herself. Our mutual friend agreed.

So here I am, the proud owner of the prettiest sweater you ever saw. It is a bright cherry red and seems to embody all that is good for both of us. That warm red is the colour of the sweater's soul. I am writing these lines before going out, wearing my new sweater. The colour of fire and flame, it has been given to me with such affection that its warmth embraces me and keeps out the chill of solitude. It is like being caressed in deep friendship. Today I am wearing it in public for the first time. The sweater is ever so slightly tight, but perhaps that is how it is meant to be worn: proudly flaunting the glorious state of womanhood. The moment I have stopped writing, I shall spray myself with my favourite perfume. My little secret. I adore secrets. And then I shall be ready to face the wintry cold outside: the real cold as well as those other chills we experience.

I am just another woman too many.

HOW TO TREAT ONE'S POSSESSIONS

There is a creature living inside me as if he were at home, and he is. He is a black horse with a shiny coat and although completely wild – for he has never lived inside anyone before nor ever been saddled – although completely wild, this gives him that primitive sweetness of a creature without fear. His nose is moist and fresh. I love kissing that nose. When I die, the black horse will be homeless and suffer a great deal. Unless he can find another home where no one will be afraid of this creature who can be savage and at the same time so gentle. I must warn you that the horse is nameless: you need only call him in order to discover his name. Or perhaps you will not discover it, but once called with tenderness and authority, he comes. If his sense of smell tells him that a body is free, he comes trotting up quietly. But I should warn you not to be afraid when he neighs: you could easily be deceived into thinking some human being is giving voice to pleasure or wrath.

A REMARKABLE LOVE STORY

There once lived a girl who spent so much time observing hens that she came to understand their souls and deep anxieties. The hen is anxious, unlike the cockerel who suffers from an almost human anguish: he is deprived of any true love from his harem. Besides, he has to keep watch all night long, awaiting the first glimmer of dawn in the distant sky before singing those sonorous notes. That is his duty and art. But coming back to the hens, the girl kept two of them as pets. One was called Pedrina: the other Petronilla.

Whenever the girl suspected one of them might have a liver infection, she would sniff under its wings as if she were a trained nurse. She believed this was the first symptom of any illness, because the stench from a live hen is no joke. She would then ask her aunt for some medicine. Only to be told: 'But there's nothing wrong with your liver.' Feeling she could confide in her favourite aunt, the girl explained why she needed the medi- ine. She also felt it wise to administer equal doses to Pedrina and Petronilla in order to prevent any contagion. There was really no point in giving them any medicine because Pedrina and Petronilla continued to spend the whole day pecking away at the soil and eating all sorts of rubbish likely to harm their livers. And the stench under their wings was something awful. It never occurred to the girl to try using deodorant because where she lived in Minas Gerais people did not use deodorants and their underwear was made of linen rather than nylon. Her aunt continued to give her the medicine, a dark brown liquid which the girl suspected might be water coloured with a few drops of strong coffee – and then there was the awkward business of forcing open their beaks in order to administer the medicine that would finally cure them of being hens. The girl was too young to understand that humans cannot be cured of being humans or hens of being hens: humans, like hens, have their failures and triumphs (the hen's triumph is to be able to lay a perfect egg), something inherent in the species. The girl lived in the heart of the countryside and there was no chemist in the neighbourhood.

There was a further crisis when the girl discovered how thin Pedrina and Petronilla had become under their ruffled feathers, despite the fact that they never stopped eating all day long. The girl had not yet realized that to fatten them up would only hasten their destiny which was to be killed and eaten. And she went on struggling to open their beaks. She could soon sense every little thing about the hens in that great farmyard in Minas Gerais. And when she grew up, she was surprised to learn that the word hen or chicken in the local jargon also meant coward. The irony of the situation escaped her:

– 'But it's the cockerel who is the nervous creature as he goes chasing after the hens! The hens give no bother! But the cockerel moves so quickly he can scarcely be seen! He is forever trying to find a hen to love him! Without success!'

One day the little girl's mother decided to take her to spend the day at a relative's house which was some distance away. And when she returned home, the hen whom she had known in life as Petronilla no longer existed. Her aunt told her:

– 'We've eaten Petronilla.'

The little girl had an enormous capacity for love: the hen had never reciprocated that love, yet she had gone on loving it without hoping for anything in return. When she learned what had happened to Petronilla she began to loathe everyone at home, everyone except the mother who did not eat poultry and the servants who preferred beef. But she could scarcely bear to look at her father, for he was particularly fond of eating chicken. Her mother realized what was happening and tried to explain:

– 'When humans eat animals, those animals become more like people because they become part of us. We are the only two people here in the house who did not eat Petronilla. More's the pity!'

Pedrina, whom the little girl had always secretly preferred, died a natural death, for she had always been a delicate creature. When the little girl found Pedrina trembling under the blazing sun, she wrapped her up carefully in a dark-coloured towel and then sat her on top of one of those large tiled stoves to be found in all the old farm-houses in Minas Gerais. Everyone warned her that Pedrina was close to death but the little girl was stubborn and insisted on settling Pedrina, all wrapped up, on top of the warm tiles. Next morning Pedrina was a stiff corpse. Weeping bitterly, the little girl was finally convinced that death had claimed her beloved pet hen.

The years passed and she adopted another hen called Eponina. This time, her love for Eponina was more down-to-earth and less romantic: the love of someone who had already suffered for love. And when the time came for Eponina to be killed and eaten, the little girl accepted the news as the inevitable destiny of any creature born a hen. The hen appears to have some premonition of its own destiny and therefore learns not to love its owners or the cockerel. A hen is alone in this world.

But the little girl had not forgotten what her mother had told her about eating animals one loved: she ate more of Eponina than the rest of the family. She ate without feeling hungry, but with an almost physical satisfaction because she now knew that Eponina would become part of her and be more hers than when she was alive. The cook had prepared Eponina in a traditional brown sauce or *molho pardo*, made with the blood and some vinegar. And so the little girl went through the pagan ritual which has been handed down throughout the ages, partaking of flesh and drinking blood. During dinner, she felt almost resentful of the others who were eating Eponina. The little girl was made for love: eventually she became a young woman and men entered her life.

EXCESS AND PRIVATION

The worst thing of all is to become suddenly tired of everything. It is rather like excess, as if one already had everything and wanted for nothing more. Tired of the Beatles. Tired, too, of those who are not the Beatles. Even tired of my inner freedom, which I gained as such great cost. Tired of loving one's neighbour. Hatred would be preferable. What could save me from this feeling of excess (is it excess or a useless freedom?) would be anger. Not that loving anger you sometimes find. But naked, uncontrolled anger. The more violent the better. Anger with those who know nothing. Anger, too, with those intelligent people who always *have something to say*. Anger with *avant-garde* cinema, and why not? And anger with the other kind of cinema as well. Anger with the affinity I share with certain people, as if this excess within me were not enough. And fury

42

with success? Success is a joke, a false reality. Fury has saved my life. Without it, what would have become of me? How could I have borne to read those headlines reporting that one hundred starving children die every day in Brazil? Is anger my deep revulsion against being human? I am tired of being human. And angry at feeling so much love. Some days I am angry just to be alive. Because anger enlivens everything. I have never felt so alert. I know this will pass and that a vital sense of need will return. Then I shall want everything, everything! Oh, how good to need only to be satisfied. Oh, how good to feel that moment of need before the moment of satisfaction. But not to be satisfied too easily. Because one can tire of things which seem easy. Is even writing becoming too easy? Why do I now write with my fingertips when I used to write from the heart? It is sinful, I know, to seek privation. Yet the privation I am speaking of is much more satisfying than this feeling of excess. I simply do not want it. I am now going to sleep because I cannot bear today's world, so full of useless things. Goodnight, forevermore. I shall be back next Saturday. And please do not write to me: I have no desire to hear the human voice. And if I am listening to myself as I take my leave, that is only because it helps to increase my fury.

But there is only one fury which is blessed: the fury of those who suffer privation.

MEMORY OF A SMALL BOY

But how should I feel about my little boy? Because I cannot summon any definite feeling about him. What should I feel? I can see his face bronzed by the sun, a face entirely unaware of its expression. Busy licking at his ice-cream, he looks like some pretty animal – delicate yet ferocious.

The ice-cream is chocolate-flavoured. My son likes it. Sometimes he finds licking takes far too long so he bites into it, and the face he makes is that of someone who is totally unaware of the awkward happiness produced by a lump of frozen ice-cream filling a warm mouth. And such a pretty mouth. I look at my little boy, inscrutable as ever, but he is used to this foolish expression of intense love. He ignores me, and does not mind being

43

observed as he performs this private ritual, so vital and delicate, as he carries on licking his ice-cream with his crimson, watchful tongue. I feel nothing other than a sense of being complete, weighed down by primary matter and solid wood. As a mother, I have no finesse. I am coarse and silent. With rude silence and vacant eyes, I watch the severe expression on my son's face. I can feel nothing because this must be crude, indivisible love. There I am, recoiling. Recoiling before so much. The enigmatic leaves me with a kind of cruel obstinacy: enigma is my name; there I am, enhanced by nature. The expression on my face must be one of obstinacy, the look in my eyes that of the foreigner who does not speak the language of the country. As if overcome by fatigue, I communicate with no one. My heart is heavy, stubborn, expressionless, and closed to any suggestions.

I am there, and I can see: my boy suddenly looks greedy – he must have found a lump of ice-cream with rather more chocolate and his practised tongue has prised it out. No one could describe me as thin: I am plump, heavy and big, with rough hands I inherited from my ancestors. I am a suspicious woman taking a pause. My son is now eating the chocolate coating. I am an immigrant who has thrown down roots on virgin territory. My searching gaze is absorbed and sombre. And what do I see? A small boy absorbed in eating ice-cream.

TERROR

The light was too strong for his eyes. Then he felt a violent tug; he was being settled in his cot but how was he to know? All he was aware of was the terror of those faces bending over him. He knew about nothing. And he could not move freely. The voices sounded like thunder, apart from one melodious voice: how comforting. But he was soon tucked in and started feeling terrified. He screamed between the cot-railings and saw colours which he later recognized as blue. A disquieting blue which made him cry. And his fear of that dreadful colic. They would open his mouth and pour down his throat some nasty liquid which he would be forced to swallow. It was somehow easier to bear when the melodious voice gave him his medicine.

On those occasions, he did not scream. The one positive thing was that he had just been born. He was five days old.

When he became a little older, he could hear without understanding: 'He's no longer any trouble but when he was born he cried and screamed such a lot. Thank goodness, he's getting easier to handle.' No, no, it was not easy. It never would be easy. Birth was the death of one being dividing into two solitary beings. It only seemed easy now that he had learned to cope with his secret terror which would last until death. The terror of being on earth yet longing for heaven.

I KNOW WHAT SPRING IS LIKE

I know it sounds rather fatuous to say in the middle of spring that I know what spring is like. But sometimes I am so reticent that friends get annoyed. My reticence stems from gratitude and is probably excessive. That childish I is uttered with a child's fear. But this time, when I saw that I was being much too reticent in expressing my happiness as spring arrived bringing showers, this time I embraced what belongs to me and to others.

I know what spring is like because I can smell the pollen in the atmosphere as if it were mine, I can feel myself tremble when a little bird sings, and feel that I am unconsciously renewing my life. Because I am alive.

Transparent and mortal, let that agonizing spring speak for me, that spring I impatiently await year after year. I know it brings turmoil to the senses, but why resist its dizzying spell? I accept this head of mine beneath the glistening showers of spring, I accept my existence and that of others because that is their privilege and without them I should die, I accept the possibility of the existence of the great Beyond despite my having prayed for so little, only to be denied.

I feel that to live is inevitable. In springtime I can sit smoking for hours, simply existing. But existing can sometimes cost blood, and there is no way of avoiding this because it is in my blood that I feel spring. And it hurts. Spring gives me things. It gives me the wherewithal to live. And I feel that I shall die on a spring day. Die of wounding love and a broken heart.

'WANTED'

This is the ideal newspaper for classified advertisements and, as I scan the items under *Wanted* or *For Sale*, my eye catches the following advertisement printed in bold type:

'Man or woman wanted to help someone to remain contented. I am so contented that I cannot keep all this happiness to myself and must share it with others. Exceptional wages offered: the right person will be repaid minute by minute with happiness. Apply at once because my happiness is as fleeting as those falling stars one only sees after they have fallen; I need this man or woman before dusk because once night falls no one can help me and it will be much too late. Applicants must not expect any free time until the horrors and dangers of Sunday have passed. Anyone who is sad may also apply because the happiness promised is so great that it must be shared before disaster strikes. I implore readers to apply, I implore them with all the humility of inexplicable happiness. There is also a house on offer, all lit up as if a ball were being held. The successful applicant will be allowed full use of the pantry, the kitchen and sitting-room.

P.S. No previous experience required. And my apologies for troubling you with this advertisement. But I swear to you that there is a divine happiness on this solemn face of mine to be shared with others.'

BRAVADO

Z.M. felt that life was slipping away between her fingers. In her humility, she was forgetting that she herself was the source of life and creation. So she rarely left the house and refused all invitations. She was not the type of woman to notice if a man was interested in her unless he declared himself – whereupon she would express surprise and accept the fact.

In the afternoon – it was Spring, the first day of Spring – she went to visit a woman friend who spoke to her bluntly. How could a grown woman like her be so humble? How could she fail to notice that several men were interested in her? Surely she realized that there was nothing like a love affair for satisfying one's vanity? She also told her that she had watched her enter a room where everyone knew each other. And, as it happened, there was no one present who could be considered her equal. Yet she entered the room looking nervous and distracted, like a timid doe with its head lowered. 'You must keep your head up and be prepared to suffer because you are different, so totally different from others. You must accept that you cannot live a bourgeois existence, so when you walk into a room you must hold your head high.' 'Even when I enter a room full of people on my own?' 'Precisely. You don't need anyone to accompany you. You should be self-reliant.'

She remembered that later that afternoon there was to be some sort of cocktail party for the primary school-teachers who were on holiday. She remembered the new attitude she wished to adopt and deliberately avoided making any arrangement to go with another teacher, male or female. She would face the ordeal alone. She put on a dress she had scarcely worn, but could not summon her courage. Then – as she realized later – she applied far too much mascara and put on so much lipstick that her face looked just like a mask. She had transformed herself into some-one else. And that someone else was incredibly flamboyant, vain and self-assured. That someone else was everything she was not. But when the moment arrived to leave, she began to weaken. Could she be asking too much of herself? All dolled up and with this painted mask covering her face – ah, *persona*, how am I to abandon you in order to be myself at last! Lacking courage, she sat in the arm-chair in that sitting-room she knew so well, her heart pleading with her to stay at home. As if her heart could foresee that she would be badly hurt, she who was no masochist. In the end she extinguished the cigarette-of-courage, got up and left.

It struck her that the torture endured by people who are timid has never been fully described. Travelling in that speeding taxi, she died a little.

And then she suddenly found herself confronted by an enorm-ous room where there were probably lots of people but who were themselves somehow lost in that vast space where the cocktail party was in full swing like some modern ritual.

For how long would she be able to hold her head high? The mask was uncomfortable and she knew she looked much prettier

47

without make-up. But without make-up her soul would be exposed. And she could not take that risk or permit herself such luxury.

Smiling, she greeted this one and that one. But, as with all cocktail parties, conversation was impossible and when she came to her senses, she was all alone once more.

She saw a man who had once been her lover. And she thought to herself: no matter how much love he may have received since, I was the one who gave him my whole body and soul. The two of them looked at each other, scrutinized each other, he no doubt startled by that painted mask. She could think of nothing to say except to ask him if he was still her friend. He replied yes, for always.

Until she felt she could no longer stand there holding her head high. But how was she to cross that enormous room and reach the door? All on her own, like some fugitive? She mumbled her plight to one of the women teachers, who escorted her across that vast expanse to the door.

And in the shadows of that spring evening she was an unhappy woman. Yes, she was different. Of course, she was shy. She was certainly hypersensitive. And yes, she had seen a former lover. The shadows and perfume of spring. The world's heart was beating in her breast. She had always known how to inhale the smell of nature. Having finally found a taxi, she got in almost crying with relief, remembering how the same thing had happened to her in Paris, only worse. She travelled home as if fleeing from the world. But it was useless hiding: the truth is that she did not know how to live. At home she felt safe. She looked at herself in the mirror as she washed her hands and saw that *persona* attached to her face. That *persona* had the fixed smile of a clown. After washing her face, she discovered to her relief that her soul was once more laid bare. After taking a sleeping pill, she lay wide awake, waiting for sleep to come and promising herself that she would face no more risks without taking some precautions. The sleeping pill had a calming effect. And the endless night of dreams began.

A KNOWING SENSIBILITY

Sometimes people wishing to pay me a compliment tell me I am intelligent. And they are surprised when I tell them that being intelligent is not my strong point and that I am no more intelligent than other people. They then accuse me of being modest.

Of course I know about certain things. I was a bright student and intelligence has helped me to cope with certain situations. And like many others, I am capable of reading and understanding books which are generally considered to be difficult.

But often this so-called intelligence of mine is so limited that one would think I was stupid. People who refer to my intelligence are, in fact, confusing *intelligence* with what I would call a *knowing sensibility*. Now that is something I really do possess.

And notwithstanding my admiration for sheer intelligence, I find a knowing sensibility much more important when it comes to living with others and trying to understand them. Nearly everyone I know could be described as intelligent. They also happen to be sensitive. They can feel things and be deeply moved. I daresay this is the kind of sensibility I exercise when I write, or in my relationships with friends. I also exercise it when I come into superficial contact with certain people whose aura I can sense immediately.

I daresay this kind of sensibility, which is capable of stirring emotions and making one think even without using the mind, is a gift. And a gift which can be diminished with neglect or perfected if exercised to the full. I have a friend, for example, who is not simply intelligent but also extremely sensitive, an essential quality in her particular profession. As a result, she possesses what I would call a *knowing heart*, so knowing that it can guide her and others as reliably as radar itself.

THE DREAM

I do not understand dreams but there was one dream which seemed to have some meaning even though I could not understand it.

49

I dreamt that, having closed the door when I went out, I found on my return that it had merged with the walls and that even the outlines had disappeared. Faced with the choice of searching for traces or making another opening, I felt it would be easier to start digging. So I set to work, determined to find a way through. But no sooner had I made a hole than I realized that no one had entered here before. This was the first door that had ever been there. And although this narrow entrance was in the same house, it was as if I were seeing the house for the first time. And my bedroom was like the inside of a cube. I could now see that I had been living inside a cube.

At this point I woke up in a cold sweat. I had been having a nightmare despite the apparent calm surrounding the events in my dream. I cannot explain what those images might have symbolized. But the idea of going through one's 'first door' fascinates and terrifies me to the extent of becoming a nightmare in itself.

REBELLION

When love is too great it becomes futile: it can no longer be put to use and not even the person loved has the capacity for so much love. I became as bemused as any child when I realized that even in love we must be sensible and show restraint. Our emotional life, alas, is extremely bourgeois.

EAT UP, EAT UP

I do not know what happens in other people's homes. In mine, everybody talks about food. 'Is that cheese yours?' 'No, help yourself.' 'Is the cereal good?' 'Excellent!' 'Mummy, ask the cook to make a prawn cocktail. I can show her.' 'When did you learn to make a prawn cocktail?' 'I've eaten them lots of times and I know how they're made.' 'Today all I want to eat is a plate of pea soup and some sardines.' 'This meat is much too salty.' 'I don't feel hungry, but if you buy some peppers, I'll eat those.'

'No, Mummy, eating out in restaurants costs a lot of money. I'd rather eat at home.' 'What's for dinner this evening?'

No, my house is not metaphysical. No one is overfed in this house but everybody likes to eat well. As for me, I spend all my time opening and closing my purse to hand out money for yet more shopping. 'I'm eating out, Mummy, but keep me some dinner.' I am a firm believer in keeping the fire lit in preparation for any eventuality. That is what a home is all about. The sacred flame of love should always be lit and the pots kept standing on the stove. Frankly, we enjoy eating. And I can say with some pride that I keep a good kitchen. As well as eating, we discuss what is happening in Brazil and in the world at large, we argue about the clothes we consider suitable for certain occasions. We are a real family.

THE BIRTH OF PLEASURE (EXTRACT)

Pleasure brings so much pain that one almost prefers familiar sorrow to unaccustomed pleasure. True happiness cannot be explained or understood. It is best compared to the beginnings of some irretrievable disaster. This complete fusion is unbearably consoling – as if death were our greatest and final good, only it is not death, it is immeasurable life which comes to resemble the splendour of death. One must absorb happiness little by little – for it is emergent life. And let those lacking in strength cover each nerve with a protective membrane, with the membrane of death, in order to withstand life. That membrane might consist of some formal act of protection, of silence or some words without meaning. For pleasure is not to be toyed with. We are that pleasure.

IF IT WERE ME

Whenever I mislay an important document and cannot find it, I ask myself: If it were me and I wanted to keep a document in a safe place, where would I put it? Sometimes this works. But at other times, I am so harassed by the phrase 'If it were me', that the search for that document becomes secondary and I begin to think. Or rather, to feel.

And I feel anything but reassured. Try it: if it were you, what would you do? From the outset one feels a certain inhibition: the lie into which we have settled has just been ever so slightly disturbed. Yet I have read biographies of certain people who suddenly started to be their true selves and completely transformed their lives. I think if I were to become truly me, my friends would stop greeting me on the street, for even my appearance would have changed. In what way? I cannot say.

I cannot reveal half the things I would do if it were left to me. I believe I might even end up in jail for certain crimes. And if it were left to me, I should give away everything that is mine and entrust the future to the future.

'If it were me' seems to sum up the greatest risk we face in life, a new entrée into the unknown. Yet I cannot help feeling that, after those first mad moments of euphoria, we would finally experience the world. We would certainly experience all the sorrow of this world. And our own sorrow too, that sorrow we have learned to ignore. But sometimes we would also be overcome by sheer ecstasy, by that utter happiness we can barely sense. Wait, I believe I am already experiencing it as I begin to smile and feel that sense of inhibition which comes when one is confronted by something momentous.

A DIALOGUE

When I studied French I would have found it much more enjoyable if my text-book had been like the one I came across recently. It contains a dialogue between a Dog and his little Puppy. The Dog asks: 'Have you been studying hard?' The Puppy: 'Yes, father.' The Dog: 'Mathematics?' The Puppy: 'No.' The Dog: 'Science?' The Puppy: 'No.' The Dog: 'Geography, philosophy or history?' The Puppy: 'No.' The Dog: 'What have you been studying then?' The Puppy: 'Foreign languages.' The Dog: 'And which foreign language have you mastered?' The Puppy: 'Miaow.'

MY CHRISTMAS

When the children were small and had to be in bed long before midnight, we decided to forgo the traditional Christmas Eve Supper and have a celebration lunch on Christmas Day itself. The children eventually grew up but we continued to exchange gifts on Christmas Morning and celebrate over lunch.

With no supper to prepare on Christmas Eve, I had the evening to myself. But for the last three or four years I have fulfilled a solemn commitment on that evening.

This came about when I asked a girl, whom I did not know all that well, how I should spend my Christmas Eve. She immediately replied: 'Do what I do on Christmas Eve. I take enough pills to make me sleep for forty-eight hours.' I was astonished and intrigued, and asked her to explain. 'Christmas always brings back sad memories. My father and mother both died at Christmas. After they were gone, I could never bring myself to celebrate Christmas again.' I pointed out the danger of taking so many pills and warned her that, instead of sleeping for forty-eight hours, she might find herself sleeping forever.

Then I had an idea: perhaps in future we could spend Christmas Eve together and dine out in some restaurant. We could meet around eight o'clock in the evening and then she would see for herself how the city's restaurants were full of people with neither a home nor anything resembling a home where they might spend Christmas Eve. After dinner she drops me off at my apartment and then goes to fetch an aunt who always accompanies her to Midnight Mass. We agreed that we would share the bill for dinner and exchange presents: presents to remind us that we have each other.

But one Christmas my friend had to cancel our arrangement and, though knowing that I was not religious, she gave me a Holy Missal. I opened it to find that she had written inside: Pray for me.

The following September, a fire broke out in my apartment which left me so badly burned that I hovered between life and death for several days. My bedroom was completely destroyed. Plaster fell from the ceiling and walls, my furniture and books were reduced to ashes.

I shall make no attempt to explain what caused the fire. But strange to relate, my Missal remained intact, apart from some slight damage to the cover.

ANNUNCIATION

At home I have a painting by the Italian artist Savelli. I valued it all the more when I learned that he had been commissioned to design the stained-glass windows in the Vatican.

However much I study the painting, I never grow tired of it. On the contrary, I always find something new to admire.

In the painting, the Virgin Mary is seated beside a window and it is clear from her swollen belly that she is pregnant. The archangel at her side is watching her. And the Virgin, as if overwhelmed by the archangel's message, prophesying her destiny and that of future generations, raises her hand to her throat with surprise and anguish.

The angel, who has entered by the window is almost human: but those long wings remind us that angels can move from one place to another without touching the ground. Those wings are quite human: they appear to be made of flesh and the angel's face is that of a man.

This is the most exquisite and harrowing truth the world has to offer.

All human beings experience annunciation. With pregnant souls we raise our hands to our throats with surprise and anguish. As if each of us had learned at a given moment in life that we have a mission to fulfil.

That mission is by no means easy: each of us is responsible for the entire world.

LEARNING TO LIVE

Thoreau was an American philosopher whose profound thoughts cannot be summarized in a newspaper article, but he wrote many things which might help us to lead a more rational, useful and agreeable life with rather less anguish.

Thoreau found it distressing, for example, to watch his fellow-men devote all their energies to making money for some distant future. That people should give some thought to their future was no bad thing. But 'Do try to improve the present', he would exclaim. Before adding: 'We are living *now*.' Thoreau sadly observed: 'Men spend all their time hoarding treasures which will be eaten by worms, eroded by rust, or fall into the hands of thieves.'

The message is clear: do not sacrifice today for tomorrow. If you are unhappy at present, do something about it *now*, because we only exist from one *now* to the next.

Besides, if we examine our consciences, we can all remember moments that were lost nevermore to return. There are moments in all our lives which we regret having ignored, allowed to pass or refused, and that regret is as painful as the deepest sorrow.

Thoreau was anxious that we should lose no time in doing what we wish to do. All his life he preached and practised the need to waste no time in doing the things we believe to be important.

For example, he would urge all those young men and women who dreamed of being writers to start writing at once instead of making excuses that they were either too busy or lacking in talent and inspiration.

Nor did he have any patience with those people who waste so much time studying life that they never get down to living. He wrote: 'It is only when we discard all knowledge that we begin to know.'

And he offered these bold words of encouragement: 'Why not abandon ourselves to the torrent, why not open the flood-gates and put our whole mechanism into action?' Those words are enough to send the blood coursing through my veins. And *now*, dear friends, means *this very minute*.

Thoreau believed that fear prevented us from exploiting the present. And our lack of self-confidence. He once wrote: 'Public opinion is a feeble tyrant when compared with the low opinion we have of ourselves.' It is true: even those people who give the impression of being self-assured have such a low opinion of themselves that they are simply concealing their fear. And this worried Thoreau, who believed that 'how a man sees himself determines, or rather reveals, his destiny.'

And, surprising as it may seem, he would urge his readers to 'take pity on yourselves' whenever they were leading a life of quiet despair. He would counsel them not to be too hard on themselves at such moments. Fear, Thoreau argued, provokes unnecessary cowardice. In that situation, people should not judge themselves too harshly. 'I believe,' he wrote, 'that we should have much greater confidence in ourselves. Nature conforms as much to our weakness as to our strength.' Appalled at our common tendency needlessly to complicate matters, he repeated incessantly: 'Aim for greater simplicity! Aim for greater simplicity!'

Not so long ago, I opened a newspaper and in an article by someone whose name I have alas forgotten, I found several quotations attributed to Bernanos which truly complement those of Thoreau, whom the French writer probably never read.

The author of the article comments at one point that Bernanos was ever prepared to castigate the falseness of the so-called 'free world'. For he was seeking a '*Salvation achieved by taking risks without which life is worthless,* and not by senile withdrawal which is not only practised by the elderly but by all those who defend their positions whether ideological or religious.'

Bernanos, the article went on, considered greed in all its forms to be the greatest sin of all. 'Greed and apathy are destroying the world.' And 'both of these vices stem from egoism', the author of the article concludes.

Overcome with the joy of living, I repeat: *Salvation is achieved by taking risks without which life is worthless!*

Happy New Year.

MIRACULOUS LEAVES

No, miracles never happen to me. I sometimes hear people discuss them and that gives me hope. But it also makes me rebel: why do they never happen to me? Why do I only hear about them? For I have heard conversations about miracles such as the following: 'He told me that if such and such a word were to be spoken, some valuable object would smash into pieces.' The objects in my house are broken in much more humdrum fashion, usually by one of the maids. I have even come to the conclusion that I am one of those people who roll stones throughout the centuries. I mean rough stones, not the smoothly polished kind. Although I do have fleeting visions before falling asleep – could those be miraculous? But it has already been patiently explained to me that this phenomenon even has a name: *cidetismo*, which means being able to project unconscious images into the sphere of hallucination.

Not exactly a miracle. But what about certain coincidences? I experience them all the time, lines which keep coinciding and crossing one another, and as they cross they form a faint, fleeting point, so faint and fleeting, so subtle and elusive that simply to speak of it is like speaking of nothing.

But yes, I have experienced a miracle. Miraculous leaves. Walking along the street the wind deposits a leaf on my hair. The incidence of millions of leaves transformed into a single leaf, the incidence of millions of people reduced to one person – me. This has happened so frequently that I have modestly come to consider myself as someone *chosen* by the leaves. Furtively, I remove the leaf from my hair and slip it into my handbag, as if it were the tiniest of diamonds. Until one day, on opening my handbag, I find a withered leaf among the objects, shrivelled up and dead. I throw it away. I have no wish to keep a dead talisman as a souvenir. Besides, I know that new leaves will coincide with me.

One day a leaf grazed my eyelashes, and I thought to myself: *God* is being extremely delicate.

ALMOST

My taxi was approaching the tunnel which goes to Leme and Copacabana when I saw the Church of St Teresa of Lisieux. My heart beat faster: I recognized in the depths of my suffering soul that I might be able to find refuge in that church.

I asked the taxi-driver to stop, paid him and got out. With humility I penetrated the cool shadows inside the church. I sat down on a pew and there I remained. The church was completely deserted. The overpowering perfume of flowers filled the air and almost suffocated me. Little by little my inner turmoil began to subside into sad resignation: I was offering my soul in exchange for nothing. For it was not peace I felt. I was conscious that my world had crumbled only to leave me standing there, a bewildered, anonymous witness.

I gradually forgot my sorrow and started looking at the statues of saints. They had all been martyred, for that is the path both human and divine. They had all renounced a greater life in favour of a deeper, more bruised existence. None of them had taken advantage of the only life we possess. All of them had been foolish in the purest sense of the word. All had become immortal in order to answer our pleas for mercy. And why, dear God, was it so necessary to sacrifice our most legitimate desires? Why this mortification in life?

I looked round the empty church in search of an answer and saw a great coffin in the centre of the main nave. I got to my feet and drew near. Lying there was the effigy of St Teresa of Lisieux, her feet covered with flowers...I stood there staring.

Yet something puzzled me. Any statue I had ever seen of St Teresa depicted her as a young nun carrying flowers in her arms. But this St Teresa was so old that her skin looked like crinkled parchment. Her eyes were closed, her white hands crossed on her breast, the bright, red flowers burgeoning at her feet like a cry of life.

I realized at once that the effigy was not made of porcelain. What could it be then? It looked like wax. But wax would melt in summer or from the heat of the candles, so it could not be wax. I had never seen this material before. I knew that if I touched the effigy I would recognize the texture at once. When I was a little girl, Rosa our maid would get annoyed at my habit of touching everything and she used to say: 'This girl's eyes must be in her paws, she can only see things by touching them.'

Only by touching would I find out what that effigy was made of, but if the parish priest were suddenly to appear and catch me he would not be pleased. I looked around me. The church was still empty, so I furtively stretched out my hand to touch St Teresa's face.

But before I could do so, two girls entered the church. Heading in my direction, they came and joined me beside the coffin. Both girls had a worried expression. We stood there in silence. Until one of the girls said to the other:

– 'I wonder when that lot are going to turn up for gran's funeral. We can't keep her lying here in church forever!'

No sooner had she spoken than I understood. Feeling quite sick, I realized this was not St Teresa after all but the corpse of an old woman. I had been about to touch a corpse. Almost. Saved just in time, when the old woman's granddaughters unexpectedly arrived.

The very idea that I had almost touched a corpse made me go weak at the knees. I struggled to the nearest pew where I slumped down, feeling faint, and barely conscious. My heart was beating in all the wrong places: in my wrists, head and knees, as well as in my breast.

I could sense the pallor of my lips beneath my lipstick. Nor could I understand all this panic simply because I had almost touched a corpse – since death is part of life. Without death, life is incomprehensible, yet I had almost fainted upon touching what was also mine. I felt I had to get out of that church but could not stand. At last, after forcing myself, I struggled to my feet and staring straight ahead of me, I made for the door.

How can I explain what I saw outside? Already feeling dazed, I felt even more dazed as I walked out into the bright sunshine and bustling atmosphere with cars rushing past and everyone alive, so alive – only the old woman was dead although I myself had almost died after inhaling the perfume of those red flowers covering the feet of death.

Out on the street, I stood for ages inhaling the smell of life. It is a combination of flesh, of body odour and petrol, sea-breezes and perspiration under armpits: the smell of what still has to die.

I then hailed a taxi to take me home. I climbed in, pale and shaken, but as much alive as a fresh rose-bud.

SEA-BATHING

My father was a great believer in sea-bathing during the summer months. And how I loved those outings to the seaside at Olinda near Recife.

My father also believed that the best time for sea-bathing was before sunrise. Difficult to describe my sense of wonder as we boarded an empty tram in the dark in order to reach Olinda before the sun came up.

Even although I had been to bed, my heart would stay awake with sheer anticipation. Feeling terribly excited, I would jump out of bed just after four and awaken my sisters. We would dress quickly and leave without breakfast. Father believed one should always bathe on an empty stomach.

We would walk through the dark streets shivering in the early morning breeze. Then wait for the tram to arrive. Until at long last we could hear it rumbling towards us from a distance. I would sit right on the edge of my seat and begin to feel happy. Crossing the city in darkness brought feelings I would never again experience. Inside the tram itself there was more light as dawn began casting its first rays upon us and upon the world.

I looked at everything: the odd person on the street, the journey through the countryside with animals to be seen everywhere. 'Look, a real pig!' I once exclaimed, and that cry of ecstasy became a family joke and thereafter my sisters would often tease me by calling out: 'Look, a real pig!'

We passed magnificent horses just standing there in the fields, waiting for dawn.

I do not know about the childhood of others. But this trip to Olinda every morning gave me such happiness. And helped me believe in future happiness. My capacity for happiness was unfolding. And amidst the unhappiness of my childhood, I clung to this daily trip as if I were travelling to some enchanted island.

Dawn broke inside the tram. And my heart would beat faster as we approached Olinda. Having finally reached our destination, we jumped down and headed for the bathing-huts, trampling soil that was already a mixture of sand and weeds. We changed in the huts. And no body ever flowered like mine as I stepped onto the beach in anticipation of what awaited me. The sea at Olinda could be dangerous. The water was shallow for a bit, then there was a sudden drop of at least two metres.

There were other people there who believed in bathing before sunrise. And a lifeguard who, for a pittance, would accompany the women into the water. He would stretch out his arms and, supporting a woman on each arm, he would protect them from the strong waves.

The smell of the sea penetrated and intoxicated me. Seaweed floated on the surface. I can see just how difficult it is to express what that sea-bathing on an empty stomach meant to me in terms of pure life as the pale sun rose on the horizon. I become so emotional that I cannot write. The sea at Olinda was salty and rich in iodine. And I did what I would always do: holding my hands together in the form of a shell I would plunge them into the sea and bring some water to my lips. I drank that water each morning, in my desire to be united with the sea.

We never stayed for long. Once the sun had risen it was time to leave, because father always arrived early for work. We dressed quickly, our clothes impregnated with brine. My hair was matted with salt.

Then we stood in the wind, waiting for the tram arriving from Recife. Back inside the tram, my hair soon dried out, caked with salt. From time to time I would lick my arm to taste that thick coating of salt and iodine.

We reached home and only then did we have our breakfast. And when I remembered that I would be going back to the seaside next morning, I grew solemn at the thought of all that adventure and good fortune.

My father believed we should not shower immediately with fresh water but insisted that we allow the effect of the salt-water to work on our skin for several hours. And I was always reluctant to take a shower which would wash away the salt and iodine and remove all traces of the sea.

Who can restore that happiness? How can I renew that sensation of radiant innocence beneath the crimson glow of sunrise? Never more?

Never more.

Never.

ANGUISHED PROTECTION

She could not bear to look at her father when he was happy. For at such moments, this strong, embittered man would become entirely innocent. And so defenceless. Oh God, how he would forget he was mortal. And oblige her, a mere child, to cope with the heavy responsibility of knowing that even our most innocent animal pleasures die. At such moments when he forgot he was going to die, her father transformed her into the *Pietà*, the mother of man.

EARTH'S SWEETNESS

I do not know if many people have made this discovery – but I know that I have. I also know that *to discover land* is a platitude which has long been divorced from what it expresses. But everyone should try at some time or other to rediscover the sensation that underlies the expression: *to discover land*.

I once had this experience in Italy while making a train journey. It need not be Italy. It could even happen in Jacarepaguá. But this was in Italy. The train was speeding along and, after a sleepless night in the company of a Swedish woman who spoke nothing but Swedish and a miserable cup of stale coffee smelling of railway stations, suddenly we were passing through countryside. The sweet Italian countryside. It was early spring, the month of March. Nor does it have to be spring. It only has to be – earth. And for that matter, we all have earth under our feet. Yet it was so strange to feel oneself living on top of a living thing. When feeling nervous, the French say they are *sur le qui-vive*. We are perpetually on top of what is living.

And to earth we shall return. Oh, why were we not allowed to discover for ourselves that we shall return to the earth? We were warned before being able to discover this for ourselves. It cost me considerable effort to discover that: to earth we shall return. The discovery caused me no sadness, it was exciting. Just thinking about it made me feel myself surrounded by the earth's silence. By this silence which we foresee and seek out before time becomes a reality.

Somehow everything is made of earth. A precious substance. Its abundance does not make it any less strange to feel – for it is so very difficult to feel that everything is really made of earth. Such unity. And why not the soul as well? My soul is woven from the finest earth. And is the flower not made of earth?

And since everything is made of earth – what a wondrous,

inexhaustible future we possess. An impersonal future which surpasses us. Just as the human race surpasses us.

Earth showed her bounty by separating us into persons – we have repaid her by being nothing other than earth. We are immortal. And I feel moved and committed.

SO SENSITIVE

This was when she went through a crisis which seemed to have nothing to do with her life – a crisis of deep compassion. Her head was so narrow, her hair so neatly combed, that it could scarcely support all that compassion. She could not bring herself to look at a tenor while he was singing. She would turn her face away, pained, unable to bear it, unable to watch the singer being applauded. And sometimes she would press her gloved hands to her bosom, overcome with remorse. She suffered without recompense, without so much as feeling sorry for herself. Until one day she was cured like a wound which had healed.

It was this same woman, who suffered from sensitivity as if it were a disease, who chose a Sunday when her husband was away from home to go out and look for a seamstress who could do fine embroidery. It was more of an outing. What could anyone have against it? Besides, she often took a stroll. As if she were still a little girl walking along the pavement. Especially when she *felt* her husband was betraying her.

So off she went one Sunday morning to look for a seamstress. She found herself walking down a muddy track full of chickens and naked urchins. The seamstress lived in a house with a brood of starving children and a husband dying of tuberculosis. She told the seamstress what she wanted but the seamstress refused to make her a blouse that needed cross-stitching. She hated doing cross-stitching!

The woman left, outraged and puzzled by the seamstress's refusal. She *felt* almost unclean in the morning heat. And ever since childhood, she had always liked to think of herself as being scrupulously clean.

Back in her own house, she had lunch, then lay down in the semi-darkness of her bedroom, thinking mature thoughts devoid of any resentment. At least for once she was not *feeling* anything. Apart from this waiting. In semi-darkness.

A HAPPY MAN

Not so long ago I took a taxi and lit a cigarette. When we stopped at the traffic lights, the driver asked me:
– Have you a match by any chance, lady?
I handed him the box and as he returned it, but before he could thank me, without really thinking I said out of habit:
– Don't mention it.
Whereupon he replied:
– I haven't thanked you yet. Why did you say 'Don't mention it'?
– Oh, it's not important.
– Excuse me, but it is important. You should have waited until I thanked you before saying 'Don't mention it'.
– It really doesn't matter, I insisted, somewhat surprised.
– Of course it matters. His tone was that of a man defending sacred laws which had suddenly been violated. It was as if he had trodden on dangerous territory. I took a closer look at him, and saw just how little freedom he enjoyed and how much he needed to feel himself imprisoned, and others, too. I then tried to make amends by speaking to him gently:
– Really, young man, it isn't all that important...
But he was not to be appeased:
– Next time, lady, you wait until you're thanked.
There was nothing more to be done. His stubborn attitude was beginning to irritate me. For the rest of the journey we did not speak. And if ever there was mute silence, that was it.

LIGHTNING INTERVIEW WITH PABLO NERUDA (II)

– Does writing make the anguish of living more bearable?
– Yes, of course. Exercising your profession, if you enjoy it, is sheer bliss. Otherwise it is sheer hell.
– Who is God?

– Sometimes everybody. Always nothing.

– How can one best describe a human being?

– Political, poetic. And physical.

– What is your idea of a beautiful woman?

– One who embodies many women.

– Write down your favourite poem, that is to say your favourite poem at this very moment.

– I am writing. Can you spare me ten years?

– Where would you like to live if you were not living in Chile?

– You may think me foolish and excessively patriotic, but as I once stated in a poem:

> Were I to be born a thousand times over,
>
> This is where I would wish to be born.
>
> Were I to die a thousand times over,
>
> That is where I would wish to die...

– What has been your greatest satisfaction as a writer?

– To be able to read my verses to ordinary people in the remotest places: to miners in the desert regions of Northern Chile, to wool-shearers in the Magellan Straits in a shed smelling of unwashed wool, sweat and solitude.

– Are your moments of creative inspiration preceded by anguish or a state of grace?

– I experience no such feelings. Yet I would not call myself an insensitive person.

– Say something to surprise me.

– 748.

(And he really did surprise me with the unexpected resonance of those numbers.)

– What are your views on contemporary Brazilian poetry? Which of our poets do you prefer?

– I admire Drummond, Vinícius de Morais and your religious poet, Jorge de Lima, who reminds me of Claudel. I am not familiar with the work of younger poets in Brazil, that is to say poets after the generation of Paulo Mendes Campos and Geir Campos. One poem I greatly admire is 'O Defunto' [The Deceased] by Pedro Nava. I read it aloud to friends everywhere.

– How do you feel about literature of commitment?

– All literature is committed.

– Which of your own books do you like best?

– The next one.

65

– Can you explain why readers often refer to you as 'The Volcano of Latin America'?

– That is news to me. They have probably never experienced a volcano.

– What is your most recent poem?

– 'Fim do Mundo' [End of the World]. It is about the twentieth century.

– How does the creative process develop in your case?

– With pen and paper. At least that is the method I follow.

– Do you find reviews by the critics constructive?

– Perhaps for others, but not for the writer.

– Have you ever written a poem to order? Could you compose one now, however short?

– Lots of them. Some of my best poems. Here is the poem you asked for.

– Was the name Neruda accidental or inspired by Jan Neruda, the poet of the Czech freedom movement?

– No one has ever been able to verify this matter.

– What is the most important thing in the world?

– To try and make the world a worthy place for everyone, not just for the privileged few.

– What do you desire most of all for yourself?

– That depends on the hour of the day.

– What is love? Any type of love?

– The best definition is simply: Love is love.

– Have you suffered much for love?

– I am prepared to suffer even more.

– How long would you like to spend here in Brazil?

– A year, but much depends on my work.

And thus ended my interview with Pablo Neruda. I wish he had been prepared to say more. I could have carried on almost indefinitely even if only to be given the briefest of replies. He offered me a copy of his book: *Cien sonetos de amor* [One Hundred Love Sonnets]. And after writing my name he wrote: 'From your friend Pablo'. I, too, felt that we could have become close friends in more favourable circumstances. On the back cover of his book, the blurb says: 'Everything is manifest with an aura of innocent, pagan sensuality: love is seen as man's vocation and poetry as his mission.'

Those words sum up the essential qualities of Pablo Neruda.

CHARLATANS

A friend of mine once remarked that there is something of the charlatan in all of us. I had to agree. I can feel the charlatan inside me, haunting me. Without getting the better of me, firstly because it is not really true, secondly because I am almost sickened by my basic honesty. There is another thing which haunts me and makes me smile: bad taste. Oh, how tempted I feel to give in to bad taste. In what way? Well, here there is plenty of scope, endless scope. It can be anything from saying the wrong thing at the worst possible moment to uttering words of great beauty and truth which catch the other person off guard and leave him speechless. In what other way? Well, the way one dresses, for example. Not simply by overdressing. I cannot describe it but know exactly what I mean by dressing in bad taste. And when it comes to writing? Here there are great temptations because the dividing line between bad taste and truth is almost imperceptible. In writing, moreover, there is an accepted standard of good taste which is actually much worse than bad taste. Just to amuse myself or, as a simple experiment, I sometimes walk that thin line between the two.

Have I ever been a charlatan? Yes, indeed I have, while believing in all sincerity that I was doing the right thing. For example, I graduated in law, thus deceiving myself and others. Perhaps myself rather than others. Yet in all sincerity I decided to study law in the hope of reforming the Brazilian penal system one day.

The charlatan sells himself short. What was I about to say? It was on the tip of my tongue, but has now escaped me. Does the charlatan harm himself? That I do not know, but what is certain is that charlatanism can be very harmful. It disrupts the most solemn moments. It makes you wish you did not exist just when you exist at your most powerful. Alas, I cannot dwell too long on this subject.

Someone told me that a certain critic had described Guimarães Rosa and me as a couple of imposters, in other words, as a couple of charlatans. The critic in question won't understand a word of what I am saying here. For I am speaking of something very profound even if it appears otherwise and I give the impression of toying a little sadly with the subject.

67

ENIGMA

She was dressed in her maid's striped uniform but spoke as if she were the mistress of the household. She watched me climb the stairs laden with parcels, pausing to sit on the stairs because both elevators were out of order. The maid worked on the fifth floor, I lived on the seventh. She walked up with me carrying some of my parcels in one hand and the milk she had just purchased in the other. When we arrived at the fifth floor, she left the milk in her own apartment, using the servants' entrance, and then insisted on helping me to carry my parcels up to the seventh.

There was something very odd about her. She spoke like the mistress of the household, and even looked the part in spite of her maid's uniform. She knew that my apartment had caught fire, expressed her sympathy that I should have suffered so much and told me: Better to feel pain than nothing at all.

– There are certain people – she went on – who never even feel depressed, and have no idea what they are missing.

She then explained, to me of all people, that depression can be very revealing.

And – believe me – she finally added: 'Life must have a sting, otherwise one is not really living.'

Those were her very words and I must confess that I like the word *sting*.

SOCIAL COLUMN

It was a ladies' luncheon. Not only the hostess but every one of her guests seemed to be pleased that it was turning out so well. As if there were always the danger of suddenly discovering that the reality of dumb-waiters, flowers, and all this elegance was a little above them – not in terms of social status but simply: above them. Perhaps because they were simply women and not just ladies. But if they were all entitled to this ambience, they still seemed apprehensive about committing some *faux-pas*. A *faux-pas* is that moment when a certain reality comes to light.

The lunch was elegantly served with no hint of the anxious

preparations in the kitchen beforehand. When the guests arrived, all the tell-tale signs of frantic activity had been carefully removed.

Which did not prevent each of the guests from having some little reservation or other about the luncheon while pretending everything was perfect. One lady in particular had to show forbearance every time the waiter served her neighbour and lightly brushed against her coiffure, giving her the kind of fright which presages catastrophe. There were two waiters. The one who was serving this lady remained invisible as he served her from behind. And there is no reason to believe he caught a glimpse of her expression. Without any likelihood of their ever getting to know each other, a relationship was established through those periodic brushes with her coiffure. And he could sense it. Through that coiffure he could feel her mounting hatred until he himself began to feel enraged.

One must assume that every one of the guests had her own little moment of crisis during this formal gathering. Each of them must have sensed, however momentarily, this acute and imminent danger of their coiffure coming apart and throwing the luncheon into chaos.

The hostess exuded an air of calm authority which rather suited her. From time to time, however, she would forget she was being observed and adopt some surprising expressions: a sudden look of weariness or annoyance. And at one point – who knows what vague and anguished thought was passing through her mind – she stared quite blankly at her neighbour on the right who was speaking to her. The woman remarked: 'The landscape there is wonderful!' And the hostess, in a dreamy tone of voice mingling disquiet and complacency, heartily replied:

– 'Yes, you're right... isn't it lovely?'

The lady who enjoyed herself most of all was Mrs X, the guest of honour, who received so many invitations that she simply treated any luncheon party as lunch. With delicate gestures and completely at her ease, she devoured everything on that French menu with relish – spooning the food into her mouth and then looking round with avid curiosity – the vestiges of childhood.

But all the other guests felt ill at ease. Perhaps if they had tried a little less hard to appear so relaxed, they might have looked more natural. None of them had the courage. Every one of them

69

felt very unsure of herself, as if capable of making the most awful social blunder should she drop her guard. No: they were determined this should be the perfect luncheon.

Nor had they any way of being themselves without the odd moment of silence. And that was not allowed. For no sooner was some topic casually raised than they all pounced ferociously, prolonging the discussion until they all became reticent. And since they exploited every topic in the same fashion – for all of them were up to date with the latest topics – and since they agreed about everything, each topic renewed the possibility of further silence.

Mrs X, a huge woman, healthy as an ox and wearing flowers in her corsage, was fifty years old and recently married. Her ready, excitable laughter was that of a woman who had married late in life. All the others appeared to be of one mind in finding her absurd. And this relieved the tension a little. But she was too obviously absurd for comfort and there had to be something more to her – if only one's chatty neighbour would stop talking and give one time to examine Mrs X more closely. But no such luck. The chatter went on and on.

The worst part of it was that one of the women invited spoke only French. This created difficulties for Mrs Y. She took her revenge when the foreign lady uttered one of those expressions which can be repeated word for word by way of reply with only the slightest change of intonation. '*Il n'est pas mal*', said the foreigner. Whereupon Mrs Y, confident that she was pronouncing it correctly, repeated the expression aloud, with all the surprise and satisfaction of someone who has suddenly discovered: '*Ah, il n'est pas mal, il n'est pas mal.*' For as another guest, who was not foreign and discussing something else, remarked: '*C'est le ton qui fait la chanson.*'

As for Mrs K, dressed all in grey, she was ever ready to listen and make conversation. She did not mind in the least being somewhat *passée*. She had discovered that discretion was her most effective weapon and exercised it with a certain freedom. 'I'm not going to change my little ways for anyone', those smiling maternal eyes of hers were saying. She had even established a dress code to highlight her discretion, as in the story about the spies who wore badges to show they were spies. And so she dressed in what were unmistakably discreet colours. And her jewellery was no less discreet. Discreet women form a kind of sisterhood. They recognize each other at a glance, and in praising each other, they are praising themselves.

The opening discussion was about dogs. And when the conversation ended with liqueurs after lunch, as if constrained by some mysterious force to close the circle, they were still discussing dogs. Their kind hostess had a dog called José. A name no member of the sisterhood of discreet women would ever have dreamed of giving her dog. They would have chosen a name like Rex, and, even then, at some discreet moment, hasten to explain: 'My little son gave the dog its name.' Members of the sisterhood of discreet women frequently refer to their children as if they were adorable little tyrants around the house. 'My son thinks I look terrible in this dress.' 'My daughter has booked seats for a concert but I don't think I'll go. She can always take her father.' As a rule, the members of the sisterhood of discreet women are only invited because of their husband, almost certainly some influential business man, or their late father, who was probably a famous lawyer.

They rise from the table. Some of the guests fold their napkins before getting to their feet as they were taught to do as children. Those who just leave them lying there unfolded have a theory about leaving them unfolded.

A cup of coffee is welcome after all that rich food, but the liqueurs begin to mix with the wines imbibed earlier, making the guests feel slightly breathless and hazy. Those who smoke, smoke. Those who do not, do not. But they all smoke. The weary hostess never stops smiling. At long last, the guests take their leave. It is already late. Some of the women return home, their afternoon spoiled. Others decide, since they are all dressed up for the occasion, to visit a friend. Who knows, perhaps to offer their condolences. It's the same the world over, people eat and people die.

On the whole, the luncheon was perfect. My turn to offer lunch next time? Not on your life.

REBELLION

When they removed the stitches from my hand after they had operated between the fingers, I screamed with pain. I screamed with pain and anger because the pain was an insult to my physical integrity. But I was no fool. I took advantage of my pain and screamed at the past and present. I even screamed at the future, dear God.

SILKEN THREADS

A friend of mine who thought Henry James was a marvellous writer suggested that I should start reading his work. Henry James can be hermetic yet at the same time so lucid. In quoting from one of his essays, I hope my readers won't find me hermetic. That would be most unfortunate. But there are certain things I feel I must express and they are not easy. I suggest you read the following passage several times:

> Experience is never limited and it is never complete; it is an immense sensibility, a kind of huge spider's web of the finest silken threads, suspended in the chambers of consciousness and catching every air-borne particle in its tissue. It is the very atmosphere of the mind; and when the mind is imaginative – more so when it happens to be that of a man of genius – it takes to itself the faintest hints of life, it converts the very pulses of the air into *revelations*.

Far from being a genius, how many revelations, how many air-borne particles I find myself catching. And that huge spider lurks in the chamber of my consciousness. Ah, how wonderful life is with its ensnaring webs.

Warn me if I start becoming too personal. That is a weakness of mine. But I am also objective. So much so that I can transform those subjective threads of the spider into objective words. Any word, for that matter, is an object and therefore objective. Moreover you may be certain that one does not have to be intelligent: the spider is not intelligent, and as for words, words are inevitable. Do you get my meaning? Never mind. Simply accept what I am offering you. Accept me with silken threads.

NON-ACCEPTANCE

Once she started ageing she preferred to remain indoors. I am convinced she actually thought it was in bad taste to be seen out and about after reaching a certain age: the air outside was so fresh and pure, her body so repugnant with its flabbiness and wrinkles. The sea in particular was so clear that it looked naked. Others did not mind her presence in public for everyone accepts that people grow old. But she herself found it distasteful. How anxiously she tried to restore the figure she had lost, distress written in those eyes which were still bright.

Another thing: in the old days her face did not betray her thoughts, only her features were accentuated. Now, when she involuntarily glances at herself in the mirror, she almost cries out in horror: I was thinking no such thing! Although it was impossible and hopeless trying to decide what her expression conveyed, just as it was impossible and hopeless trying to explain what she herself was thinking.

All around her things were fresh, a story was about to unfold, and there was wind, wind...Meanwhile her belly sagged and her legs thickened, and her hair had settled into natural drabness.

PERILOUS NIGHT

I swear to you – the drawing-room was in darkness – but the music drew me to the centre of the room – something was on the alert there – the entire room darkened within darkness – I found myself in shadows – felt that, notwithstanding the darkness, the room was bright – I took refuge in fear – just as I once took refuge in you – and what did I find? simply that light was filling the room without making things any brighter – and that I was trembling amidst this difficult light – believe me, even though I cannot explain it – I am something perfect and fragile – as if I had never seen a flower – and it frightened me to think of that flower as the soul of someone who had just died – and I watched that bright centre which kept moving – and the flower disturbed me as though there were a dangerous bee hovering round it – a bee paralysed with terror before the ineffable beauty of that quivering flower – and then the flower became paralysed before the bee sweetened by the flower it sucked in darkness – believe me, even if I cannot understand – an inevitable ritual was being enacted – the room was filled by a penetrating smile as the shadows began to disperse – no evidence remained – I can offer no proof – I am my only proof – that is all I can tell you about this illness of mine which has landed me in hospital and which others do not understand – I do not know how anyone can be frightened by a rose – they experimented with violets which are somewhat more delicate – but I was afraid – they smelled like flowers in a graveyard – and the flowers and bees are already calling me – I cannot resist their call – I truly desire to go. Do not mourn my death. I have decided what I must do here in hospital. My love, it will not be suicide. I value life much too dearly and therefore would never contemplate suicide. I am going, but in order to become fleeting light, to feel the taste of honey and, if so ordained, to become a bee.

UNWELCOME COMPASSION

Y with her great wisdom and understanding, trying hard not to be human, in the sense that to be human also means having faults and outbursts of temper. She tries hard to understand by forgiving others. That heart is bereft of me because it expects me to be admirable. Everyone turns to her when they have a problem she, 'the self-appointed comforter', understands, understands, understands. But my great pride dictates that I should be found on the street.

SHARING BREAD

It was Saturday and we had been forced into accepting an invitation to dinner. But each of us valued our Saturday evening far too much to waste it on a couple whom we found rather boring. Each of us had experienced happiness at some time or other and been left with the mark of desire. As for me, I desired

74

everything. And there we were, trapped, as if our train had been derailed and we had been left stranded among strangers. No one there loved me and I had no love for them. As for my Saturday – which swayed outside my window amongst acacias and shadows – I preferred to fritter it away, to hold that lost Saturday in my clenched fist and crumple it like a handkerchief. Waiting for dinner to be served, we drank dispiritedly, toasting resentment. The next day would be Sunday. I have no desire to be with you, our dry expression was saying, as we slowly blew smoke from a dry cigarette. The meanness of not sharing our Saturday gradually began to erode and advance like rust to the point where any happiness would have been an affront to greater happiness.

Only the mistress of the household did not appear to prefer to spend her Saturday in better company. She, whose heart had nevertheless known other Saturdays. How could she have forgotten that one wants more and more? She did not so much as lose her patience with this mixed gathering of people, dreamy and resigned, who sat there in her house as if waiting for the first train to leave – any train – rather than remain in that empty station or curb that horse which was straining at the bit in its anxiety to gallop off and join other horses.

We finally moved into the dining-room for a supper without the blessing of hunger. The sight of that table took us by surprise. This could not be for us...It was a table for men of good will. Who were the missing guests for whom this was really intended? We ourselves. So that woman gave of her best without discrimination? She happily washed the feet of the first stranger to appear. Fidgeting awkwardly, we stood there staring.

The table was covered with solemn abundance. Sheaves of corn had been piled up on the white table-cloth. And there were red apples, enormous yellow carrots, round tomatoes with skins ready to burst, juicy green courgettes, pineapples of a malign ferocity, tranquil, golden oranges, gherkins bristling like porcupines, cucumbers stretched tight over watery flesh, hollow red peppers that made our eyes smart – were all entangled in moist whiskers of maize, tinged with crimson like outlined lips. And bunches of grapes. The purplest of black grapes anxiously awaiting the moment to be crushed. Nor did they mind who should crush them – like the mistress of the household in times gone by. The tomatoes were not round for anyone: for the atmosphere, the circular atmosphere. Saturday was for anyone who might turn up. And the orange would sweeten the tongues of the first to arrive. Beside the plate of each unwanted guest, the woman who washed the feet of strangers had placed – without choosing or loving us – a sheaf of wheat, a bunch of fiery radishes or a red slice of water-melon with its glossy seeds. All broken up by the Spanish acidity of green lemons. In the earthenware jugs there was milk, as if it had been transported across a rocky desert with the goats. Wine that was almost black after all that pressing, shuddered in earthenware bowls. Everything was set before us. Everything cleansed of perverse human desire. Everything as it is and not as we would wish it to be. Simply existing and intact. Just as a field exists. Just as mountains exist. Just as men and women exist, but not us with our greed. Just as Saturday exists. Simply existing. It exists.

On behalf of nothing, it was time to eat. On behalf of no one, it was good. There was no dream. And along with the night, we gradually became anonymous, growing, rising above the height of possible existence. Then, like landed aristocracy, we accepted that table.

There was no holocaust: everything there was as anxious to be eaten as we were to eat it. Putting nothing aside for the following day, there and then I offered up my feelings to whatever had provoked them. This was a moment of existence for which I had not paid in advance with anxious waiting, the hunger that comes as we raise the food to our lips. For now we felt hungry, with an all-consuming hunger which took in everything, even the very crumbs. Those who were drinking wine kept a watchful eye on the milk. Those who were slowly sipping milk could taste the wine the others were drinking. And outside, the presence of God amongst the acacias. Acacias which existed. We ate. Like someone giving water to a horse. The carved meat was passed round. Any exchanges were homely and down to earth. No one spoke ill of anyone because no one spoke well of anyone. It was a harvest reunion and any social niceties were dispensed with. We ate. Like a horde of locusts, we gradually covered the earth. As absorbed as those who cultivate existence, by planting and harvesting, by living and dying and eating. I ate with the honesty of someone who does not belie what he is eating. I ate that food and not its name. God was never possessed by what He is. Brusque, contented and austere, the food was saying: eat, eat and share among you. Everything there was mine. This was the father's table. I ate without affection, I ate without any feelings of compassion. And without giving way to hope. I ate without any trace of regret. And I was wholly deserving of that food. For I cannot always be my brother's keeper, nor can I be my own keeper. Alas, I no longer love myself. I have no desire to forge life because existence already exists. It exists like the ground we tread. Without a word of love. In total silence. But your satisfaction is akin to mine. We are strong and we eat. Bread is love between strangers.

SUPERNATURAL LIFE

After some reflection I came to the rather startling conclusion that thoughts are as supernatural as past history after death. I simply discovered to my surprise that thinking is unnatural. I then reflected a little more and discovered that I have no day-to-day existence. It is a life-to-life existence and life is supernatural.

THE EGG AND THE CHICKEN (I)

In the morning the egg is lying on the kitchen table.

I see the egg at a single glance. I immediately perceive that I cannot be simply seeing an egg. Seeing an egg is always in the present: No sooner do I see the egg than I have seen an egg, the same egg which has existed for three thousand years. The very instant an egg is seen, it becomes the memory of an egg. The only person to see an egg is someone who has seen it before. Like a man who, in order to understand the present, must have had a past. Upon seeing the egg, it is already too late: an egg seen is an egg lost. A vision that passes like a sudden flash of lightning. To see the egg is the promise of being able to see the egg again one day. A brief glance which cannot be divided. Does thought intervene? No, there is no thought: there is only the egg. Vision is the essential faculty and, once used, I shall cast it aside. I shall remain without the egg. The egg has no *itself*. Individually, it does not exist.

It is impossible actually to see the egg. The egg is supravisible just as there are supersonic sounds the ear can no longer hear. No one is capable of seeing the egg. Can the dog see the egg? Only machines can see the egg. The windlass sees the egg. In ancient times an egg settled on my shoulder. Nor can anyone feel love for the egg. My love for the egg is suprasensitive and I have no way of knowing that I feel this love. One is unaware of loving the egg. In ancient times I was the depository of the egg and I walked on tiptoe in order not to disturb the egg's silence. When I died, they carefully removed the egg inside me: it was still alive. Just as we ignore the world because it is obvious, so we fail to see the egg because it, too, is so obvious. Does the egg no longer exist? It exists at this moment. Egg, you are perfect. You are white. To you I dedicate this beginning. To you I dedicate this first moment.

To the egg, I dedicate the Chinese nation.

The egg is something in suspense. It has never settled. When it comes to rest, it is not the egg that has come to rest. A surface has formed beneath the egg. I vaguely glance at the egg in the kitchen in order not to break it. I take the greatest care not to understand it. It cannot be understood and I know that if I were to understand the egg, it could only be in error. To understand is proof of error. Never to think about the egg is one way of having seen it. Could it be that I know about the egg? Of course I know about it. Like this: I exist, therefore I know. What I do not know about the egg is what really matters. What I do not know about the egg gives me the egg itself. The Moon is inhabited by eggs ...

The egg is an exteriorization: to have a shell is an act of giving. The egg exposes the kitchen. It transforms the table into a slanting plane. The egg exposes everything. Anyone who fathoms the egg, who can penetrate the egg's surface, is seeking something else: that person is suffering from hunger.

The egg is the chicken's soul. The awkward chicken. The stable egg. The startled chicken. The placid egg. Like a missile suspended in mid-air. For the egg is an egg in space. An egg

78

against a blue background. Egg, I love you. I love you like something that does not even know it loves another thing. I do not touch it. It is the aura of my fingers that sees the egg. I do not touch it. But to devote myself to the vision of the egg would be to renounce my earthly existence which I continue to need, both yolk and white. Can the egg see me? Is it trying to fathom me? No, the egg only sees me. And it is immune to that painful understanding. The egg has never struggled to be an egg. The egg is a gift. It is invisible to the naked eye. From egg to egg, one reaches God Who is invisible to the naked eye. Perhaps the egg was once a triangle which turned so much in space that it ended up being oval. Is the egg basically a sealed jar? Perhaps the first jar to be modelled by the Etruscans? No. The egg originated from Macedonia. There it was designed, the fruit of the most deliberate spontaneity. On the sands of Macedonia a mathematician traced it out with a rod in one hand. And then erased it with his bare foot.

An egg needs careful handling. That is why the chicken is the egg's disguise. The chicken exists so that the egg may traverse the ages. This is what a mother is for. The egg lives like a fugitive because it is always ahead of its time: it is more than contemporary: it belongs to the future. Meanwhile the egg will always be revolutionary. It lives inside the chicken so that no one may call it white. The egg is really white but must not be called white. Not because this would harm the egg which is immune from danger, but those people who state the obvious by describing the egg as white renege on life. To call something white which is white can destroy humanity. Truth is always in danger of destroying humanity. A man was once accused of being what he was and referred to as That Man. They were not lying: he was man. But we have not recovered since. This is the universal law so that we may go on living. One may say 'a pretty face' but anyone who says 'face' will die for having exhausted the subject.

In time the egg became the egg of a chicken. It is not. But once adopted, the surname is used. One should say 'the egg of the chicken'. If people simply say 'egg', the topic is exhausted and the world goes back to being naked. An egg is the most naked thing in existence. Regarding the egg, there is always the danger that we may discover what could be termed beauty, in other words, its utter veracity. The egg's veracity has no semblance of truth. If its beauty were to be discovered, people might try to make it rectangular. The egg is in no danger, it would not become rectangular. (Our guarantee is that it cannot: and that is the egg's great strength: its supremacy stems from the greatness of being incapable, which spreads like reluctance.) But as I was saying, the egg would not become rectangular and anyone struggling to make it rectangular would be in danger of losing his own life. And so the egg puts us at risk. Our advantage is that the egg is invisible to the vast majority of people. And as for the initiated, the initiated conceal the egg as in a freemasonry.

As for the chicken's body, the chicken's body is the clearest attempt to prove that the egg does not exist. Because one look at the chicken is enough to see that the egg could not possibly exist.

And what about the chicken?

The egg is the chicken's great sacrifice. The egg is the cross the chicken bears in life. The egg is the chicken's unattainable dream. The chicken loves the egg. She does not know that the egg truly exists. Were she to know she has an egg inside her, would she be saved? Were she to know she has an egg inside her, would she lose her function as a chicken? To be a chicken is the chicken's only chance of surviving mentally. Survival means salvation. For it would appear that the act of living does not exist. Living ends in death. While the chicken goes on surviving. And to survive is to keep up the struggle against mortal existence. This is what it means to be a chicken. The chicken always looks ill at ease.

The chicken must not know she is carrying an egg. Otherwise she might be saved as a chicken – although there is no guarantee – but at the same time she would lose her egg in a premature birth to rid herself of that exalted ideal. Therefore she does not know. The chicken only exists on behalf of the egg. She had a mission to fulfil which she enjoyed. And this was the chicken's undoing. Enjoyment has nothing to do with birth. To enjoy being alive is painful.

As for what came first, it was the egg that discovered the chicken would make the perfect disguise. The chicken was not even summoned. The chicken is directly chosen. She exists as in dreams. She has no sense of reality. She gets nervous because people are always interrupting her daydreams. The chicken is one great slumber. She suffers from some strange malaise. Her strange malaise is the egg. She cannot explain: 'I know the fault lies with me'. She calls her life a mistake. 'I no longer know what I feel', etc.

What clucks all day long inside the chicken is etc. etc. etc. The chicken has considerable resources of inner life. If truth be told, inner life is all she possesses. Our vision of her inner life is what we refer to as *chicken*. The chicken's inner life consists of behaving as if she understood. The slightest threat of danger and she screeches her head off. All this simply to ensure that the egg does not break inside her. The egg which breaks inside the chicken has the appearance of blood.

The chicken watches the horizon.

THE EGG AND THE CHICKEN (II)

The chicken watches the horizon. As if she were watching an egg slowly advance from the distant horizon. Apart from being a means of transport for the egg, the chicken is stupid, idle and short-sighted. How can the chicken understand herself when she is everything the egg is not? The egg is still that same egg which originated in Macedonia. But the chicken is always a recent tragedy. She is continuously being designed anew. Yet no more apt form has been found for the chicken. As my neighbour answers the telephone, he absentmindedly sketches a chicken with his pencil. But nothing can be done for the chicken: it is in her nature to be of no use to herself. And since her destiny is more important than the chicken herself and her destiny is the egg, her private life is of no interest to us.

The chicken neither recognizes the egg when it is still inside her nor when it has been laid. When the chicken sees the egg, she thinks she is confronting the impossible. And suddenly I see the egg in the kitchen and all I see there is food. I do not recognize it. My heart is beating fast. Something is changing inside me. I can no longer see the egg clearly. Apart from each individual egg, apart from the egg one eats, the egg no longer exists for me. I can no longer bring myself to believe in an egg. I find it more and more difficult to believe, I am weak and dying.

81

Farewell. I have been looking at an egg for so long that it has hypnotized me and sent me to sleep.

The chicken had no desire to sacrifice her life. She who had chosen to be 'happy'. She who had failed to perceive that if she were to spend her life designing the egg inside herself like an illuminated manuscript, she would be doing all that could be expected of her. She remained true to herself. She who thought her feathers were to cover her precious skin, unaware that those feathers were only intended to lighten her burden while she carried the egg, because the chicken's deep suffering might put the egg at risk. She who thought satisfaction was a gift rather than a ploy to keep her totally distracted until the egg had been formed. She who did not know that 'I' is only one of the words people jot down on paper when answering the telephone, a mere attempt to find some more convenient form. She who thought that *I* means to possess a *selfness*. The chickens in greatest danger of harming the egg are those who pursue a relentless *I*. Their *I* is so persistent that they cannot pronounce the word egg. But who knows, perhaps this is precisely what the egg needs. Because if they were not so distracted and were to pay closer attention to the great life forming inside them, they might disturb the egg.

I began discussing the chicken, yet for some time now I have said nothing about the chicken. I am still talking about the egg. Only to realize that I do not understand the egg. All I understand is a broken egg: broken in the frying pan. And this is how I indirectly pledge myself to the egg's existence. My sacrifice is to reduce myself to my inner self. I have concealed my destiny with my joys and sorrows. Like those in the convent who sweep floors and wash linen, serving without the glory of any higher office, my task is to live my joys and sorrows. It is essential that I should possess the modesty of living. In the kitchen I take one more egg and break its shell and form. And from this very moment the egg no longer exists. It is most important that I should be kept occupied and distracted. I am essentially one of those who renege. I belong to the freemasonry of those who, once having seen the egg, reject it as a form of protection. Anxious to avoid destruction, we destroy ourselves. Agents in disguise and assigned to discreet enquiries, we occasionally recognize each other. A certain manner of looking, a certain way of shaking hands, help us to recognize each other, and we call this love.

Then there is no further need for disguise. Though one does not speak, one does not hear either; though one may be telling the truth, there is no further need for pretence. Love prospers, especially between a man and woman, when one is allowed to share a little more. Few people desire true love because love shakes our confidence in everything else. And few can bear to lose all their other illusions. There are some who opt for love in the belief that love will enrich their personal lives. On the contrary: love is poverty, in the end. Love is to possess nothing. Love is also the deception of what one believed to be love. And it is not a prize likely to make one conceited. Love is not a prize. It is a state conceded only to those who would otherwise contaminate the egg with their private sorrow. This does not make an honourable exception of love. It is conceded precisely to those unworthy agents who would spoil everything unless they were allowed some vague intuition.

All the agents enjoy many advantages in order to ensure the egg is formed. There is no cause for envy, because even the worst of the conditions imposed on some agents happen to be the ideal conditions for the egg. As for the satisfaction of the agents, they receive that, too, without conceit. They quietly savour any satisfaction. This is the sacrifice we make so that the egg may be formed. We have been endowed with a nature which has a considerable capacity for satisfaction, which helps to make satisfaction less painful. There are instances of agents who commit suicide: they discover that the handful of instructions at their disposal are insufficient and sense a lack of support. There was the case of the agent who publicly revealed his identity because he could not bear not to be understood, just as he found it intolerable not to be respected by others. He died after being run over as he was leaving a restaurant. There was another agent who did not even need to be eliminated: he slowly burned himself up in disgust, a disgust which overwhelmed him when he discovered that the few instructions he had been given explained nothing. Another agent was also eliminated because he thought 'the truth should be spoken courageously', and he set about searching for that truth. People say he died in the name of truth, but in fact he simply obscured truth, he was so ingenuous. His seeming courage was mere folly and his desire for loyalty was

83

naïve. He had failed to understand that loyalty is not something pure, that to be loyal is to be disloyal to all the rest. These extreme cases of death are not provoked by cruelty. There is a job to be done which one might term cosmic, and unfortunately individual cases cannot be taken into consideration. For those who succumb and become individuals, there are instructions, there is charity, there is an understanding which does not discriminate between motives – our human life, in short.

THE EGG AND THE CHICKEN (III)

The eggs sizzle in the frying pan and, lost in a dream, I prepare breakfast. Without any sense of reality, I call the children who jump out of bed, draw up their chairs and start eating and the work of the day which has just dawned begins, with shouting and laughter and food, the white and the yolk, happiness amidst squabbles, the day is our salt and we are the salt of the day, life is quite tolerable, life occupies and distracts, life provokes laughter.

It makes me smile in my mystery. The mystery of my being which is simply a means, and not an end, has given me the most dangerous freedom of all. I am not stupid and I use it to my advantage. I even do considerable harm to others. I take advantage of the phoney job they have given me to conceal my identity and turn it into my real occupation. I have even misused the money they pay me on a daily basis to make life easier while the egg is being formed. Having changed the money on the black market, I have misused it and only recently bought shares in a brewery which has made me a rich woman. I still refer to all this as the essential modesty of living. They have also allowed me time so that the egg may form inside me at its leisure but I have frittered away my time in illicit pleasures and sorrows, completely forgetting about the egg. That is my simplicity as a human agent.

Or is this precisely what they wanted to happen so that the egg may be formed? Is this freedom a coercion? For I am now beginning to see that every error on my part has been exploited. My grievance is that in their eyes I count for nothing, I am simply useful. With the money they pay me I have started drinking.

No one knows how you feel inside when you are hired to pretend you are a traitor and you end up believing in your own betrayal. A job which consists of forgetting day after day. Being expected to feign dishonour. My mirror no longer reflects a face which can even be called my own. Either I am an agent or this is truly betrayal. But I sleep the sleep of the just in the knowledge that my futile existence does not impede the march of infinite time. On the contrary: it would appear that I am expected to be utterly futile, that I should even sleep the sleep of the just. They want me occupied and distracted, by whatever means. For with my wandering thoughts and solemn foolishness I might impede what is happening inside me. Strictly speaking, I myself have only served to impede. The notion that my destiny exceeds me suggests that I might be an agent. At least, they might have allowed me to perceive as much, for I am one of those people who do a job badly unless I am allowed some insight. They made me forget what I had been allowed to perceive, but I still have this vague notion that my destiny exceeds me and that I am the instrument of their work.

In any case, I could only be the instrument because the work could never be mine. I have already tried to establish myself in my own right without success; my hand has never stopped trembling to this day. Had I insisted a little more, I should have lost my health for good. Since then, after that abortive experience, I have tried to reason as follows: I have already received a great deal and they have made me every possible concession. And the agents, far better than me, have also worked only for what they did not know. And with the same meagre instructions and, like me, they were modest civil servants or otherwise. I have already received a great deal. Sometimes overcome with emotion at being so privileged yet without showing any gratitude! My heart beating with emotion, yet without understanding anything! My heart beating confidently, yet leaving me baffled.

But what about the egg? This is precisely one of their little ruses. As I was talking about the egg, I forgot about the egg. 'Keep on talking, keep on talking,' they told me. And the egg remains completely protected by all those words. 'Keep on talking' is one of their guiding rules. I feel so weary.

Out of devotion to the egg I forgot about it. Forgetfulness born out of necessity. Forgetfulness born out of self-interest. For the egg is an evasion. Confronted by my possessive veneration, the egg could withdraw never to return and I should die of sorrow. But suppose the egg were to be forgotten and I were to make the sacrifice of getting on with my life and forgetting about it. Suppose the egg proved to be impossible. Then perhaps – free, delicate, without any message whatsoever for me – the egg would move through space once more and come up to the window I have always left open. And perhaps with the first light of day the egg might descend into our apartment and move serenely into the kitchen. As I illuminate it with my pallor.

FIVE STORIES ON A SINGLE THEME

This story could be called *The Statues*. Another possible title would be *Murder*. Or even *How to get rid of Cockroaches*. So I shall tell at least three stories and all of them true, because none of the three will contradict the others. Although they constitute one story, they could become a thousand and one, were I to be granted a thousand and one nights.

The first story, *How to get rid of Cockroaches*, begins like this: I was complaining about the cockroaches. A woman heard me complain. She gave me a remedy for killing them off. I was to mix together equal quantities of sugar, flour and plaster of Paris. The flour and sugar would attract the cockroaches, the plaster of Paris would dry up their insides. I followed her advice. The cockroaches died almost immediately.

The next story is really the first, and is called *Murder*. It begins like this: I was complaining about the cockroaches. A woman heard me complain. The remedy is prepared. And then murder ensues. The truth is that I had only complained in abstract terms about the cockroaches for they were not even mine: they came from the ground floor and climbed into our apartment through the pipes in the building. It was only when I prepared the mixture that they became mine, too. On our behalf, therefore, I began to measure and weigh the ingredients with somewhat greater concentration. I was gripped by a vague sense of rancour, by a sense of outrage. During the day the cockroaches were invisible and no one would have believed in the hidden evil that was invading

86

our tranquil household. But if the cockroaches, like some dark secret, slept by day, there I was preparing their nightly poison. Meticulous and eager, I prepared the elixir of prolonged death. A nervous fear and my own guilty secret guided me. Now I chillingly desired only one thing: to kill every cockroach in existence. Cockroaches crawl up the pipes while weary humans dream. And now the mixture was ready, white as white could be. As if I were dealing with cockroaches as wily as myself, I cautiously spread the powder which seemed to have become part of my nature. Lying there in bed in the silence of night, I could imagine those cockroaches climbing up one by one into the kitchen where darkness slumbered, a solitary towel watching from the clothes-line. I awoke hours later, startled at having overslept. Dawn had broken. On a nearby hill a cockerel crowed.

This third story I am now about to tell is entitled *The Statues*. It opens with my complaint about the cockroaches. Then the same woman turns up. And so it goes on until I wake up at first light feeling drowsy and make my way to the kitchen. The pantry floor looks even more drowsy with its tiled perspective. And in the shadows of dawn, there is a purplish hue which distances everything. Looking down, I see blobs of white and shadows at my feet: a multitude of rigid statues scattered everywhere. Cockroaches which had petrified from the core outwards. Some are lying upside down. Others arrested in the midst of some movement which they will never complete. In the mouths of some of the cockroaches there are still traces of white powder. I am the first person to see dawn breaking over Pompeii. I know what this night has been. I am aware of the orgy enacted in the dark. The plaster of Paris must have hardened gradually in many of them as in some vital process, and the cockroaches, with increasingly painful movements, must have eagerly intensified the night's frenzied pleasures as they tried to escape from their insides. Until they finally turned to stone with innocent terror and an expression, but such an expression, of sorrowful reproach. Others, suddenly assailed by their own core, unaware that their insides were turning to stone, suddenly crystallized like the truncated phrase: I love... Invoking the name of love in vain, the cockroaches sang on a summer's night. While that cockroach over there, the one with its brown antennae powdered white, must have realized much too late that it had become mummified simply because it had not known how to use things with the spontaneous grace of the *in vain*: 'Alas, I looked too closely inside myself! Alas, I looked too closely inside...' From my impassive height as a human being, I witness a world's destruction. Dawn breaks. Here and there, the stiff antennae of dead cockroaches quiver in the breeze. The cockerel from the previous story begins to crow.

The fourth story marks a new era in the house. The story begins in the usual fashion: I was complaining about the cockroaches. It continues up to the moment when I discover those statues made of plaster of Paris. Dead, of course. I glance at the pipes where this very night another swarm will appear, advancing slowly upwards in Indian file. Should I administer the lethal sugar night after night? Like someone who can no longer sleep without satisfying this craving for the nightly ritual. And should I spend my sleepless nights on the terrace? Eager to discover those statues my humid nights have erected? I trembled with perverse satisfaction at the vision of my dual existence as a sorceress. I also trembled at the sight of that hardening plaster of Paris, the depravity of existence which would shatter my inner form.

The cruel moment of choosing between two paths which I thought would divide, convinced that any choice would mean sacrificing either myself or my soul. I made my choice. And today I secretly wear the badge of virtue on my heart. 'This apartment has been disinfected.'

The fifth story is called *Leibnitz and the Transcendence of Love in Polynesia*. It begins as follows: I was complaining about the cockroaches.

THE PRINCESS (I)

If I were to be asked about Ofélia and her parents, I should reply with decorous honesty: I scarcely knew them. Before the same jury I should testify: I scarcely know myself – and to each member of the jury I should say, with the same innocent look of someone who has hypnotized herself into obedience: I scarcely know you. But sometimes I wake from a long sleep and turn submissively towards the delicate abyss of disorder.

I am trying to speak about that family which disappeared years ago without leaving any traces in me, and of which all that remains is a faded and distant image. My sudden willingness to know was provoked today when a little chick appeared in the house. It was brought by a hand which wanted to have the pleasure of giving me some living thing. Upon releasing the chick from its box, its charm overwhelmed us. Tomorrow is Christmas Day, but the moment of silence I await all year came on the eve of Christ's birth. Something chirping by itself arouses the most gentle curiosity which, beside a manger, becomes adoration. Well, whatever next, said my husband. He felt much too big and clumsy. Scruffy and with gaping mouths, the children approached. Feeling somewhat courageous, I gave in to feelings of happiness. As for the chick, it went on chirping. But tomorrow is Christmas, the older boy said self-consciously. We smiled, disarmed and curious.

But sentiments are like sudden water. Presently – just as water changes and loses some of its force when it attempts to devour a stone, and changes once more when we bathe our feet – presently there is no longer simply an aura and glow on our faces. Feeling good and anxious, we gathered round the distressed chick. Soft-heartedness leaves my husband cold and morose, something to which we have become accustomed; he tends to torment himself. For the children, who are much more serious, kindness is a passion. As for me, kindness inhibits me. Very soon the same water had changed, and we watched, ill at ease, entangled in our clumsiness as we struggled to be good. And now the water had changed, the expression on our faces gradually betrayed the burden of our desire, our hearts weighed down by a love which was no longer free. The chick's fear of us also made us feel uncomfortable; there we were, and not one of us worthy of appearing before a chick; with every chirp it was driving us away. With each chirp, it was reducing us to helplessness. Its persistent terror accused us of thoughtless mirth which by now was no longer mirth, but annoyance. The chick's moment had passed, and with increasing urgency it was expelling us without letting go. We adults quickly suppressed our feelings. But the children were silently indignant. They accused us of doing nothing for the chick or for humanity. The chick's persistent chirping had already left us, the parents, uncomfortably resigned: such is life. Only we had never said so to the children, for we were ashamed; and we postponed indefinitely the moment when we should summon them and tell them straight that this is how things are. It became increasingly difficult, the silence grew, and they were slow to respond to our anxiety to give them love in return. If we had never discussed such things before, all the more reason why we should hide from them now the smile that came to our faces as we listened to the desperate squawks coming from that beak; a smile as if it were up to us to bless the fact that this is the way things are, and we had just given them our blessing.

As for the chick, it was chirping. Standing on the polished table, it dared not make a move as it chirped to itself. I never realized there could be so much terror inside a creature made only of feathers. Feathers covering what? Half a dozen fragile little bones put together for what purpose? To chirp terror. Mindful of our inability to understand each other and out of respect for the children's revolt against us, we watched impatiently in silence. It was impossible to comfort the chick with words of reassurance, to console that tiny creature which was terrified just to have been born. How could we promise that everything would be all right? A father and a mother, we knew just how brief the chick's life would be. The chick also knew, in the way that living creatures come to know; through profound fear.

Meanwhile, there was the chick with all its charm, an ephemeral, yellow thing. I also wanted the chick to experience the joys of life, just as we were expected to experience them, for its only joy was to make others happy. That the chick should feel it was superfluous, unwanted – one of the chicks is bound to be useless – and had only been born for the greater glory of God and, therefore, for the happiness of mankind. But in loving our dear little chick, did we wish it to be happy simply because we loved it? I also knew that only a mother determines birth, and ours was the love of those who take pleasure in loving; I rejoiced in the grace of having devoted myself to loving; bells, bells were pealing because I know how to adore. But the chick was trembling, a thing of terror rather than beauty.

The younger boy could stand it no longer:
– Do you want to be its mummy?

Startled, I answered yes. I was the messenger assigned to that creature which did not understand the only language I knew: I was loving without being loved. My mission might founder and the eyes of four children waited with the intransigence of hope for my first real sign of love. I recoiled a little, smiling and aloof; I looked at my family and wanted them to smile. A man and four little boys were staring at me, incredulous and trusting. I was the mistress of that household, the provider. I could not understand the impassiveness of these five males. How often I would founder, so that, in my hour of fear, they would look at me. I tried to isolate myself from the challenge of those five males, so that I, too, might expect love from myself and remember what love is like. I opened my mouth, I was about to tell them the truth: exactly how, I cannot say.

But what if a woman were to appear to me in the night holding a child in her arms. And what if she were to say: Take care of my child. I would reply: How can I? She would repeat: Take care of my child. I would reply: I cannot. She would insist: Take care of my child. Then – then, because I do not know how to do anything and because I cannot remember anything and because it is night – I would then stretch out my hand and save a child. Because it is night, because I am alone in another's night, because this silence is much too great for me, because I have two hands in order to sacrifice the better of the two, and because I have no choice.

THE PRINCESS (II)

It was at that moment that I saw Ofélia again in my mind's eye. And at that same moment I recalled that I had been the witness of a little girl.

Later, I remembered how my neighbour, Ofélia's mother, had the dark complexion of an Indian woman. The dark shadows round her eyes made them very beautiful and gave her the sort of languorous appearance which caused men to take a second look. One day, when we were seated on a bench in the park, while the children were playing, she told me with that resolute expression of someone scanning the desert: 'I have always wanted to take a course in confectionery.' I remembered that her husband – who was also dark-skinned, as if they had chosen each other for their complexion – wanted to make a fortune in his particular line of business: he was the manager or perhaps even the owner of an hotel, I was never quite sure. This gave him an air of refinement but distinctly cool. When we could not avoid meeting in the lift, he tolerated an exchange of words with that haughty tone of voice which he had acquired in greater battles. By the time we reached the tenth floor, the humility his cold manner had forced from me placated him a little: perhaps he might even arrive home a little more amiable. As for Ofélia's mother, because we lived on the same floor she feared we might become too intimate, and started avoiding me, unaware that I was also on my guard. The only intimacy between us had been that day on that bench in the park, where, with those dark shadows round her eyes and those thin lips, she had talked about learning how to decorate cakes. I did not know what to say and ended up by confiding, so that she might know that I liked her, that I, too, would like to take a course in confectionery. That one moment of mutual intimacy divided us even more, out of fear that any mutual understanding might be abused. Ofélia's mother was even rude to me in the lift: the next day I was holding one of my children by the hand, the lift was going down slowly and, feeling oppressed by the silence which gave the other woman strength – I said in an affable tone of voice, which I myself found repugnant even as I spoke:

– We're going to visit his grandmother.

Whereupon to my horror, she snapped in reply:

– No one asked you where you're going. I never poke my nose into other people's affairs.

– Well I never, I mumbled in a low voice.

This led me to believe there and then that I was being made to pay for that moment of intimacy on the park bench. This in turn made me think that she was afraid of having confided more than she actually had that day. And in turn made me wonder if she had not told me more, in fact, than either of us had realized. By the time the lift finally reached the ground floor, I had reconstituted that obstinate, languid air of hers on the park bench – and I gazed with new eyes at the proud beauty of Ofélia's mother.

'I won't tell a soul that you want to learn how to decorate cakes', I thought to myself, giving her a furtive glance.

The father hostile, the mother keeping her distance. A proud family. They treated me as if I were already living in their future hotel and as if I had offended them by not paying my bill. Above all, they treated me as if I did not believe, nor could they prove, who they were. And who were they? I sometimes asked myself that question. Why was that slap imprinted on their faces and why was that dynasty living in exile? Nor could they forgive me for carrying on as if I had been forgiven. If I met them on the street, outside the zone to which I had been confined, it terrified me to be caught out of bounds: I would draw back to let them pass, I gave way as the dusky, well-dressed trio passed as if on their way to Holy Mass – a family that lived under the sign of some proud destiny or hidden martyrdom – purple as the flowers of the Passion. Theirs was an ancient dynasty.

But contact was made through the daughter. She was a most beautiful child with her long hair in plaits. Ofélia with the same dark shadows round her eyes as her mother, the same gums looking a little inflamed, the same thin lips as if someone had inflicted a wound. But how those lips could talk. She started coming to visit me. The door-bell would ring, I would open the spy-hole without seeing anyone, and then I would hear a resolute voice:

– It's me, Ofélia Maria dos Santos Aguiar.

Disheartened, I would open the door. Ofélia would enter. She had come to visit me, for my two little boys were far too small then to be treated to her phlegmatic wisdom. I was a grown-up and busy, but it was me she had to visit. She would arrive dispensing with any formalities, as if there were a time and place for everything. She would carefully lift her flounced skirt, sit down and arrange the flowers – and only then would she look at me. In the midst of duplicating my files, I carried on working and listening. Ofélia would then proceed to give me advice. She had very decided opinions about everything. Everything I did was not quite right in her opinion. She would say 'in my opinion' in a resentful tone, as if I should have asked her advice and, since I had not asked, she was giving it. With her eight proud and well-lived years, she told me that, in her opinion, I did not rear my children properly: for when you give children an inch, they take a mile. Bananas should not be served with milk. It can kill you. But of course, you must do what you think is best: everyone knows their own mind. It was rather late for me to be wearing a dressing-gown: her mother dressed as soon as she got up, but everyone must live as they see fit. If I tried to explain that I still had to take my bath, Ofélia would remain silent and watch me closely. With a hint of tenderness and then patience, she added that it was rather late to be taking a bath. I was never allowed the last word. What last word could I possibly offer when she informed me: vegetable patties should not be covered. One afternoon in the baker's shop, I found myself unexpectedly confronting the useless truth: there stood a whole row of unco-vered vegetable patties. 'But I told you so', I could hear her say, as if she were standing there beside me. With her plaits and flounces, with her unyielding delicacy. She would descend like a visitation into my sitting-room, which was still waiting to be tidied up. Fortunately she also talked a lot of nonsense, which made me smile, however low I might be feeling.

The worst part of this visitation was the silence. I would raise my eyes from the typewriter and wonder how long Ofélia had been watching me in silence. What could possibly attract this child to me? Personally, I found myself exasperating. On one occasion, after another of her lengthy silences, she calmly said to me: you are a strange woman. And as if I had been struck on the face without any form of protection – right on the face which is our inner self and therefore extremely sensitive – struck full on the face, I thought to myself in a rage: you are about to see just how strange I can be. She who was so well protected, whose mother was protected, whose father was protected.

THE PRINCESS (III)

However, I still preferred her advice and criticism. Much less tolerable was her habit of using the word *therefore* as a way of linking sentences into a never-ending chain. She told me that I bought far too many vegetables at the market – therefore – they would not fit into my small fridge and – therefore – they would go bad before the next market day. A few days later I looked at the vegetables, and they had gone bad. Therefore – she was right. On another occasion, she saw fewer vegetables lying on the kitchen table, as I had secretly taken her advice. Ofélia looked and looked. She seemed prepared to say nothing. I waited, standing there fuming but saying nothing. Ofélia said phlegmatically:

– It won't be long before there's another market day.

The vegetables had run out towards the middle of the week. How did she know? I asked myself bewildered. Probably she would reply with 'therefore'. Why did I never, never know? Why did she know everything, why was the earth so familiar to her, and here was I without protection? Therefore? Therefore.

On one occasion, Ofélia actually made a mistake. Geography – she said, sitting before me with her hands clasped on her lap – is a kind of study. It was not exactly a mistake, it was a slight miscalculation – but for me it had the grace of defeat, and before the moment could pass, I said to her mentally: that's exactly how it's done! just go on like that and one day it will be easier or more difficult for you, but that's the way, just go on making mistakes, ever so slowly.

One morning, in the midst of her conversation, she announced peremptorily: 'I'm going home to get something but I'll be right back.' I dared to suggest: 'If you've got something to do, there's no need to hurry back.' Ofélia looked at me, silent and questioning. 'There is a very nasty little girl', I thought firmly to myself so that she might see the entire sentence written on my face. She kept on looking at me. A look wherein – to my surprise and dismay – I saw loyalty, patient confidence in me, and the silence of someone who never spoke. When had I ever thrown her a bone – that she should follow me in silence for the rest of my life? I averted my eyes. She gave a tranquil sigh. 'I'll be right back.' What does she want? – I became nervous – why do I attract people who do not even like me?

Once when Ofélia was sitting there, the door-bell rang. I opened the door and came face to face with Ofélia's mother. Protective and unbending, she had come in search of her daughter.

– Is Ofélia Maria here by any chance?

– Yes, she is, I said, excusing myself as if I had abducted her.

– Don't do that again – she said to Ofélia with a tone of voice that was meant for me: then turning to me, she suddenly sounded peevish: I'm sorry if you've been troubled.

– Not at all, your little girl is so clever.

The mother looked at me in mild surprise – but suspicion flickered across her eyes. And in her expression I could read: what do you want from her?

– I have already forbidden Ofélia to come bothering you, she now said with open distrust. And firmly grabbing the little girl by the hand to lead her away, she appeared to be protecting her from me. Feeling positively degenerate, I watched them through the half-opened spy-hole without making a sound: the two of them walked down the corridor leading to their apartment, the mother sheltering her child with murmured words of loving reproach, the daughter impassive with her swaying plaits and flounces. On closing the spy-hole, I realized that I was still in my dressing-gown and that I had been seen like this by the mother who dressed the moment she got up. I thought somewhat defiantly: Well, now that her mother despises me, at least there will be no more visits from the daughter.

But naturally, she came back. I was much too attractive for that child. I had enough defects to warrant her advice, I was apt terrain for exercising her severity, I had already become the property of that slave of mine: of course, she came back, lifted her flounces and sat down.

As it happened, Easter was approaching, the market was full of chicks and I had brought one home for the children. We amused ourselves with it, then the chick was put in the kitchen while the children went out to play. Soon afterwards, Ofélia appeared for her daily visit. I was typing and from time to time I would express assent, my thoughts elsewhere. The girl's monotonous voice, the singsong of someone reciting from memory, made me feel quite dizzy, her voice infiltrating between the words typed on the paper, as she talked and talked.

Then it struck me that everything seemed to have come to a sudden standstill. Aware that I was no longer being tortured, I looked at her hazily. Ofélia Maria's head was erect, her plaits transfixed.

– What's that? she asked.

– What's what?

– That! she said stubbornly.

– What?

We might have remained there forever in a vicious circle of 'that!' and 'what?', were it not for the extraordinary will-power of this child, who, without saying a word, but with an expression of intransigent authority, obliged me to hear what she herself was hearing. Forced into attentive silence, I finally heard the faint chirping of the chick in the kitchen.

– It's the chick.

– The chick? she said, most suspiciously.

– I bought a chick, I replied submissively.

– A chick! she repeated, as if I had insulted her.

– A chick.

THE PRINCESS (IV)

And there the matter would have rested had I not seen something which I had never noticed before.

What was it? Whatever it was, it was no longer there. A chick had flickered momentarily in her eyes only to disappear, as if it had never existed. And a shadow had formed. A dark shadow covering the earth. From the moment her trembling lips almost involuntarily mouthed the words: 'I want one, too' – from that moment, darkness intensified in the depths of her eyes into remorseful desire which, if touched, would close up like the leaf of the opium poppy. She retreated before the impossible, the impossible which had drawn near, and which, in a moment of temptation, had almost become hers; the darkness of her eyes changed colour like gold. Slyness crept into her face – and had I not been there, she would slyly have stolen something. In those eyes, which blinked with cunning knowledge, in those eyes there was a marked tendency to steal. She gave me a sudden look betraying her envy: you have everything; and censure: why are we not the same, then I would have a chick? and possessiveness – she wanted me for herself. Slowly I slumped into my chair, her envy was exposing my poverty and left my poverty musing: had I not been there, she would have stolen my poverty as well. She wanted everything. After the tremor of possessiveness subsided, the darkness of her eyes revealed her suffering.

I was not only exposing her to a face without protection. I was now exposing her to the best of the world: to a chick. Without seeing me, her moist eyes stared at me with an intense abstraction, which made intimate contact with my intimacy. Something was happening which I could not understand at a glance. And desire returned once more. This time her eyes were full of anguish, as if they had nothing to do with the rest of her body, which had become detached and independent. And those eyes grew wider, alarmed at the physical strain as her inner being began to disintegrate. Her delicate mouth was that of a child, a bruised purple. She looked up at the ceiling – the dark shadows round her eyes gave her an air of sublime martyrdom. Without stirring, I watched her. I knew about the high incidence of infant mortality. The great question she was asking concerned me as well. Is it worthwhile? I do not know, my increasing composure replied, but it is so. There, before my silence, she surrendered to the process, and if she was asking me the great question, it must remain unanswered. She had to surrender – and without anything in return. It had to be so. And without anything in return. She held back, reluctant to surrender. But I waited. I knew that we are that thing which must happen. I could only be her silence. And, bewildered and confused, I could hear her heart, which was not mine, beating inside me. Before my fascinated eyes, like some mysterious emanation, she was being transformed into a child.

Not without sorrow. In silence, I watched the sorrow of her awkward happiness. The lingering colic of a snail. She slowly ran her tongue over her thin lips. (Help me, her body said, as it painfully divided into two. I am helping, my paralysis replied.) Slow agony. Her entire body became swollen and deformed. At times, her eyes became pure eyelashes, avid as an egg in the process of being formed. Her mouth trembling with hunger. Then I almost smiled, as if stretched out on an operating table, and insisting that I was not suffering much pain. She did not lose sight of me: there were footprints she could not see, no one had passed this way before, and she perceived that I had walked a great deal. She became more and more distorted, almost the image of herself. Shall I risk it? Shall I give way to feeling? she asked herself. Yes, she replied to herself, through me.

And my first yes sent me into rapture. Yes, my silence replied to her, yes. Just as when my first son was born and I had said: yes. I had summoned the courage to say yes to Ofélia, I who knew that one can die in childhood without anyone noticing. Yes, I replied enraptured, for the greater danger does not exist: when you go, you go together, you yourself will always be there: this, this you will carry with you whatever may become of you.

The agony of her birth. Until then I had never known courage. The courage to be one's other self, the courage to be born of one's own parturition, and to cast off one's former body. And without being told whether it was worthwhile. 'I', her body tried to say, washed by the waters. Her nuptials with self.

Fearful of what was happening to her, Ofélia slowly asked me:

— Is it a chick?

I did not look at her.

— Yes, it's a chick.

From the kitchen came a faint chirping. We remained silent, as if Jesus had just been born. Ofélia kept on sighing.

— A tiny little chick? she confirmed, with some uncertainty.

— Yes, a little chick, I said, guiding her carefully towards life.

— Ah, a little chick, she said pensively.

— A little chick, I repeated, trying not to be unkind.

For some minutes now, I had found myself in the presence of a child. The transformation had taken place.

— It's in the kitchen.

— In the kitchen? she repeated, pretending not to understand.

— In the kitchen, I repeated, sounding authoritarian for the first time, and without saying anything more.

— Ah, in the kitchen, said Ofélia, shamming and looking up at the ceiling.

But she was suffering. Feeling almost ashamed, I became aware that I was taking my revenge at last. Ofélia was suffering, shamming, looking up at the ceiling. Her mouth, those shadows around her eyes.

— Why don't you go into the kitchen and play with the little chick?

— Me...? she asked slyly.

— Only if you want to.

I know that I should have ordered her to go rather than expose her to the humiliation of such intense desire. I know that I should not have given her any choice, and then she could say that she had been forced to obey. At that moment, however, it was not out of revenge that I tormented her with freedom. The truth is that this step, this step, too, she had to take alone. Alone and without delay. It was she who had to go to the mountain. Why — I wondered – why am I trying to breathe my life into her purple mouth? Why am I giving her my breath? How can I dare to breathe inside her, if I myself...is it only that she may walk, that I am giving her these painful steps? Am I only breathing my life into her so that one day she may momentarily feel in her exhaustion that the mountain has come to her?

Perhaps I had no right. But there was no choice. This was an emergency, as if the girl's lips were becoming more purple by the minute.

THE PRINCESS (V)

— Go and see the little chick only if you want to, I then repeated with the extreme harshness of someone saving another.

We stood there facing each other, dissimilar, body separated from body; united only by hostility. I sat still and composed in my chair so that the girl might cause pain to some other being, unyielding so that she might struggle inside me; I felt increasingly strong as I saw Ofélia's need to hate me, her determination that I should resist the suffering of her hatred. I cannot live this for you – my coldness told her. Ofélia's struggle came ever closer and then inside me, as if that creature who had been born and endowed me with the most extraordinary strength, were drinking from my weakness. In using me, she bruised me with her strength: she clawed me as she tried to cling to my smooth walls. At last the words came out in simmering rage:

— I'm off to see the chick in the kitchen.

— Yes, off you go, I said slowly.

She withdrew hesitantly, conscious of her dignity, even as she turned her back on me.

She re-emerged from the kitchen immediately – she looked startled, shamelessly holding out the chick in one hand and examining me from head to foot in her bewilderment.

— It's a little chick! she said.

She looked at the chick in her outstretched hand, then looked at me, then looked once more at her hand – and suddenly she became nervous and worried, which automatically made me feel nervous and worried.

– But it's a little chick! she said, and reproach flickered in her eyes at once as if I had not told her what was chirping.

I laughed. Ofélia looked at me, deeply offended. And suddenly – suddenly she laughed. Then we both laughed, somewhat stridently.

When we stopped laughing, Ofélia put the chick down on the floor to see it walking. When it ran, she went after it. She seemed to be giving the chick its freedom in order to provoke desire, but if it cowered, she rushed to its aid, pitying it for being subjected to her power: 'Poor little thing, he's mine': and when she held the chick, it was with a hand deformed by delicacy. – Yes, it was love, tortuous love. He's very little and needs a lot of attention. One mustn't fondle him for that could be really dangerous; don't let people handle him unless they promise to be careful, and do as you think best, but corn is far too big for his little open beak; for he's very fragile, poor little thing, and so tiny; therefore, you shouldn't let your children play with him; I'm the only one who knows how to look after him; he keeps slipping all over the place, so the kitchen floor is clearly no place for a little chick.

For the last half hour I had been trying to get back to my typewriter in order to make up for lost time, while Ofélia's voice droned on. Little by little, she was only speaking to the little chick, and loving for love's sake. For the first time she had abandoned me, she was no longer me. I watched her, pure gold, and the chick, pure gold, and the two of them were humming like distaff and spindle. For me this also meant freedom at last and without any malice. Farewell. And I smiled with longing.

It was only much later that I realized that Ofélia was talking to me.

– I think – I think I'll put him in the kitchen.

– Off you go then.

I did not see her leave, nor did I see her return. At a given moment, quite by chance and somewhat distracted, I realized that there had been silence for some time. I suddenly looked at her. She was sitting with her hands folded on her lap. Without quite knowing why, I looked at her a second time.

– What is it?

101

– I…?
– Do you want to go to the lavatory?
– I…?

I gave up and carried on with my typing. Some time later, I heard a voice:

– I must go home now.
– Of course.
– If you don't mind.

I looked at her in surprise: Now then, if you wish…
– Well then, she said, I'll be going.

She walked away slowly and closed the door quietly behind her. I went on staring at the closed door. What a strange child you are, I thought to myself. I went back to my typing.

But I was stuck at the same sentence. Well – I thought impatiently, looking at my watch – now what's the matter? I sat there, searching restlessly in my mind, searching in my mind to discover what was troubling me. Just as I was about to give up, I saw that impassive face again: Ofélia. Something started to cross my mind, when to my surprise, that face was leaning over me in order to be able to hear what I was feeling. I slowly pushed away the typewriter. Reluctantly, I began moving chairs out of the way, until I came to a halt in the doorway of the kitchen. On the floor lay the dead chick. Ofélia, I impulsively called after the girl who had fled.

From an infinite distance, I saw the floor. Ofélia. From afar, I tried in vain to reach the heart of that silent girl. Oh, don't be so frightened! Sometimes people kill for love, but I promise you that one day you will forget everything, I promise you! People do not know how to love, do you hear me, I repeated as if I might reach her before she should proudly serve nothingness in refusing to serve the truth. I who had forgotten to warn her that without fear there was the world. But I swear that this is breathing. I was very tired. I sat down on the kitchen stool.

Where I am still sitting, slowly beating the mixture for tomorrow's cake. Sitting, just as if throughout all these years I had been patiently waiting in the kitchen. Beneath the table today's chick shudders. The same yellow, the same beak. As we are promised at Easter, He will return in December. It is Ofélia who has not returned: she grew up. She went away to become the Indian princess whose tribe awaited her in the desert.

RACING AGAINST THE TYPEWRITER

The world is so enormous, dear God, and to think that one day I shall have to die. How many moments have I left before death comes? I plead for more than moments. Not because those moments are so brief but because they are so rare and loving them can kill. Do I love you, precious moments? Reply, for life is slowly killing me. Do I love you, precious moments? Yes or no? I wish others to know what I shall never understand. I prefer to understand rather than be given explanations. Shall I have to spend my entire life waiting for Sunday to pass? And what about the charwoman from Raiz de Serra who gets up at four in the morning to work all day in the city before returning late at night to Raiz de Serra, where she falls into bed to be up at four next morning to go through the same exhausting routine. I shall tell you my mortal secret: living is not an art. Those who made such claims were lying. Ah! there are certain days when everything becomes so dangerous. But the typewriter goes faster than my fingers. The typewriter writes inside me. And I have no secrets apart from mortal ones. Those are all I need in order to become a creature with eyes, who will die one day. How can I explain what has just occurred to me? For I can now see that there is a price to be paid for everything, and that life is so costly it can even bring about death. To stroll through the countryside with a phantom-child is to walk hand-in-hand with what we have lost and, for all their beauty, those unending fields are of no help: hands clasp like claws for fear of getting lost. Perhaps it would be better to kill the phantom-child in order to be free? But what would then become of those great fields where no flowers have been planted other than that cruel little phantom-child? Cruel, because a child and demanding. Ah! I am too much of a realist. I walk alone with my own ghosts.

THE LEARNED MAN

He now manages a shoe-shop. Not because he likes the job, but it was all he could find. He was forever asking himself: where did I go wrong? He meant in planning his future. There is no

103

great mystery about becoming the manager of a shoe-shop. But once he himself poses the question and shows customers shoes as if he were not of this world, there is a reason for asking. Why, in fact? After all, he had been the brightest student of history at school and taken a keen interest in archaeology. But what he appeared to lack was any genuine appreciation of history or archaeology. All he had was learning. But no real understanding of prehistoric times when the world was uninhabited and fish had not yet been transformed into amphibians to provide food for humans. And to this day he sells shoes with the air of a scholar, as if his feet never touched this rough earth which wears out the soles of shoes.

THE HAUNTED ROOM

I want to tell you about the little room I put under a spell with my imaginings. It was in a rented apartment which was furnished. But let me say first of all that when reality is unmasked without fear, nothing in the world could be more agreeable and *real*. Reality, even if imaginary, has no dream and almost no future: its every moment belongs to the present. And there is no fear. It is extraordinary. In this reality unmasked by the imagination without fear, the richness is no longer behind us like some memory or about to appear from some desired future. It is there, and breathing.

Let me try to describe in the simplest possible words something which is far from simple. The little room, as I told you, was furnished. It was difficult to say if the arrangement of the furniture was intentional or whether, in fact, any arrangement existed. In all probability the first woman to occupy the apartment had decorated it without any conscious plan, making life easier for subsequent tenants. For the abundance in that sitting-room had nothing to do with our past or our reminiscences – it was there. There was no austerity in that room. On the contrary, it had a certain chic and charm. But the room was haunted. Oh, there was no ghost. It was haunted in its own right. The light – the light in the room was real enough – the light of space or the sky above – without any suggestion of shadows. And yet the objects in the room were obscured by the light.

And such a lack of comfort. There was not a single chair in that room where a person could sit in comfort. Perhaps that is why visitors behaved as if they were being bitten, kept moving from chair to chair, jumping to their feet, and looking out of the window and up at the ceiling as if in search of some means of escape. And no guarantee of safety anywhere. That was the problem. There was no guarantee of safety in that room. Either one accepted being lit up in some way by one's own ghost, or refused. There were no promises of any recompense.

There was a mirror in the room. It had been hung up in a silly position directly opposite the window – not to capture any view but simply the empty sky framed by the window – the mirror had nothing to reflect, repeat or copy: the window had become a rectangle of light hanging on a wall.

That room offered no reassurance. But if anyone fearlessly accepted being lit up, they sat for a moment on the edge of that uncomfortable chair like this – they sat there and glowed.

People saw things in such different ways. We became as wicked as champagne. It was not exactly a nice feeling: the room became stifling. And mischievous as we were, we did not know how to react to all that splendour except by bubbling. And by laughing our heads off at the slightest thing.

Even when there were few visitors the room looked crowded. But never to the extent of people knocking into each other. Visitors entering that room for the first time were so intrigued by the objects there that they scarcely noticed each other as they peered first at one object, then another, inquisitive and contemptuous. There were moments of silence. And then water could be heard spurting from a tap. The noise was coming from the kitchen sink which was in need of repair. No one appeared to mind the silence. Everyone seemed to be holding back a smile or some item of news, as the room grew brighter and brighter.

Upon reflection, I cannot recall ever having seen a child in that room. Only people who were mature enough to drop from the tree and be squashed in all that brightness. No, there was not a child in sight. What I did see was a fat man who could not squeeze into those narrow chairs. Spurned and crestfallen, he became our great beetle in the light. I also saw a frail, abandoned woman enter. Her blue eyes were bulging and she clearly had thyroid trouble. As she entered, those bulging eyes momentarily distorted my vision: the room was that woman, that woman was the room. They merged like waters from the same waterfall. How could she close those enormous blue eyes when it was time to sleep? And what about the room? Where could it store all that light when it went to sleep? If only we could switch that room off for a second – what would happen? What great darkness made up of dead shadows would descend?

But the room had no place to store its light. Because I forgot to mention that the room was quite bare, despite the objects, furniture and people. There was no place to conceal oneself in that room. Everything was exposed.

One thing in particular happened to us. Richness was no longer behind us nor did we expect it any more for we were not adolescents: *today* had become such a perfect word that another second would have destroyed it. *Today* would only have to leave the room in order to disintegrate. That room was neither *yesterday* nor *tomorrow*. And whenever we uttered the word *today*, it was as if a secret had been unmasked.

Wounded by the intense light of that bloated room, strange quarrels broke out amongst those present. Muted, short-lived quarrels about trivial things: flashes of lightning on a summer's day. For example, paper could not be found to wrap a gift for the landlady. What did a sheet of paper cost? Yet harsh words were exchanged. On another occasion, we spotted a grape-pip shining like a diamond on the floor. Joking among ourselves, we went down on our hands and knees and jostled each other in an attempt to claim the pip on the pretext that it would make a handsome tie-pin or brooch. At first we fought in jest, but friction soon broke out, tiny sparks were flying and there were angry explosions on all sides. Until I finally claimed the pip on the grounds that I had seen it first, only to be met by stony silence from the others. Needless to say, I threw it away the moment I left the room because the pip had been lying there for ages and was covered in grime. Only the odd trace of moisture had allowed it to glisten under the light.

What a cheerful room that was. We did everything possible to be invited there. We would arrive panting like a dog which had run for miles and come to die at its master's feet. Panting, our mouths became dry with all this happiness. Wide-eyed, curious and exhausted. But with no cause for complaint. The room had never made any reassurances or promised any rewards. It was simply life.

PEN DRAWING OF A LITTLE BOY

How can one ever come to know a little boy?

In order to know him, I must wait for him to drop his guard, and only then will he be within my grasp. There he is, a point in infinity. No one will know his today. Not even the little boy himself. As for me, I look, and it is useless: I cannot understand anything which is simply existent, totally existent. But I do know what it means to be a child. He is the little boy whose first teeth have just started to appear, and the same little boy who one day will become a doctor or a joiner. In the meantime – there he is, sitting on the floor, and I prefer to call his reality vegetative in order to be able to understand. There are thirty thousand such little boys sitting on the floor. Will they have the chance to build another world, one that will take into account that absolute reality to which we once belonged? In union there will be strength. There he sits, initiating everything anew, but for his own future projection, and without any real opportunity of initiating anything.

I do not know how to sketch the little boy. I know that it is impossible to sketch him in charcoal, for even pen and ink stains the paper beyond that subtle line of extreme actuality within which he lives. One day we shall domesticate him into a human being and then we shall be able to sketch him. For this is what we have done with ourselves and with God. The little boy will assist in his own domestication; he is keen and co-operative. He co-operates without knowing that the assistance we expect of him is for his own self-sacrifice. Recently, he has had a lot of practice. And so he will go on progressing until little by little – because of the essential good nature with which we achieve our salvation – he will pass from present time to continuous time, from meditation to expression, from existence to life. Making the great sacrifice of not being mad. I am not mad out of solidarity with the thousands of people who, in order to construct the possible, have also sacrificed the truth which would be madness.

107

But meanwhile, there he sits on the floor, immersed in a deep void.

From the kitchen his mother calls out anxiously: What are you up to through there? Once called, the little boy gets up with difficulty. He totters, unsteady on his feet, all his attention concentrated within, his balance wholly internal. Once that has been achieved, all his attention turns outwards: he observes what the effort of getting to his feet has provoked. For getting up has had one effect after another: the floor moves unsteadily, the chair towers over him, the wall confines him. And on the wall there is a portrait of THE LITTLE BOY. It is difficult to look up at the portrait without leaning against a piece of furniture, and that is something he has still to learn. But his own awkwardness gives him support: what keeps him on his feet is precisely focusing his attention on the portrait above; looking up serves as a hoist. But he makes one mistake: he blinks. Blinking detaches him for a fraction of a second from the portrait which was supporting him. He loses his balance – and all at once, he falls on his bottom. His mouth gaping from all that human effort, the clear spittle trickling on to the floor. He examines the spittle at close quarters, as if it were an insect. He raises his arm and brings it forward in slow mechanical stages. Then suddenly, as if he were capturing something ineffable, with unexpected violence he squashes the spittle with the palm of his hand. He blinks and waits. Finally, having allowed sufficient time to pass, he carefully removes his hand and looks down at the floor, examining the fruit of this action. The floor is empty. With another brusque movement, he examines the palm of his hand: the spittle is stuck there. He has learned something new. Then, with his eyes wide open, he licks the spittle which belongs to the little boy. He thinks aloud: little boy.

– Who are you calling? his mother enquires from the kitchen.

With effortless charm he looks round the room and looks for the person his mother says he is calling; he turns his head and falls backwards. As he sobs, the room becomes distorted and refracted by his tears, the white volume grows until he cries out – Mummy! – he is gathered into strong arms, and suddenly the little boy finds himself in mid-air, cradled in an embrace which is warm and consoling. The ceiling is much closer now: the table down below. Overcome with exhaustion, the pupils of his eyes roll before sinking beneath the horizontal line of his eyes. He closes them over the final image, the wooden bars of his cot. The little boy falls asleep, worn out and peaceful.

The saliva has dried in his mouth. A fly beats against the window-pane. The little boy's sleep is streaked with light and warmth, his sleep vibrates in the atmosphere. Until in a sudden nightmare, one of the words he has learned comes to mind; he shivers violently, opens his eyes. And to his horror, he sees nothing but the warm, clear emptiness of air – and no mother. His thoughts explode into sobs which fill the entire house. As he sobs, he starts to recognize himself, transforming himself into that child whom his mother will recognize. He grows almost weak from so much sobbing: he must transform himself immediately into something which can be seen and heard, otherwise he will remain alone, he must transform himself into something comprehensible, otherwise no one will understand him, no one will respond to his silence, no one will know him if he does not speak for himself. I shall do everything necessary so that I might belong to the others and the others belong to me; I shall skip over my real happiness which will only bring neglect; and I shall be good, anything for the sake of being loved. For what could be more magical than to weep in exchange for a mother?

Until that familiar noise comes through the door and the little boy, silent and intrigued by what a little boy can provoke, stops sobbing: Mummy. Mummy is: not to die. And he is reassured in the knowledge that he has a world to betray and to sell, and that he will sell it.

Yes, it is Mummy with a clean nappy in her hand. The minute he sees the nappy, he begins to sob once more.

– But you're soaking wet!

The news alarms him, curiosity is reawakened, but now his curiosity is comfortable and guaranteed. He looks blindly at his own wetness and, in a new phase, looks at his Mummy. But suddenly, he stops and listens with his whole body, his heart pounding in his tummy: honk-honk! he recognizes the noise with a sudden cry of victory and terror – the little boy has just recognized something!

– That's right! his mother says proudly, that's right, my darling, honk-honk has just passed along the street, I shall tell Daddy what you've learned today, that's just what it sounds like: honk-

honk, my darling! his mother repeats, bouncing him up and down on her lap, lifting him by his legs, throwing him backwards, and then bouncing him up and down again. In all these postures, the little boy keeps his eyes wide open. They are as dry as a fresh nappy.

IMPASSE

She was sobbing. And as if the bright glare of the afternoon were not enough, she had red hair.

In the empty street, the stones vibrated with heat – the little girl's head was aflame. Seated on the steps in front of the house, she was bearing up. The street was deserted except for a solitary figure waiting in vain at the tram-stop. As if her submissive and patient gaze were not enough, her sobs kept coming back, causing her chin to tremble as it rested meekly on one hand. What was to be done with a sobbing little girl with red hair? We looked at each other in silence, dismay confronting dismay. In the deserted street there was no sign of a taxi. In a land of brunettes, to have red hair was an involuntary act of rebellion. Who cared if one day this red hair of hers would cause her to raise her woman's head with an air of defiance? For the present, she was seated on the doorstep which was sparkling under a hot sun at two o'clock in the afternoon. What saved her was a woman's discarded handbag, with a broken strap. She held it as if experienced in conjugal love, pressing it to her knees.

At that moment she was approached by her other half in this world, a soul-mate in Grajaú. The possibility of communication arose on a street-corner in a haze of sweltering heat; accompanying a woman and embodied in the image of a dog. It was a beautiful and wretched little basset-hound, sweet beneath the spell of its destiny. It was a red-haired basset.

There he came, trotting, ahead of his owner, dragging that long body of his. Suspecting nothing, tame dog.

The little girl opened her eyes in astonishment. Gently prepared, the dog stopped in his tracks before her. His tongue quivered. They eyed each other.

Among so many creatures who are ready to become the owners of another creature, there was the little girl who had come into this world to possess that dog. He trembled nervously without barking. She looked at him from under her fringe, spellbound and solemn. They seemed to be there for ages. A great sob shook her whole body as she watched him defiantly. The basset did not so much as flinch. She, too, overcame her sobbing and continued to stare at him.

Both of them had short, red hair.

What did they have to say to each other? No one knows. All we know is that they communicated rapidly with each other, for there was no time to lose. We also know that, without speaking, they entreated each other. They entreated each other with urgency, embarrassment and surprise.

Trapped among so many vague obstacles under that hot sun, there was the solution for the red-haired girl. And among so many streets to be trotted, so many bigger dogs, and so many dry sewers – there was a little girl like the flesh of his own rod flesh. They stared hard at each other, infatuated, remote from Grajaú. Another second and their hovering dream would shatter, yielding perhaps to the solemnity with which they entreated each other.

But they were both pledged. He to his imprisoned nature. She to her impossible childhood, the centre of that innocence which could only open out when she became a woman.

The dog's owner waited impatiently beneath her parasol. The red-haired basset finally detached himself from the little girl and trotted off as if in a dream. She remained there terrified, holding on to this encounter, stunned into a silence which neither a father nor a mother could understand. She accompanied the basset with black eyes, watching him in disbelief, slumped over the handbag pressed against her knees, until she saw him disappear round the next corner.

But he was stronger than she was. He did not look back even once.

BRAINSTORM

Oh, if I had only known. I would never have been born, oh, if I had only known, I would never have been born. Madness borders on the most humiliating wisdom. By absorbing madness, I became

111

quietly hallucinated. The glass ring you gave me shattered into pieces but love did not end there. It was replaced by the hatred of those who love. For me, the chair is an object. Useless so long as I am looking at it. What is the time, please, so that I may know if I am living this moment? Creativity stems from some origin but today it eludes me and all I have is this incipient madness which is in itself a valid creation. I have no further interest in valid things. I am liberated or lost. I shall let you into a secret: life is mortal. We conveniently suppress this secret otherwise we should make each instant mortal. Ibrahim Sued claimed to be an unrobed member of the French Academy. As an object, the chair has always interested me. This one in the Empire style is an antique bought from an antique dealer in Berne. It would be difficult to envisage simpler lines, in contrast with the red upholstery. I love objects in so far as they do not love me. If I do not know what I am talking about, I am not to blame. I must talk because talking can be one's salvation. Yet I do not have a single word to say. The words already spoken have sealed my lips. What does one person say to another? Apart from 'How are you?' If people were suddenly to start being frank, what might they say to each other? Not to mention what they might say to themselves. But it would mean salvation, even though frankness is determined at a conscious level, and any horror of frankness comes from the part it plays in this vast unconsciousness which binds us to the world and to the world's creative unconsciousness. Tonight there will be stars in the sky: as promised by this sad evening which could be saved by a human voice. The most awful blindness is that of people who do not know they are blind. I open my eyes wide but it is useless: I can only see. But I neither see nor feel what is secret. The gramophone is broken, it is costly to mend, and to live without music is to betray the human condition which is surrounded by music. Besides, music is an abstraction of thought, I refer to the music of Bach, Vivaldi and Handel. *That Sweet Embrace*, how that song gets on my nerves with its cloying words of affection. I can only write if I am free, and free of criticism, otherwise I give up. I look at the chair in the Empire style but this time I fancy it has been watching me. The future is mine so long as I am living. In future, there will be more time for living, and haphazardly for writing. In future, one will say: If I had known, I would never have been born. Marly de Oliveira, I scarcely ever write to you because I only know how to be intimate. I only know how to be intimate, whatever the circumstances: therefore I tend to be silent. Will we one day achieve all the things we have never done? Future technology threatens to destroy all that is human in man, but technology cannot touch madness: and so that is where all that is human in man can take refuge. I see flowers in a vase: they are wild flowers and were planted by no one. They are yellow and beautiful. But all my cook could say was: What ugly flowers. Simply because it is difficult to understand and appreciate anything which is spontaneous and austere. To understand complicated things is no advantage, but to love things which invite love is to progress up the human ladder. I am forced into telling so many lies. But I refuse to be obliged to lie to myself. For what would that leave me? Truth is the residue of all things and in my unconscious lurks the world's truth. The moon, as Paul Eluard once described it, is *éclatante de silence*. Who knows if we shall see the moon tonight for it is already late and there is nothing to be seen in the sky. I once accompanied my father to a spa in Minas Gerais. I looked up at the night sky, turning my head as I looked upwards, and the sight of all those stars made me feel quite dizzy. For there in the open countryside the sky is clear. If one thinks about it, there is no logic in the perfectly balanced illogicality of nature. And the same is true of human nature. What would become of the world or the universe if man did not exist? If I could always write as I am writing now, I would be in that mental turmoil people call a *brainstorm*. Who could have invented the chair? Someone who cared for himself. So he invented something for his greater comfort. The centuries passed and no one took any more notice of the chair which people take for granted. It takes courage to have a *brainstorm*: one can never tell what might turn up and give us a fright. The sacred monster died and in its place a little girl was born who lost her mother. I really must break off at this point not because words fail me, but because these are things, not to mention the ones I only thought about, which I never put into words. And things one does not publish in newspapers.

Was it an afternoon of sensitivity or susceptibility? I was walking hurriedly along the street, deep in thought, as sometimes happens. When suddenly, there was a tugging at my skirt. Thinking my skirt had got caught on something, I turned round and saw a grubby little hand. It belonged to a small boy whose squalor and the blood coursing through his veins brought a glow to his cheeks. The child was standing in the doorway of a large pâtisserie. It was his eyes, rather than his half-garbled words, which made me aware of his patient distress. Too patient by far. I vaguely perceived a plea, before understanding what it really meant. Somewhat perplexed, I looked at him, still uncertain whether my thoughts had really been interrupted by that child's hand.

– Something to eat, lady, buy me something to eat.

I finally woke up. What had I been thinking of before encountering this child? The fact is that his plea seemed to fill a void, to offer a reply which could serve for any question, just as a heavy downpour of rain can quench the thirst of someone who only wanted a few drops of water.

Without looking around me, perhaps because I felt embarrassed, I carefully avoided looking at the tables inside where some acquaintance might be seated having tea or eating ice-cream, I went up to the counter and said with a firmness only God can explain: Give this child a pastry.

What was I afraid of? I was not looking at the child and wanted to get this humiliating episode over and done with as soon as possible. I asked him: Which pastry do you...?

Before I could finish, the boy told me, quickly pointing with his finger: that one there with chocolate on top.

Bewildered for a second, I quickly recovered and brusquely ordered the assistant to serve him.

– What else would you like? I asked the swarthy child.

Impatiently fidgeting with his hands and mouth as he waited to be served the first pastry, he paused, looked at me for a moment and said with unbearable delicacy, baring his teeth: I don't want another one. He was sparing my generosity.

– Go on, have another one, I insisted eagerly, pushing him forward. The child hesitated, then said: the yellow one made

114

with egg yolks. He received a pastry in each hand and held them above his head as if afraid of crushing them. Even the pastries were out of the reach of that dark-skinned boy. And without even looking at me, he did not so much disappear as escape. The assistant was looking on:

– So he found a charitable soul at long last. That little fellow has been hanging round the door for over an hour begging from passers-by, but they all ignored him.

I walked away, flushed with shame. But was it really shame? I tried without success to revive my earlier thoughts. I was swamped by feelings of love, gratitude, rebellion and shame. But as the saying goes, the Sun shone brighter than ever. I had had the opportunity of...An opportunity provided by a thin, dark-skinned child...by a child to whom others had denied a pastry.

And what about the people having tea and eating ice-cream? Now then, what I wanted to know with self-inflicted cruelty was this: had I been afraid that the others might have seen me or that the others might not have seen me? The fact is that when I crossed the street, what could have been compassion had already been stifled by other feelings. And now that I was alone, my earlier thoughts slowly returned but they were meaningless.

Instead of taking a taxi, I caught a bus. I found a seat.

– Are my parcels in the way?

– The woman who spoke had a baby on her lap and various parcels wrapped in newspapers at her feet. Not at all, I reassured her. 'De dum, de dum, de dum' prattled the baby girl, stretching out her tiny hand and grabbing the sleeve of my dress. 'He likes you', the mother said smiling. I returned her smile.

– I've been on the road all morning, the woman informed me. I went to visit some friends but they were not at home. One had gone out to lunch, the other was off somewhere with her family.

– And what about your little girl?

– He's a boy, she corrected me, he's dressed in girl's clothes but he's a boy. I've fed him. But I haven't had anything to eat yet.

– Is he your grandson?

– My son, he's my son, I have three more. The child's taken a fancy to you...Play with the lady, my little one! Would you believe that we live in what is no more than a narrow corridor and it costs us a fortune. We still owe last month's rent. And

115

we'll soon be at the end of *this* month. The landlord wants us out. But God willing, I'll find the two thousand *cruzeiros* I still owe him. I've got the rest. But he won't accept it. He thinks that if I pay him some in advance, he'll never see the rest.

That unfortunate woman was experienced in the ways of mistrust. There was nothing she did not know, but felt obliged to act as if she knew nothing – the reasoning of the powerful banker. She reasoned as a cautious landlord would reason without allowing things to upset her.

But I suddenly turned cold. The penny had dropped. The woman went on talking. Whereupon I took two thousand *cruzeiros* from my bag and, filled with self-loathing, I handed the notes to the woman. Without a moment's hesitation, she grabbed the notes and pushed them into a secret pocket concealed between her various skirts, almost dropping the baby boy-cum-girl in her haste.

– May the Good Lord reward you, she blurted out as readily as a beggar-woman.

Turning crimson, I continued to sit there with folded arms. The woman went on sitting beside me.

But we no longer spoke. She had more dignity than I suspected. Once she had got the money, she had nothing more to say to me. And I was no longer allowed to fuss over that little boy dressed as a girl. I deserved at least that little pleasure, having paid for it in advance.

What I am trying to say is that a certain uneasiness had descended upon the woman and myself.

– Leave the lady in peace, Zezinho, she scolded the child.

We avoided any contact with our elbows. There was nothing more to be said, and it was a long journey. Dismayed, I looked at her out of the corner of my eye. She looked weary and unwashed. And the woman knew I had given her a furtive look.

Then an atmosphere of resentment sprang up between us. Only that tiny hybrid infant continued to glow with happiness, his gentle prattling resounding throughout the bus: 'De dum, de dum, de dum.'

THE IMMORTAL MAN

Forgive me if I seem always to be writing about taxi-drivers. One of these days, I shall end up marrying a taxi-driver to avoid listening to any more of their tall stories. The conversation went like this:

– I'm going to sell up and emigrate to the United States.

I said nothing.

– There's too much red-tape here in Brazil.

I continued to say nothing.

– Well, that's not exactly true. I'm emigrating because I want them to freeze me.

– What?

– When people die in the States, they freeze the corpse and then defrost it later. And I'm scared of dying. Aren't you?

The answer was no. I felt much more scared of him.

– And what happens when they defrost you?

– I'll come back to life.

– But surely only to die again?

– Then they'll freeze me again.

– So, you'll never die?

– That's right.

FREEDOM

My relationship with a friend has become so simple and free that I often telephone her and, when she picks up the receiver, I explain I am not in the mood for conversation. So I say goodbye, replace the receiver and occupy myself with something else.

CRUELTY

When I think of the eager enjoyment with which we sit down to that Brazilian delicacy, chicken cooked in its own blood, I begin to realize how cruel we humans are. Personally, I could never kill a chicken for I adore watching them as they stretch

117

their ugly necks and scratch for worms. So should we avoid eating chicken cooked in its own blood? Of course not. We must never forget that we are cannibals. We must respect our cruelty. For who knows, perhaps if we were to stop eating chicken cooked in its own blood, we might start devouring human beings instead. My cowardice about eating chickens, even if I am prepared to eat them once they have been cooked, leaves me puzzled and bothered, yet I accept it. Life is cruel. We are born in blood as the umbilical cord is cut. And so many human beings die shedding their blood. We must believe in blood as part of life. Cruelty. But also love.

INTERROGATION

Are we using our life or not when we fritter it away? What precisely am I trying to find out?

THE EXPEDIENTS OF A PRIMITIVE BEING

I once read that hysterical behaviour is a reaching out for liberation by means of wild gestures. Unaware of the movements needed to secure their release, animals become hysterical and lose all control. And in their frenzy they often discover the right gesture to gain their freedom.

This reminds me of the liberating advantages of a primitive existence which is purely emotional. However hysterical, the primitive person draws upon so many contradictory feelings that the one capable of bringing a sense of freedom finally comes to the surface, even if that person does not know it.

A MISCHIEVOUS LITTLE GIRL (I)

Whatever his previous occupation had been, he had abandoned it, changed his profession and drifted half-heartedly into teaching in a primary school: that was all we knew about him.

The teacher was burly, tall and silent, with rounded shoulders. He wore a jacket that was far too short and rimless spectacles, with a thin band of gold bridging his great Roman nose. And I was attracted to him. Not in love with him, but drawn by his silence and his self-control as he tried to teach us. Watching him conceal his impatience made me resentful. I started to misbehave in class. I talked in a loud voice, pestered my classmates and interrupted the lesson with silly jokes until the teacher, turning red in the face, would say:

– Be quiet or I'll send you out of the room.

Wounded but triumphant, I would answer back defiantly: Send me out then! But he didn't send me out, for that would have made him look foolish. I exasperated him so much that it had become painful for me to be an object of hatred for that man whom I somehow loved. I did not love him like the woman I would be one day; I loved him like a child awkwardly trying to protect an adult, with the anger of someone who has not yet become a coward and sees a strong man with such round shoulders. He bothered me. At night, before I went to sleep, he bothered me. I was scarcely nine years old, a difficult age like the unbroken stem of a begonia. I goaded him and when I finally succeeded in making him lose his temper, I could taste, in glorious martyrdom, the unbearable acidity of the begonia when crushed between the teeth; and I bit my nails in triumph. In the morning, as I walked through the school gates, feeling refreshed, nourished on coffee and milk, and with my face washed, it startled me to meet in the flesh the man who had clouded my thoughts for one abysmal moment before falling asleep. On the surface of time it was only a moment, but in the depths of time they were bygone centuries of the darkest sweetness. In the morning – as if I had not counted on the real existence of that man who had unlocked my black dreams of love – in the morning, confronted by that enormous man with his short jacket, I was thrown into a state of confusion, bewilderment, and alarming hope. Hope was my greatest sin.

Each day I renewed the futile struggle which I had begun in order to save that man. I wanted what was good for him, and in return, he hated me. Bruised, I became his demon and tormentor, the symbol of the hell it must have been for him to teach that smirking, inattentive class. Never to give him a moment's peace had become a sadistic pleasure. The game, as always, fascinated me. Without knowing that I was observing time-honoured traditions, yet with that insight with which the wicked are born – those wretches who bite their nails in terror – without knowing that I was conforming to one of the most common situations in the world, I was playing the whore and he the saint. No, perhaps not. Words rush ahead of me, they seduce and transform me, and if I am not careful it will be too late: things will be said before I have even uttered them. Or, at least, it was not only that. My confusion stems from the fact that a rug is woven from so many threads that I cannot resign myself to pursuing one only; my confusion stems from the fact that a story is made up of many stories. And I cannot narrate all of them, for the resounding echoes of some greater truth might bring my vast glaciers toppling down the precipice. So I shall say no more about the maelstrom that raged within me as I daydreamed before falling asleep. Otherwise, even I will begin to think that it was only that subdued whirlpool which drew me towards him, forgetting my desperate sacrifice. I became his temptress, a duty which no one had imposed on me. It was sad that the task of saving him by means of temptation should have fallen into my clumsy hands because, of all the adults and children there, probably no one was less capable. 'These aren't flowers for smelling', as our maid used to say. But it was as if, finding myself alone with a mountaineer paralysed by his terror of the precipice, I could not but try to help him descend, however ill-equipped I might feel. The teacher had suffered the misfortune of finding himself alone in his wilderness with the most foolhardy of his pupils. Whatever the risk, I felt obliged to pull him over to my side because his was fatal. And that was what I did, like a tiresome child tugging at the tails of a grown-up's jacket. He did not look back nor ask what I wanted, and shook me off with a slap. I went on tugging at his jacket, for persistence was my only weapon. He only noticed that I was tearing his pockets. The truth is, I myself was scarcely aware of my behaviour. My life with the teacher was invisible. Yet I sensed that my role was wicked and dangerous: it drove me to a craving for a real existence that was slow in coming. More than clumsy, I even enjoyed tearing his pockets. Only God could forgive what I was, because He alone knew of what matter He had made me and for what purpose. So I allowed myself to be His matter. Being God's matter was my only virtue. And the source of a nascent mysticism. Not mysticism for Him, but for His matter, for a raw life filled with pleasure. I worshipped. I accepted the vastness of things beyond my understanding and confided therein the secrets of the confessional. Was it towards the dark depths of ignorance that I was luring the teacher with the zeal of a cloistered nun? A happy and monstrous nun, alas! Not even of this could I boast: in the classroom we were all equally monstrous and sweet, the avid matter of God.

But if the teacher's heavy round shoulders and his tight jacket moved me, my outbursts of laughter only made him all the more determined to pretend that he had forgotten me, and all that self-control made him look even more deflated. The hatred this man felt for me was so strong that I began to hate myself. Until my outbursts of laughter finally supplanted my impossible waywardness.

A MISCHIEVOUS LITTLE GIRL (II)

As for learning, I did not learn anything during those lessons. The game of making him unhappy had taken much too great a hold over me. Enduring with undisguised resentment my lanky legs and my ever shabby shoes, mortified at not being a flower, and, above all, tortured by an enormous childhood which I feared would never end – I was determined to make him even more unhappy and I flaunted my only wealth: the flowing hair which I planned to have beautifully permed one day and, in anticipation of the future, I tossed my hair at every opportunity. As for studying, I did not study. I trusted in my idleness which had never let me down and which the teacher accepted as one more provocation from a horrid little girl. In that he was mistaken. The truth is that I had no time to study. Happiness kept me occupied, remaining attentive took up days and days of my time: there were the history books which I read passionately, biting my nails to the quick, a refinement which I had recently discovered in my first ecstatic moments of sadness. There were the boys whom I had chosen but who had not chosen me. I spent hours suffering because they were unattainable, and yet more hours suffering by tenderly accepting them, for man was my King of Creation; there was the hopeful threat of sin, and I occupied myself with anxious waiting; not to mention how I was constantly preoccupied with wanting or not wanting to be what I was. I could not decide which part of me I did want, but I could not accept all of me; having been born was to be full of errors that needed correcting. No, it was not to irritate the teacher that I did not study; I only had time to grow. Which I did on all fronts, with a gracelessness that suggested some miscalculation; my legs did not go with my eyes and my mouth twitched while my grubby hands dangled at my sides – in my haste I grew without any sense of direction.

A photograph from that time reveals a healthy girl, savage and gentle, with thoughtful eyes under a heavy fringe, and this real image does not belie me, yet it portrays a ghostly stranger whom I would not understand even if I were her mother. Only much later, after I had finally accepted my physical presence and become essentially more secure, could I bring myself to study a little; before that, however, I could not risk learning, I did not wish to unsettle myself – I took intuitive care with what I was, since I did not know what I was, and I proudly cultivated the integrity of ignorance. What a pity the teacher was never to see the person I unexpectedly became four years later: at thirteen, with clean hands, freshly bathed, quite self-possessed and pretty, he would have seen me looking like a Christmas poster displayed on the veranda of a large house. But, instead of the teacher, a former chum of mine walked by and called out my name, without realizing that I was no longer a tomboy but a dignified young lady whose name could not be called out along the city pavements. 'What is it?' I asked the intruder coldly. I then received the news aloud that the teacher had died that morning. Pale, and with wide eyes, I looked at the street swirling beneath my feet. My composure shattered like a broken doll.

Going back four years. Perhaps it was because of everything I have just narrated, mixed up and jumbled together, that I wrote the composition the teacher had assigned, the dénouement of this story and the nucleus of others. Or perhaps it was only because I wanted to finish my work as quickly as possible and play in the park.

– I am going to tell a story, he said, and you will write a

composition. But use your own words. When you have finished, you may go out to play without waiting for the bell.

This was the story: a very poor man dreamed that he had discovered treasure and had become very rich. On awakening, he packed his bundle and went in search of the treasure but travelled the wide world without finding anything. Weary of travelling, he returned to his modest house and, since he had nothing to eat, he started to plant seeds in his poor little yard; he planted so much, reaped so much, and began to sell so much, that he ended up a very rich man.

I listened with disdain, blatantly playing with my pencil, as if I wanted to make it quite clear that his stories did not fool me and that I knew everything there was to know about him. The teacher told the story without looking even once in my direction. Clumsy in my efforts to love him, I took pleasure in persecuting him, I pursued him with my gaze: I answered everything he said with a simple direct glance, which nobody in all conscience could have condemned. The look I affected was quite angelic and pure, completely open, like innocence confronting crime. And it always achieved the same result: perturbed, he avoided my eyes, and began to stutter. And this filled me with a sense of power that condemned me. And with pity. Which, in its turn, irritated me. It irritated me that he should force a nasty little brat like me to understand a man.

It was almost ten in the morning and the recreation bell was about to ring. My school was a rented building in one of the city parks and had the biggest playground I had ever seen. It afforded me as much pleasure as it might have given a squirrel or a horse. It had trees scattered here and there, rising and falling expanses of lawn. It seemed never-ending. Everything there was incredibly spacious, made for the long legs of a little girl, with space for piles of bricks and wood of unknown origin, for thickets of sour begonias which we ate, for sunlight and shadows where bees made honey. There was room there for an abundance of fresh air. And we lived life to the full; we rolled down every slope, whispered earnestly behind every pile of bricks, ate the different varieties of flowers, and into all the tree trunks we carved with our penknives dates, sweet obscenities and hearts pierced with arrows: girls and boys made their honey there.

I was finishing my composition and the scent of the hidden shadows was already beckoning me. I hurried. Since I only knew how 'to use my own words', writing was simple. What also made me hurry was the desire to be the first to walk down to the front of the classroom – the teacher had ended up banishing me to the back row – and to hand in my composition defiantly, just to show him how quick I could be, a quality which struck me as being essential in order to live and which, I felt sure, the teacher could not fail to admire.

I handed him my notebook and he took it without even looking at me. Offended that he should not have praised my quickness, I skipped out into the big park.

The story which I had transcribed into my own words was exactly the same as the one he had narrated. Except that even then I was beginning to 'extract the moral of the story', which made me feel virtuous but later threatened to smother me, I was becoming so inflexible. Anxious to impress him, I added on several phrases of my own at the end. Phrases which hours later I read and re-read to see what there was in them that had finally succeeded in provoking that man when I myself had so far failed. Probably what the teacher had wanted to make implicit in his sad tale was that hard work is the only way to make a fortune. Facetiously, I drew the opposite moral: something about the hidden treasure, which exists where one least expects to find it, which is only waiting to be discovered. I think I talked about squalid backyards with hidden treasure. I cannot remember, I do not know if those were my precise words. I cannot imagine with what childish phrases I expressed a simple idea which somehow turned into something complicated. I suppose that by wilfully contradicting the real meaning of the story, I had some-how promised myself in writing that idleness rather than work would yield me many gratuitous rewards, the only rewards to which I aspired. It is also possible that even then the theme of my existence was irrational hope, and that my perverse stub-bornness was already manifest. I would give everything I posses-sed for nothing, but I wanted everything in return for nothing. Unlike the labourer in the story, in my composition I shrugged off all responsibilities and came away free and poor and carrying treasure in my hands.

I went out to play, only to find myself alone with the useless reward of having been the first to finish, raking the soil with my foot, waiting impatiently for my classmates who, one by one, emerged from the classroom.

In the midst of our rowdy games, I decided to look for something or other in my satchel to show to the park-warden, my friend and protector. Dripping with perspiration, flushed with an irrepressible happiness which, had I been at home, would have earned me a few slaps – I fled in the direction of the classroom, crossed it at a run, so flustered that I did not see the teacher leafing through the notebooks piled on his desk. The object I had gone to fetch was already in my hand and I was just about to run out again – when my eyes met his. Standing alone by his desk, he looked at me.

It was the first time we had come face to face on our own. He was staring at me. My steps faltered almost to a standstill.

For the first time I found myself alone with him, without the whispered support of my classmates, without the admiration that my insolence aroused. I tried to smile, feeling the blood rushing to my cheeks. A bead of sweat ran down my forehead. He was looking at me. His look was like a soft, heavy paw resting on me. But if that paw was soft, it froze me like a cat's paw as it quickly catches a mouse by the tail. The bead of sweat ran down over my nose and on to my mouth, cutting my smile in half. Just that: his face drained of any expression, he was staring at me. I began to skirt the wall with lowered eyes, taking refuge in my smile, the only feature left in a face which had otherwise become blurred. I had never noticed before just how long the classroom was; only now, at the slow pace of fear, could I judge its real dimensions. Lack of time had not allowed me to perceive until that moment just how bare and high and solid those walls really were. I could feel the solid wall against the palm of my hand. In a nightmare, in which smiling played some part, I scarcely believed that I could reach the doorway – from where I would run, oh, how I would run! and hide amongst the other children. As well as concentrating on my smile, I was most careful not to make any noise with my feet, and thus I adhered to the intimate nature of a danger about which I knew nothing more. With a shudder, I caught a sudden glimpse of myself as if in a mirror: a perspiring thing pressed against the wall, advancing slowly on tiptoe, my smile becoming brighter. My smile had frozen the room into silence and even the sounds that came from the park reverberated on the outer shell of silence. I finally reached the door, and my unruly heart began to beat so loudly that it threatened to awaken the immense world from its sleep.

That was when I heard my name.

Suddenly rooted to the spot, my mouth parched, I stood there with my back to him, much too scared to turn round. The breeze which came from the open door had dried the perspiration on my body. I turned round slowly, restraining within my clenched fists the urge to run.

A MISCHIEVOUS LITTLE GIRL (IV)

At the sound of my name the room had become dehypnotized.

And very slowly I began to see the teacher in his entirety.

Very slowly I saw that the teacher was huge and ugly, and that he was the man of my life. A new and greater fear. Small, sleep-walking, alone, I confronted what my fatal freedom had finally brought me to. My smile, which was all that remained of my face, had also been obliterated. I was a pair of numbed feet too paralysed to move, and a heart so parched that I might die of thirst. There I stood, out of the man's reach. My heart was dying of thirst, yes. My heart was dying of thirst.

As calm as if he were about to commit a murder in cold blood, he said:

– Come closer...

How did a man avenge himself?

Was I about to receive like a smack in the face, the ball of the world which I myself had thrown to him and which none the less I did not understand?

Was I about to retrieve a reality which would not have existed if I had not rashly perceived it, thus giving it life? To what extent was that man, a mountain of compact unhappiness, also a mountain of fury? But my past was too remote now. A stoic repentance kept my head erect. For the first time ignorance, which until then had been my faithful guide, abandoned me. My father was at work, my mother had been dead for several months. I was the only me.

– Take your notebook, he added.

I looked at him suddenly in surprise. Was this all, then? The unexpected relief was almost more alarming than my former fear. I took a step forward, and hesitantly held out my hand.

But the teacher remained still and made no attempt to hand over my notebook.

To my sudden distress, without averting his gaze the teacher slowly began to remove his spectacles. He looked at me with naked eyes fringed with thick eyelashes. I had never noticed his eyes before. Those thick eyelashes made them look like two sweet cockroaches. He stared at me. And I did not know how to react in the presence of a man. Evasively I gazed at the ceiling, the floor, the walls, and kept my hand outstretched because I did not know how to withdraw it. He looked at me gently, inquisitively, eyes bleary as if he had just woken up. Would he crush me with an unexpected hand? Or demand that I kneel and beg forgiveness? My thread of hope was that he might not know what I had done to him, just as I myself no longer knew, and, indeed, had never known.

– How did you get the idea of the hidden treasure?

– What treasure? I murmured sheepishly.

We stood there looking at each other in silence.

– Oh, the treasure! I blurted out, not really understanding, anxious to admit some fault, imploring him that my punishment should be simply to feel forever guilty, that eternal torture should be my punishment, anything but this unknown life.

– The treasure which is hidden where you least expect to find it. That is only waiting to be discovered. Who told you that?

The man has taken leave of his senses, I thought to myself, for what has all this got to do with the treasure? Stunned, unable to understand and passing from one surprise to another, I sensed, nevertheless, that I was on less dangerous ground. In our school races I had learned to carry on running after a fall, however serious, and I regained my composure at once: 'It was the composition about the treasure! So that was my mistake!' Feeling weak, and still treading carefully on this new and slippery re-

127

assurance, I had recovered sufficiently from my fall to be able to toss, in imitation of my former arrogance, this hair of mine which one day would have a permanent wave.

– Gosh, nobody…, I replied haltingly. I made it up myself, I said nervously, but already beginning to sparkle once more.

If I felt some relief at having something concrete to battle with at last, I was also aware of something much worse. The teacher's sudden lack of anger. Puzzled, I looked at him askance. And little by little, with deep suspicion. His lack of anger began to frighten me, it implied new threats which I could not fathom. His staring eyes refused to leave me – eyes devoid of anger…I was perturbed, and for no good reason I was losing my enemy and my support. I looked at him in surprise. What did he want from me? He made me feel uneasy. And those eyes without anger began to irk me more than the brutality which I had feared. A gentle fear, cold and moist, gripped me by degrees. Slowly, lest he should notice, I backed away until my shoulders touched the wall, and then drew back my head until I could go no further. From the wall where I had embedded my entire body, I looked at him furtively.

And my stomach filled with waves of nausea. I cannot describe it.

A MISCHIEVOUS LITTLE GIRL (V)

Suddenly my heart was pounding with disillusionment. I could not bear it a minute longer – without taking the notebook, I ran out to the park, one hand over my mouth as if someone had smashed my teeth. With my hand over my mouth, horror-stricken, I ran and ran as if I would never stop. The fervent prayer is that which asks for nothing, the most fervent prayer is that which asks for nothing more. Terrified, I ran and ran.

Contaminated, I was relying on grown-ups for my redemption. The need to believe in my future goodness led me to venerate grown-ups whom I had made in my image, but an image of me cleansed at last by the penance of growing, delivered at last from the impure soul of a little girl. And now the teacher was destroying all this, he was destroying my love for him and for me. There could be no salvation for me: for that man was also me. My bitter idol who had ingenuously fallen into the snares of a confused and wilful child, and who had meekly allowed himself to be guided by my diabolical innocence...Pressing my hand to my mouth, I ran through the dust of the park.

When it finally dawned on me that I was well out of the teacher's reach, I came to an exhausted halt; close to collapsing, I leaned my full weight against a tree trunk, panting furiously. I stood there, gasping for breath with my eyes closed, swallowing the bitter dust from the tree trunk, my fingers mechanically stroking the rough grooves...forming a heart and arrow. Closing my eyes tightly, I let out a sudden moan, as I began to see things more clearly: was he trying to say that...that I was a hidden treasure? That treasure hidden where one least expects to find it...Oh, no, not at all, poor King of Creation, so much in need... of what? What was he in need of...that even I should have been turned into treasure?

I had enough strength to run even further. Forcing my dry throat to recover its breath, and angrily pushing against the tree trunk, I set off once more in the direction of the world's end.

But the shadowed edges of the park were still invisible and my steps were growing slower and slower from sheer exhaustion. I could go no further. Perhaps because I was so tired, I finally gave up. My steps became slower and slower and the foliage of the trees swayed slowly. My steps became confused. Hesitantly, I came to a halt, the trees circled overhead. The strangest sweetness left my heart weary. I paused in fear. I was alone on the lawn, unsteady on my feet, and without any support. My hand over my weary breast like some virgin in an annunciation scene. Weary, lowering to that first sweetness a head that was submissive at last, and that from a distance might even suggest the head of a woman. The crest of the trees swayed to and fro. 'You're a very funny child, and a foolish little girl', he had said. It was almost like being in love.

No, I was not funny. Unconsciously, I was most serious. No, I was not a foolish little girl, reality was my destiny, and it was that part of me which offended others. And, by God, I was not a treasure. But if I had already discovered in myself all the vicious poison with which human beings are born and use to destroy life – only at that moment of honey and flowers did I discover how I would cure whoever loved me, whoever suffered on my account. I was dark ignorance with its hunger and laughter, with small deaths nourishing my inevitable life – what was I to do? I already knew that I was inevitable. But if I was worthless, I was all the man possessed at that moment. For once at least, he was being obliged to love, and without loving anyone – to love through someone. And I alone was there. Even if this were his sole advantage: having only me, and being forced to start by loving the wicked, he had started with something few achieve. It would be much too easy to desire the pure; the ugly was beyond love's reach; to love the impure was man's deepest longing. Through me, someone difficult to love, he had charitably received the substance of which we are made. Did I understand all this? No. Nor do I know what I understood at the time. But just as for one brief moment I had seen with horrified fascination the world in my teacher – and to this day I do not know what I saw, only that forever and in one brief moment I saw – and so understood both of us, even though I shall never know what I understood. I shall never know what I understand. Whatever I understood in the park was, to my pleasant surprise, understood by my ignorance. An ignorance which stood there – in the same numbed solitude as the surrounding trees – an ignorance which I fully recovered with its incomprehensible truth. There I stood, the girl who was too knowing by far, and behold how all that was unworthy in me served both God and man. All that was unworthy about me was also my treasure.

Yes, just like a virgin in an annunciation scene. In allowing me to make him smile at last, the teacher had brought about this annunciation. He had just transformed me into something more than the King of Creation: he had made me the wife of the King of Creation. For suddenly it had fallen to me, armed with claws and dreams as I was, to pluck the barbed arrow from his heart. Suddenly it became clear why I had been born intransigent, why I had been born without aversion to pain. Why do you have such long nails? All the better to claw you to death and pluck out your fatal thorns, the wolf-man replies. Why do you have such cruel and hungry jaws? All the better to bite you with before blowing on the wound to ease the pain, my beloved. For alas, I must hurt you. I am the inevitable wolf and for this reason I was given life. Why do you have such fiery, menacing claws? So that we may go hand in hand, for my need is so great, so great, so great – the wolves howled, looking nervously at their own claws before snuggling up to one another to make love and sleep.

…Thus it came about that in the large park surrounding my school, I slowly began to learn how to be loved, while enduring the sacrifice of not being worthy, if only to lessen the pain of one who does not love. No, that was only one of the reasons. Others make up different stories. In some, other claws, filled with cruel love, have plucked the barbed arrow from my heart, indifferent to my screams of pain.

THE PARTY

The imaginings which frighten me. I imagined a party – without food or drink – a party simply to be looked at. Even the chairs have been hired and transported to an empty third-floor apartment on the Rua da Alfândega, an ideal place for a party. I would invite all my former friends of both sexes, with whom I have now lost touch. Only former friends, excluding any of the mutual friends of friends. Individuals who shared my life and whose life I shared. But how could I climb those dark stairs to a rented room on my own? And how would I get back from the Rua da Alfândega at night? For I knew the pavements would be dry and hard.

I preferred another imagining. It began by mingling affection with gratitude and rage: only afterwards did the two wings of a bat unfold, like something coming from afar and getting closer; but those wings were also shining. Perhaps a tea-party this time – on a Sunday afternoon in the Rua do Lavradio – to which I would invite all the housemaids I had ever employed. Those whom I had forgotten would indicate their absence with an empty chair. just as they exist inside me. The others would be seated, their hands folded on their laps. Silent. Until each of them should open her mouth and, restored to life, a resuscitated corpse, should recite what I can remember of their conversation. Almost like a tea-party for society ladies, except that at this tea-party there would be no talk about housemaids.

– I wish you every happiness – one of them gets to her feet – May you be blessed with what no one can give you.

– Whenever I ask for anything – another rises from her chair

131

– I can't stop laughing, so people never take me seriously.

– I like films with a gun fight. (And that was all I could remember about an entire person.)

– Plain, everyday home-cooking, madam. I only know how to cook for the poor.

– When I die, one or two people will miss me. But that's all.

– My eyes fill with tears when I speak to a lady, it must be all this spiritualism.

– He was such a pretty child that I really felt like giving him a good thrashing.

– Early this morning – the Italian maid told me – when I was coming to work, the leaves started falling along with the first snow. A man on the street said to me: 'It's raining gold and silver.' I pretended I hadn't heard him because, if I'm not careful, men always get their way with me.

– Here comes Her Ladyship – the oldest of all my former house-maids gets up, the one who only managed to show soured affection and who taught me so early in life how to forgive love's cruelty. – Did Your Ladyship sleep well? Being a lady means enjoying every luxury. She is full of whims: she wants this, she doesn't want that. To be a lady means being white.

– I want three days off during the Carnival, madam, for I'm tired of playing Cinderella.

– Food is a question of salt. Food is a question of salt. Food is a question of salt. Here comes Her Ladyship: may you be blessed with what no one can give you, that's all I ask when I die. Then the man said that the rain was gold, and no one can give you that. Unless you don't mind standing in the dark, bathed in gold, but it has to be in the dark. Her ladyship has seen better days: leaves or the first snow. To taste the salt in what you are eating, not to give a pretty child a good thrashing, to avoid laughter when you are asking for something, never to pretend that you haven't heard when someone says: It's raining, my good woman, it's raining gold and silver. It really is!

KEEPING AN EYE ON THE WORLD

I am an extremely busy person. I keep an eye on the world. Each morning I look down from my terrace at the strip of beach with the sea beyond. Sometimes the spray seems whiter and I can tell that the restless waters have advanced during the night leaving their mark on the sand. I watch the almond trees on the street below. Before falling asleep, and keeping an eye on the world in my dreams, I examine the night sky to see if there are stars twinkling against a blue background, because on certain nights the sky is not black but ultramarine. The world keeps me fully occupied, because I recognize that God is the cosmos, and that is a responsibility I would be prepared to forgo.

I see a little boy who cannot be more than ten, dressed in rags and unbelievably thin. A future case of tuberculosis, if he is not already infected.

When I visit the Botanical Gardens I soon become weary. There I have to keep an eye on thousands of plants and trees, especially the gigantic water-lilies.

Take note that I have said nothing about my emotional reactions: I spoke only of some of the thousands of things and people I keep an eye on. Nor does anyone pay me to do this job. I simply keep the world under observation.

Is it hard work keeping an eye on the world? Most certainly. I can remember the terrifying face of one woman I saw in the street, a face devoid of any expression. I also keep an eye on thousands of slum-dwellers on the nearby slopes. I observe the seasonal changes in myself: I inevitably change with every season.

You must be wondering why I keep an eye on the world. I was born with this mission. And I am responsible for everything in existence, even for those wars and crimes which cause so much physical and spiritual havoc. I am even responsible for this God Who is in a perpetual state of cosmic evolution towards greater perfection.

Since childhood I have kept an eye on a swarm of ants: they crawl in Indian file, carrying a tiny particle of leaf which does not prevent them from pausing to chat whenever they meet another procession of ants coming from the opposite direction.

I once read a standard textbook about bees and I have observed them ever since, especially the queen bee. Bees fly and nourish themselves on flowers: that much I have learned.

But ants have such a neat little waistline. Yet tiny as they are, they embrace a whole world, which eludes me unless I examine them closely: an instinctive sense of organization, a language which goes beyond the supersonic to our ears and probably attuned to instinctive feelings of love-cum-sentiment, for ants can speak. I kept a watchful eye on these insects when I was little and now that I so dearly long to see them again, I cannot find a single ant. I know they have not been exterminated otherwise I should have been told. Keeping an eye on the world also requires a lot of patience: I must wait for the ants to reappear. Patience. While watching the flowers open imperceptibly, little by little.

But I still have not found the person to whom I should report my findings.

A VARIATION ON THE DISTRACTED MAN

He is wearing his spectacles all the time as he goes searching for them throughout the entire house. Now and then he says to himself with satisfaction: How fortunate I am to be able to see everything so clearly today. This should make it easier to find my spectacles. Sometimes, in the middle of searching, he begins to think to himself: I can see so well today that I might not need my spectacles for reading any more. He only realizes that he has been wearing his spectacles all the time when he adjusts them to read before going to sleep. He feels so bitterly disappointed: No wonder I thought I did not need my spectacles any more.

GENTLE WEEPING

...I caught a sudden glance and the man was so incredibly handsome and virile that I could feel the joy of creation. Not that I wanted him for myself, just as I do not crave the Moon at night when it becomes as delicate and impassive as a pearl. Just as I do not long for that nine-year old boy I saw chasing a ball and whose ringlets reminded me of the Archangel. All I wanted was to be a spectator. The man gave me a passing glance and smiled quietly: he knew he was handsome and clearly recognized that I did not want him for myself. He smiled at me because he did not feel threatened. (Exceptional human beings are more exposed to danger than ordinary people.) I crossed the street and hailed a taxi. The breeze ruffled my hair from behind and, although it was autumn, appeared to herald a new spring as if the tedious summer deserved the freshness of budding flowers. But for the moment it was autumn and the leaves were turning yellow on the almond-trees. I felt such joy that I snuggled apprehensively into a corner of the taxi because happiness, too, can be painful. And all this had been provoked by the vision of a handsome man. I continued not to want him for myself, yet somehow he had given me a great deal with that friendly smile in token of our mutual understanding. The taxi was now approaching the viaduct near the Museum of Modern Art. I no longer felt happy. Autumn had become menacing and hostile. I felt like weeping gently.

THE ITALIAN WOMAN

Rosa lost her parents when she was small. Her brothers and sisters were dispersed throughout the world and she was sent to an orphanage attached to a convent. There she led an austere and deprived existence with the other inmates. During the winter the great mansion was permanently cold, and the work never ceased. Rosa did the washing, she swept out the rooms, and mended clothes. Meantime, the seasons passed. With her head shaved and wearing a long tunic made of coarse material, she often interrupted her sweeping to gaze out of the window. Autumn was the season she liked best, for she could savour it without going outdoors: through the window-panes she would watch the yellowing leaves fall into the courtyard, and that was autumn.

In this particular Swiss convent, whenever a man crossed the doorway, the floor had to be scrubbed and alcohol burned over the spot where he had been standing.

Then winter would return once more and Rosa's hands became inflamed and covered with chilblains. Her bed was so cold that it was impossible to sleep. In that darkened dormitory, with her open eyes peering over the sheet, she would espy those tiny glancing thoughts. In some strange way those thoughts were paradise.

How and why, at the age of twenty, Rosa suddenly decided to leave the convent, I cannot say, nor could she herself explain. But she had made up her mind, although everyone opposed the idea. Her resolve was firm, her resistance passive. The nuns were horrified and warned her that she would go to Hell. But because Rosa made no attempt to justify her decision, she got her way. She left the convent and found employment as a housemaid.

She left carrying her small bundle of possessions, her head shaved, her skirt down to her ankles.

'The world struck me as being...' but she could not explain.

With her Southern Italian features, her oval eyes, and curves which were slow in asserting themselves, Rosa went to live with a family which had been recommended. There she remained day and night, month after month, never going out. She explained to me that at that time she did not know how 'to go out'. She contemplated the wonders of winter from the windows without venturing out into that Paradise: she observed everything through those windows and no one could say for certain whether she was happy or sad. Her face was still incapable of expressing emotion. She looked through those windows with the rapt attention of someone at prayer, her arms folded, her hands tucked into her sleeves.

One afternoon when everything struck her as being much too vast – a free afternoon without any household chores was almost sinful – she felt that she should apply herself to something, adopt a much more disciplined, even pious attitude. She went downstairs, went into the drawing-room and selected a book from the bookcase. She went back upstairs and sat bolt upright in a chair, for she was unaccustomed to seeking comfort and pleasure. She began to read with concentration. But her spherical head – where tufts of vigorous hair had begun to sprout – her head became muddled. She closed the book, lay down, and closed her eyes.

The family waited for her to serve dinner, but Rosa did not appear. They went to look for her. Her eyes were swollen, inflamed, expressionless: she was burning with fever. The mistress of the house spent that night looking after her, but there was nothing anyone could do: Rosa complained of nothing and asked for nothing as the fever gripped her. Next morning, she looked thinner, her eyes half-closed. And she passed another day and night in the same condition. The family sent for the doctor.

He enquired what had happened, for there were clear symptoms of a nervous disorder. Rosa made no reply, nor did it occur to her to answer the doctor's questions, for she was not accustomed to speaking up for herself. At this point, the doctor chanced to look at the bedside table and his eye caught sight of the book. He examined it, and looked at her with some alarm. The book was entitled *Le corset rouge*. He warned Rosa that she should not read such a book under any circumstances. She had barely left the convent, and her innocence constituted a threat. Rosa said nothing. The doctor continued:

– You must not read such books because they are false.

Rosa opened her eyes a little more widely for the first time. The doctor swore to her that the book was full of lies. He had sworn...

Rosa sighed and shyly gave a wistful smile:

– I thought that everything which was written and published in a book was the truth, she said, looking modestly at the first honest man she had ever known.

The doctor said – and one can imagine in what tone of voice:

– Nonsense.

Rosa slept, thin and pallid. Her fever abated and she was soon back on her feet. With time, people began to notice: what lovely black hair you have, they told her. Touching her hair, Rosa would reply: really!

How Rosa could be so happy at the age of forty continues to be a mystery. How she laughed. I know that on one occasion she tried to commit suicide. Not because she had left the convent. But because of a love affair. She explained that, when she fell in love, she had no idea that 'things were really like that'. Like what? She made no attempt to answer my question. Ten years older than her lover, she laughs under that great mane of black hair and insists: I really cannot explain why I prefer autumn to the other seasons. I think it's because in the autumn things wither so quickly.

She also insists: I'm not very bright. I have the impression that

137

Madam is much more intelligent than I am. She also asks me: 'Has Madam ever cried like a fool without knowing why? for I have!' – and she bursts into laughter.

AN UNTRANSLATED EPIGRAPH

As an epigraph for my novel *A Paixāo segundo G.H.* [The Passion according to G.H.] I chose, or rather, miraculously came across, after finishing the book, a quotation from the art historian Bernard Berenson. Even though it had little to do with my novel, I could not resist using the phrase.

But in my enthusiasm, I made one mistake. I made no attempt to translate the epigraph but left it in English, forgetting that the Brazilian reader is not obliged to understand another language. It would be difficult, however, to capture the beauty and perfection of Berenson's own words in any other language:

> A complete life may be one ending in
> so full an identification with the non-self
> that there is no self to die.

OLD-FASHIONED TASTES

Not so long ago I experienced an anguished sense of loss. Without giving the matter much thought, I made a sudden decision and told my hairdresser Luís Carlos to crop my hair. As he began cutting and locks of hair fell limply on to the floor, I looked in the mirror only to be confronted by an expression of alarm at my own rashness. And I experienced a sudden feeling of loss. Why loss? This feeling is so ancient that it recedes through the depths of time to a prehistoric age. A woman never cuts her hair because her femininity resides in those long tresses. Besides, when my boys were children they used to enjoy playing with my long hair. And recently when I visited a friend, her little girl who is five took great delight in endlessly combing my hair. There was something nice about the way those tiny hands communicated a sense of satisfaction. But now I had to accept

138

having cropped hair and I promised myself that I would let it grow again. No sooner was I back home than I changed my mind. Long hair takes a long time to dry, it needs a lot of brushing and frequent visits to the hairdresser, where one has to endure the sheer torture of sitting underneath one of those absurd hair-dryers. Short hair, on the other hand, I can wash myself, then sit in the sun for a while and that is that. As I sat there daydreaming, I thought to myself: Have I lost my strength like Samson? Well, perhaps not my strength as such, but my power as a woman.

SWIMMING AGAINST THE TIDE

I have struggled all my life to cure this tendency to daydream, lest it should carry me into remote waters. But the effort of swimming against this gentle current takes away some of my vital strength. And if, in fighting off daydreams, I gain in terms of action, I inwardly lose something very precious which can never be replaced. But one of these days I shall have to go, without worrying where I might end up.

THE MAKING OF A NOVEL

I can no longer recall where it began but I know I did not start at the beginning. It was, in a manner of speaking, all written simultaneously. Everything was there, or appeared to be there, as if within the temporal space of an open piano with its simultaneous keys.

I wrote with the utmost care as the narrative began to take shape inside me, and only after the fifth version had been patiently drafted did I become fully aware of the text. Only then did I begin to understand more clearly what was waiting to be expressed.

My great fear was that, out of impatience with my slowness in understanding myself, I might arrive at some meaning with undue haste. I had the impression, or rather felt certain that the more time I gave myself, the more spontaneously would the narrative begin to surface.

Increasingly I find that it is all a matter of patience, of love begetting patience, of patience begetting love.

The book came together simultaneously as it were, emerging more here than there, or suddenly more there than here: I would interrupt a sentence in Chapter Ten, let us say, in order to write Chapter Two, which I would then abandon for months on end while I wrote Chapter Eighteen. I showed endless patience: putting up with the considerable inconvenience of disorder without any reassurance that I would finish the book. But then order, too, can bring a sense of disquiet.

As always, the greatest difficulty is waiting. (I'm feeling rather odd, a woman will tell her doctor. You're going to have a baby. And here was me thinking I was dying, the woman replies.) My deformed soul growing and swelling, while I remain uncertain whether something is about to come to light.

In addition to this tiresome waiting, it requires infinite patience to reconstitute in gradual stages that initial vision which came in a flash. Recovering that vision is extremely difficult.

And to make matters worse, I am quite hopeless when it comes to editing. I am incapable of narrating an idea, and do not know how to 'embellish an idea with words'. What I write does not refer to past thought, but to thought in the present: whatever comes to the surface is already expressed in the only possible words, or simply does not exist.

As I write them down, I am convinced once more that, however paradoxical it may sound, the greatest drawback about writing is that one has to use words. It is a problem. For I should prefer a more direct form of communication, that tacit understanding one often finds between people. If I could write by carving on wood or by stroking a child's head or strolling in the countryside, I would never resort to using words. I would do what so many people do who are not writers, and with the same joy and torment as those who write, and with the same bitter disappointments which are beyond consolation. I would live and no longer use words. And this might be the solution. And as such, be most welcome.

WRITING

Writing for a newspaper is not so demanding: it is light, it must be light, even superficial. Those who read newspapers have neither the will nor time to read in depth.

But to write something intended for a book often demands more strength than one seems to possess.

Especially if it means devising one's own writing habits, as in my case. When I consciously decided in my early teens that I wanted to become a writer, I immediately found myself in a void. And there was no one to help or advise me.

I had to emerge from that void, to try and understand myself, and to forge, as it were, my own truth. I made a start, but not even at the beginning. The sheets of paper began piling up — nothing I wrote seemed to make sense, my frustration as I struggled to write something worthwhile became one more obstacle in the path of success. What a pity I destroyed the interminable narrative I then started writing under the influence of Hermann Hesse's *Steppenwolf*. I tore it up, contemptuous of my almost superhuman efforts to master the craft of writing and come to terms with myself. And no one knew my secret. I did not tell a soul. I lived through that sorrow alone. One thing, however, did occur to me. It was important to carry on writing without waiting for the right moment, because the right moment never comes. Writing has never been easy for me. I knew from the outset this was my vocation. Having a vocation is not the same as having talent. One can have a vocation and no talent – in other words, feel compelled to write without knowing where to start.

INSPIRATION

Ample bosom, broad hips, eyes chaste, brown, and dreamy. Now and then she would cry out suddenly. Speaking so quickly that she could scarcely be heard, she confided cheerfully with an air of impatience:

'I thought that I could never be a writer, I have so...so...little to say.'

One day, however, as if hidden from herself, she had an idea and jotted down some sentences about the beauty of the Sugar Loaf Mountain in her notebook. Just a few words, for she was so concise. Time passed and one evening when she was alone she remembered that she had made a few notes about something or other – the Sugar Loaf Mountain? The sea? She went to look for her notebook. She searched the entire house. She systematically went through every drawer and cupboard. She even opened shoe-boxes in the hope of having been so secretive as to have hidden her notes in a shoe-box. What a good idea. Gradually the sensation of choking grew worse. She ran her hand over her forehead – now she was searching for something more than her notebook, she was searching for what inspiration had dictated. Let us see, let us be patient and have another look. What could she have written in her notebook? She remembered it was something very spiritual about something very picturesque. For her there was nothing like the picturesque. Let's have another look. It's a question of willpower, of getting hold of it somehow. What a calamity – she said, standing motionless in the middle of the room, not knowing where to turn, where to look. What a calamity. The room, tranquil in the evening light. And somewhere there was something written, some intimate thought, of that she was certain. She unbuttoned the collar of her blouse. Don't be down-hearted, she whispered to herself, look amongst your papers, amongst your letters, amongst the cuttings and reviews people keep sending you. Ah, she reasoned illogically, if only they had written to her more often, then she would have more papers to search through. But her orderly life was exposed, she had few places for hiding things, her existence was tidy. Her only hiding place was herself, her own soul which she had once bared in her notebook. But how happy she felt to have pieces of furniture and boxes where she might discover things by chance. She had places where she could go on searching indefinitely.

Now and then she would make another search. From time to time, she would remember her notebook and be seized with fresh hope. Until one day, after several more years had passed, she remarked modestly:

– When I was younger, I used to do a little writing.

142

IDLE CONVERSATION

I was having a cup of coffee in the kitchen when I heard the maid through in the scullery humming the loveliest melody. A melody without words, a sort of cantilena and full of harmony. I asked her who had written the music. She told me: Nobody, it's just a silly tune I made up myself.

She did not know she was creative. Just as the world does not know it is creative. I stopped drinking my coffee and began speculating: will the world become even more creative? The world is unaware of itself. We are so backward in relation to ourselves. Even the word *creative* will no longer be used or even mentioned: things will simply be created. We are not to blame – I went back to my coffee – if we are thousands of years behind. To think of 'thousands of years hence' almost made me dizzy, for I cannot even be sure what colour the earth will be. Posterity exists and will eliminate our present. And if the world recreates itself in cycles, let us say, are we likely to revert to the Stone Age so that everything may repeat itself all over again? It wounds me almost physically to think that I shall never know what this world will be like thousands of years hence. On the other hand, I continued to reflect, we may be crawling but we crawl in haste. And the tune the maid was humming will dominate this new world: for people can be creative without even knowing it. Meanwhile, we are as parched as a dried fig which has scarcely any moisture left.

Meanwhile the maid is hanging out the washing on the clothes-line, still humming that tune without words. The melody pervades me. The maid is dark and skinny, and lodged inside her is an 'I'. A body separate from other bodies, and that is called an 'I'? It is strange to have a body in which to lodge, a body where liquefied blood flows incessantly, where the mouth can sing, and the eyes must have wept so often. She is an 'I'.

FEAR OF ETERNITY

I shall never forget my dramatic and harrowing contact with eternity.

As a little girl I had never chewed bubble-gum and in Recife it was not easy to find. I simply had no idea what bubble-gum looked like. My pocket-money was meagre and for the price of bubble-gum I could have bought lots of sweets.

My sister managed to save up enough money to buy some. On our way to school, she gave me a piece and warned me: Be careful not to lose it, because you can chew it forever. Bubble-gum lasts for ages.

– What do you mean, it lasts for ages? I stopped in my tracks, completely bewildered.

– It lasts forever and that's that.

I was easily impressed and felt as if I had been transported to a never-never land inhabited by princes and good fairies. I grabbed that small pink object which promised eternal pleasure and carefully examined it, suspicious of its miraculous powers. Like most children, I would sometimes take a boiled sweet out of my mouth after the first few sucks, to keep it for later. And here I was in possession of this pink object, so innocent in appearance yet capable of realizing this impossible world of which I had just been made aware.

With the utmost delicacy, I finally popped the bubble-gum into my mouth.

– And now what am I supposed to do? – I asked my sister, for fear of spoiling whatever ritual might be expected of me.

– Suck the bubble-gum until you begin to taste the sweetness and then you can start chewing. And after that you can go on chewing for as long as you like. Unless you happen to lose it. I've lost mine several times.

Lose eternity? Never.

The bubble-gum had a nice enough taste but nothing out of the ordinary. And I was still puzzled as we made our way to school.

– It doesn't taste sweet any more. Now what?

– Now you carry on chewing.

For some strange reason I felt nervous. I began chewing and that rubbery gum in my mouth had now turned grey and tasted of nothing. I chewed and chewed but felt sadly disappointed. It would have been a lie to say I was enjoying that bubble-gum. And the fact that it lasted forever filled me with fear, the kind of fear one experiences when confronted with the idea of eternity or the infinite.

I was reluctant to admit that I was not up to eternity. The very idea distressed me. But meanwhile, I obediently carried on chewing without stopping.

Until I could stand it no longer and as I went through the school gates I managed to let it drop on to the ground.

– Oh, look what's happened! – I said, feigning alarm and disappointment. Now I can't chew it any more. I've lost my bubble-gum!

– How many times do I have to tell you! my sister rebuked me – bubble-gum lasts forever. Unless you're silly enough to lose it. You can even chew it in bed at night, and then stick it on the head-board before you fall asleep. Never mind, one day I'll give you another piece if you promise not to lose it next time.

My sister's generosity filled me with remorse. And I began to regret that I had lied to her by insisting the bubble-gum had dropped by accident. But I felt so relieved. No longer burdened by the weight of eternity.

CREATING BRASÍLIA

Brasília is built on the line of the horizon. – Brasília is artificial. As artificial as the world must have been when it was created. When the world was created, it was necessary to create a human being especially for that world. We are all deformed through adapting to God's freedom. We cannot say how we might have turned out if we had been created first, and the world deformed afterwards to meet our needs. Brasília has no inhabitants as yet who are typical of Brasília. – If I were to say that Brasília is pleasant, you would realize immediately that I like the city. But if I were to say that Brasília is the image of my insomnia, you would see this as a criticism: but my insomnia is neither pleasant nor awful – my insomnia is me, it is lived, it is my terror. The two architects who planned Brasília were not interested in creating something beautiful. That would be too simple; they created their own terror, and left that terror unexplained. Creation is not an understanding, it is a new mystery. – When I died, I opened my eyes one day and there was Brasília. I found myself alone in the world. There was a taxi standing there. No sign of the driver. – Lúcio Costa and Oscar Niemeyer are two solitary men. – I look at Brasília the way I look at Rome: Brasília began with the starkest of ruins. The ivy had not yet grown. – Besides the wind there is another thing that blows. It can only be recognized in the supernatural rippling of the lake. – Wherever you stand, you have the impression of being on the edge of a dangerous precipice. Brasília stands on the margin. – Were I to live here, I should let my hair grow down to my feet. – Brasília belongs to a glorious past which no longer exists. That type of civilization disappeared thousands of years ago. In the 4th century BC, Brasília was inhabited by men and women who were fair and very tall, who were neither American nor Scandinavian, and who shone brightly in the sun. They were all blind. That explains why there is nothing to collide with in Brasília. The inhabitants of Brasília used to dress in white gold. The race became extinct because few children were born. The more beautiful the natives of Brasília, the blinder, purer, and more radiant they became, and the fewer children they produced. The natives of Brasília lived for nearly three hundred years. There was no one in whose name they could die. Thousands of years later, the location was discovered by a band of fugitives who would not be accepted in any other place; they had nothing to lose. There they lit a bonfire, set up their tents, and gradually began excavating the sands which buried the city. Those men and women were short and dark-skinned, with shifty, restless eyes, and because they were fugitives and desperate, they had something to live and die for. They occupied the houses, which were in ruins, and multiplied, thus forming a human race which was much given to contemplation. – I waited for night, like someone waiting for shadows in order to steal away unobserved. When night came, I perceived with horror that it was hopeless: wherever I went, I would be seen. The thought terrified me: seen by whom? – The city was built without any escape route for rats. A whole part of myself, the worst part, and precisely that part of me which has a horror of rats, has not been provided for in Brasília. Its founders tried to ignore the importance of human beings. The dimensions of the city's buildings were calculated for the heavens. Hell has a better understanding of me. But the rats, all of them enormous, are invading the city. That is a newspaper headline. – This place frightens me. – The construction of Brasília: that of a totalitarian state. This great visual silence which I adore. Even my insomnia might have created this peace of never-never-land. Like those two hermits, Costa and Niemeyer, I would also meditate in the desert where there are no opportunities for temptation. But I see black vultures flying high overhead. What is perishing, dear God? – I did not shed a single tear in Brasília. – There was no place for tears. – It is a shore without any sea. In Brasília there is no place where one may enter, no place where one may leave. – Mummy, it's nice to see you standing there with your white cape fluttering in the breeze. (The truth is that I have perished, my son.) – A prison in the open air. In any case, there would be nowhere to escape to. For anyone escaping would probably find himself heading for Brasília. They captured me in freedom. But freedom is simply what one achieves. When they beat me, they are ordering me to be free. – The human indifference which lurks in my nature is something I discover here in Brasíia, and it flowers cold and potent, the frozen strength of Nature. Here is the place where my crimes (not the worst of them, but those I would not understand), where my crimes would not be crimes of love. I am off to commit those other crimes which God and I understand. But I know that I shall return. I am drawn here by all that is terrifying in my nature. – I have never seen anything like it in the world. But I recognize this city in the depths of my dream. In those depths there is lucidity. – For as I was saying, Flash Gordon... – If they were to photograph me standing in Brasília, when they came to develop the film only the landscape would appear. – Where are the giraffes of Brasília? – A certain twitching on my part, certain moments of silence, cause my son to exclaim: 'Really, grown-ups are the limit!' – It is urgent. Were Brasília not populated, or rather, over-populated, it would be inhabited in some other way. And should that happen, it would be much too late: there would be no place for people. They would sense they were being quietly expelled. – Here the soul casts no shadow on the ground. – During the first two days I had no appetite. Everything had the appearance of the food they serve on board aeroplanes. – At night, I confronted silence. I know that there is a secret hour when manna falls and moistens the lands of Brasília. – However close one may be, everything here is seen from afar. I could find no way of touching. But at least there is one thing in my favour: before arriving here, I already knew how to touch things from afar. I never became too desperate: from afar, I was able to touch things. I possessed a great deal, and not even what I have touched knows of this. A rich woman is like this. It is pure Brasília. – The city of Brasília is situated outside the city. – '*Boys, boys come here, will you. Look who's coming on the street, all dressed up in modernistic style. It ain't nobody but...*' (*Aunt Hagar's Blues*, played by Ted Lewis and his Band, with Jimmy Dorsey on the clarinet.) – Such astonishing beauty, this city traced out in mid-air. – Meantime, no samba is likely to be born in Brasília. – Brasília does not permit me to feel weary. It almost hounds me. I feel fine. I feel fine. I feel fine. I feel just fine. Besides, I have always cultivated my weariness as my most precious passiveness. – All this is but today. Only God knows what will happen to Brasília. Here the fortuitous takes one by surprise – Brasília is haunted. It is the motionless outline of something. – Unable to sleep, I look out of my hotel window at three o'clock in the morning. Brasília is a landscape of insomnia. It never sleeps. – Here the organic being does not deteriorate. It becomes petrified. – I should like to see five hundred eagles of the blackest onyx scattered throughout Brasília. – Brasília is asexual. – The first instant you set eyes on the city you feel inebriated: your feet do not touch the ground. – How deeply one breathes in Brasília. As you breathe here you begin to experience desire. And that is out of the question. Desire does not exist here. Will it ever exist? I cannot see how. – It would not surprise me to encounter Arabs on the street. Arabs of another age and long since dead. – Here my passion dies. And I gain a lucidity which makes me feel grandiose for no good reason. I am wonderful and futile, I am of the purest gold. And almost endowed with the spiritualistic powers of a medium. – If there is some crime which humanity has still to commit, that new crime will be initiated here. It is so very open, so well suited to the plateau, that no one will ever know. – This is the place where space most closely resembles time. – I am certain that this is the right place for me. But I have become much too corrupted on earth. I have acquired all of life's bad habits. – Erosion will strip Brasília to the bone. – The religious atmosphere which I sensed from the outset, and denied. This city was achieved through prayer. Two men beatified by solitude created me here, on foot, restless, exposed to the wind. How I should love to set white horses free here in Brasília. At night, they would become green under the light of the moon – I know what those two men wanted: that slowness and silence which are also my idea of eternity. Those two men created the image of an eternal city. – There is something here which frightens me. When I discover what it is, I shall also discover what I like about this place. Fear has always guided me to the things I love; and because I love, I become afraid. It was often fear which took me by the hand and led me. Fear leads me to danger. And everything I love has an element of risk. – In Brasília you find the craters of the Moon. – And the beauty of Brasília is to be found in those invisible statues.

IRRESISTIBLE INCARNATION

Sometimes when I see someone whom I have never seen before, and I observe that person at length, I begin to identify with her and take steps to get to know that person. And this intrusion into another person's life, no matter who she may be, never ends in self-accusation. Once I have identified with the other woman, I understand her motives and forgive her. Needless to say, I have to be careful not to be drawn into some dangerous or glamorous existence which might dissuade me from reverting to being myself.

One day on a plane...Oh, dear God, I implored, I beg of You, anything but *that*; I have no desire to be a missionary!

But it was hopeless. I knew that after having to spend three hours in her presence, I would become a missionary myself for several days. The missionary's austerity and polite gestures had already taken possession of me. And it is always with a certain curiosity, a sense of wonder and weariness that I finally succumb to the life I am about to experience for several days. There is also some apprehension from a practical point of view: I am much too preoccupied with my work and leisure to be able to cope with the additional burden of some strange new existence whose evangelical zeal is already weighing upon me. In the plane itself I noticed that I had already started imitating the solemn movements of the lay missionary: then I began to understand her patience, that self-effacing gait, her feet scarcely touching the ground, as if to tread more firmly would disturb the other passengers. I, too, had turned pale, my lips unpainted, my expression meek, and wearing the unmistakable head-dress of a lay missionary.

When the plane touches down, I thought to myself, I shall probably wear that expression of suffering-overcome-by-the-peace-of-having-a-mission. And on my face will be imprinted the sweetness of moral hope. Because I have suddenly become extremely moral. Yet when I boarded the plane I was so wholesomely amoral. I was, no, I am! I cried out in protest against the missionary's prejudices. It was useless: all my energy was being sapped so that I might become delicate. I pretended to be reading a magazine, while she read her Bible.

We were about to make a short landing. The air-steward distributed boiled sweets. And the missionary blushed the moment the young steward approached.

Back on the ground, I was a missionary waiting in a windy airport. I kept a firm grip on the long skirt of that imaginary habit for fear of that threatening wind. I understand, I thought, oh I understand so well how lost she must be feeling during these hours when she is not fulfilling her mission. Like the little missionary, I, too, disapproved of those short skirts worn by the other women passengers, which could only be tempting to men. And when I did not understand, it was with the same purified fanaticism of this pale woman who blushed the moment the young air-steward returned to announce the plane was ready to leave.

I knew that it would be some time before I could hope to regain my own identity. Which perhaps was never really mine apart from the moment I was born, only to be followed by one reincarnation after the other. But no: I am a person. And when my own ghost takes possession of me, the encounter is one of such bliss and rejoicing that in a manner of speaking we weep on each other's shoulder. Then, wiping away our tears of joy, my ghost fully embodies itself with me and we go out into the world with our head held high.

Once, on another trip, I came across a prostitute reeking of cheap perfume who smoked with her eyes half-closed while staring at a male passenger who was soon hypnotized. I began imitating her to see what would happen. I lit a cigarette and with half-closed eyes began staring at the only man nearby. But the fat man I had chosen in my efforts to identify with the prostitute, was far too engrossed in the *New York Times*. Besides, my perfume was much too discreet. A complete fiasco.

SATURDAY

I find Saturday is the rose of the week; on Saturday afternoon curtains blow in the breeze, and someone empties a bucket of water over the terrace. Saturday with a breeze blowing is the rose of the week. Saturday morning I associated with the yard, the bee flying from plant to plant, and the breeze: a bee-sting, a swollen face, blood and honey, the bee has left its mark. Other bees will follow the scent and on the following Saturday morning I shall see if the yard is full of bees. It was on a Saturday that the ants swarmed over paving-stones in the backyards of my childhood. It was on a Saturday that I saw a man sitting in the shade on the pavement, eating stew and manioc meal out of a gourd. It was Saturday afternoon and we had already bathed in the sea. At two o'clock, a bell announced in the breeze the matinée performance at the local cinema: Saturday with a breeze was the rose of the week. If it rained, I alone knew that it was Saturday; Saturday transformed into a drenched rose? In Rio de Janeiro, just when you think the exhausted week is about to die, the week suddenly opens out into a rose. On the Avenida Atlantica a car slams on its brakes and, suddenly, before the startled breeze can blow once more, I sense it is Saturday afternoon. It has been Saturday, but is no longer the same. I say nothing, seemingly resigned. But I have already gathered my things and moved on to Sunday morning. Sunday morning is also the rose of the week. Although not to be compared with Saturday. I shall never know why.

151

Those who have never stolen would not understand. And those who have never stolen roses would never be capable of understanding me. For when I was a little girl, I used to steal roses.

In Recife there were lots of streets with large villas on either side, surrounded by extensive gardens, where rich people lived. I used to play a game with another little girl in order to decide who owned those villas. 'That white one is mine.' 'No, it isn't, we've already agreed the white ones are mine.' But that one isn't all white for the windows are green. Sometimes we would stand there for ages, our faces pressed against the railings as we peered in.

The stealing began as follows. We were playing this game of ours one day when we stopped in front of a villa which looked like a little castle. At the far end there was an enormous orchard. And in front of the villa there were neat flower-beds full of flowers.

And all alone in the middle of one of the beds there was a bright pink rose which had just started to open. I stood there gaping, lost in admiration for that proud rose which was not yet in full bloom. And then suddenly it happened: I wanted that rose with all my heart. I wanted it, just for me, oh, how I wanted it. And there was no way of getting it. Had the gardener been there I should have asked him for the rose, although most likely he would have chased us away as if we were street-urchins. But there was no gardener around, not a soul to be seen. And to keep out the sun, the blinds were drawn. No trams passed along this street and there were few cars. In the midst of my silence and that of the rose, there was my desire to possess it just for myself. I wanted to touch it. I wanted to smell it until I became intoxicated by its perfume.

Until I could bear it no longer. Overcome with desire, I lost no time in drawing up a plan. And determined to succeed, I gave clear instructions to my little friend and carefully explained the part she was to play. She would keep an eye on the windows and watch out for the gardener, who might suddenly appear, or for any passers-by. Meanwhile, I slowly eased open the gates which were rather rusty, fully expecting them to creak a little. I eased them open just enough for my skinny frame to squeeze through. And then, moving quickly, I tiptoed over the paving-stones between the flower-beds. My heart was beating fast and it seemed to take forever to reach that rose.

At last, the rose was within reach. I paused for a second, perilously, because close up, it looked even lovelier. Reaching out to break the stem, I scratched my hand on the thorns and licked the blood from my fingers.

Then suddenly – I held that entire rose in my hand. I crept back to the gate as quietly as possible and I slipped through the gate which I had left ajar, clutching my prize. And then the rose and I, both of us deathly pale, took to our heels and ran away from the villa as fast as my legs could carry us.

What did I do with my rose? Now that it was mine, this is what I did:

I took it home and put it in a glass of water where it triumphed in all its beauty, the petals thick and velvety in various shades of pink. The colour deepened in the middle until it turned almost crimson.

It was such a wonderful feeling.

That rose gave me so much pleasure that I simply began stealing more and more roses. The ritual never varied: the other little girl kept a lookout while I went in, snapped the roses from their stems and made my escape. With my heart beating fast and forever with that sense of triumph no one could take from me.

I also stole cherries. There was a Presbyterian church near my home. The grounds were enclosed by a green hedge, which was so tall and dense that it was impossible to see the church apart from one tiny corner of the church steeple. The hedge consisted of Surinam cherry bushes and the cherries of this species are concealed amongst the branches. No cherries could be seen from the road. So, after looking carefully, first right then left, to make sure no one was coming, I pushed my hand through the railings, and fumbled inside the hedge until I could feel the moist cherries. In my haste, I often squashed the overripe ones, staining my fingers with their blood-red juice. I picked a handful which I ate on the spot, although some were too green and had to be thrown away.

No one ever caught me. And to this day I feel no remorse. Anyone who steals roses and cherries deserves a hundred years' pardon. Besides, cherries would prefer to be eaten once they ripen rather than be allowed to rot on the branch, their virginity intact.

SELF-INFLICTED SORROW

Having been through the experience of having a skin-graft, I realize that any idea of a skin-bank is impracticable because a donor's skin will not adhere for very long to the skin of another person. It is essential that the skin should be removed from another part of the patient's body and then be grafted on immediately wherever needed. In other words, skin-grafting means donating one's own skin to oneself.

This led me to consider other instances where people have to donate things to themselves. And this might bring solitude, riches, conflict. I began thinking about kindness which we would naturally like to receive from others. – Yet sometimes only the kindness we extend to ourselves exonerates us from a sense of guilt. Just as it is useless to win the acceptance of others so long as we are unwilling to accept ourselves for what we are. And as for our frailty, this is the strongest part of our nature, and brings us reassurance and satisfaction. And there are certain sorrows which only our own sorrow, if intensified, can, paradoxically, assuage.

Fortunately, when it comes to love, riches come with mutual donation. Which does not imply there is no struggle: we have to grant ourselves the right to receive love. But the struggle is worthwhile. Just as certain problems, simply because they are difficult, heat our blood, and fortunately this is something we can donate.

And that reminds me of something else we can donate to ourselves: artistic creation. For this also initially involves one in removing skin from one part to graft on somewhere else. And only once that grafting has succeeded can there be any donation to others. Perhaps I am getting confused. Artistic creation is a mystery which happily eludes me. Better not to know too much.

THE ADVANTAGES OF BEING FOOLISH

– The fool who pursues no ambitions has time to see, hear and touch the world.

– The fool can remain seated for hours on end without stirring. And when anyone asks him if he cannot find something to do, he replies: 'But I *am* doing something. I am thinking.'

— To be a fool sometimes offers an escape route because the astute only think of escaping through their astuteness, while the fool is original and ideas come to him spontaneously

— The fool has the chance to see things the astute fail to see.

— The astute are always so busy paying attention to the wiles of others that they relax in the presence of fools and the latter simply regard them as human beings.

— The fool gains the freedom and wisdom to live.

— The fool never seems to get the chance to shine. Yet the fool is often a Dostoevsky.

— Obviously there can be disadvantages. A foolish woman, for example, trusted the advice of a stranger when buying a second-hand air-conditioning system. He assured her the equipment was almost new and had scarcely been used because he had moved to Gávea where there was plenty of fresh air. So the foolish woman bought the machine without even inspecting it. As a result, it did not work. She then called in a technician who warned her the machine was so badly damaged that it would cost a fortune to repair it: much safer to buy new equipment.

— In compensation, however, the fool always acts in good faith, never mistrusts anyone and lives a tranquil life. While the curious man cannot sleep at night for fear of being deceived. The astute man pays for winning with a stomach ulcer. The fool does not even notice when he has won.

— Warning: do not confuse fools with donkeys.

— Disadvantage: the fool might receive a knife in the back when he least expects it. This is one of the hazards the fool cannot foresee. Caesar ended up by uttering those famous words: 'You, too, Brutus?'

— The fool voices no protest. But how he shouts!

— Incorrigible buffoons, all fools must go to heaven.

— If Christ had been astute, he would not have been crucified.

— The fool is so endearing that some astute men even try to pass for fools.

— The fool has to be creative but, like any creative act, playing the fool is not easy. That explains why the astute do not succeed in passing for fools.

— The astute gain at the expense of others. In compensation, fools are simply rewarded with life.

– Blessed are the fools because they know without anyone suspecting. Nor do they care if people know that they know.

– Certain places are more congenial for the fool (not to be confused with donkey or simpleton or good-for-nothing). Minas Gerais, for example, is most receptive to fools. Oh, it is amazing how many people lose out because they were not born in Minas!

– Chagall is a fool when he puts a cow into space, flying over roof-tops.

– It is almost impossible to avoid the excess of love a fool arouses. For only a fool is capable of excessive love. And only love makes the fool.

FORGIVING GOD

I was strolling along the Avenida Copacabana and looking distractedly at buildings, a strip of sea, people on the pavement, thinking of nothing in particular. I still had not realized that I was not really distracted but effortlessly observing things. I was being something very rare: free. I was looking at everything and at my leisure. Little by little I began to realize I was perceiving things. My freedom became a little more intense without ceasing to be freedom. It was not a *tour de propriétaire*, nothing of what I perceived was mine nor did I covet it. Yet it seems to me that I felt deeply satisfied with what I saw.

Just then, I experienced a feeling which I had never heard of before. Out of sheer affection, I felt myself to be the mother of God Who was both earth and the world. Out of sheer affection, without any suggestion of arrogance or vanity, without the slightest hint of superiority or equality, I had become the Mother of all that exists. And I knew that if all this were what I *really* felt and not some false sentiment, then God would allow Himself to be loved by me without pride or pettiness and without any compromise. He would find the intimacy with which I loved Him acceptable. This feeling was new to me but unmistakable and, if it had not occurred to me before, that was simply because it could not be. I know that one loves what we call God with grave and solemn love, with respect, fear and reverence. Yet no one ever told me about loving Him as a Mother. And just as this

156

maternal love does not diminish God but makes Him greater, so being the Mother of the World released my love.

Just at that moment I stepped on a dead rat. I bristled immediately with the terror of being alive; in a second I felt shattered by fear and panic, struggling to suppress the piercing scream inside me. Almost running, oblivious to everyone around me, I ended up leaning against a lamp-post, my eyes firmly closed and refusing to look any more. But the sight of that dead rat was engraved in my mind: a reddish-brown rat with an enormous tail, its claws crushed, as it lay there dead, silent, reddish-brown. My uncontrollable fear of rats.

Shivering from head to foot, I somehow managed to go on living. Totally bewildered, I walked on, the expression on my lips almost childish, such was my surprise. I tried to sever the connection between the two facts: what I had been feeling some moments earlier and then the rat. But it was useless. They were linked at least by their proximity. The two facts were illogically connected. It terrified me to think that a rat should harmonize with me. Repugnance suddenly overwhelmed me: was I unable to surrender to sudden love? What was God trying to tell me? I am not the sort of person who needs to be reminded that there is blood in everything! Far from ignoring that blood, I acknowledge and desire it. There is too much blood in me to allow me to forget blood. For me, words such as spiritual and earthly have no meaning. There was no need to confront me so brutally with a rat. Especially at such a moment, when I felt so exposed and vulnerable! You should have considered the terror that has haunted me since childhood; those rats have already persecuted and mocked me. From ancient times those rats have been devouring me with impatience and loathing! So, was it to be like this? My walking through life asking for nothing, wanting for nothing, loving with a pure and innocent love, and God confronting me with His rat. God's cruelty wounded and outraged me. God was a brute. Walking with a heavy heart, my disappointment as inconsolable as those disappointments I suffered as a child. A child grown prematurely to escape the injustices of childhood. I carried on walking, trying to forget. All I could think of was revenge. But what revenge could I hope for against an Almighty God, against a God Who only needed a rat crushed to death in order to crush me? While all I had was my vulnerability as a mere mortal. In my thirst for revenge, I could not even confront Him. Nor did I know where to find Him or where He might be concealed. Looking with hatred at some thing, would I finally see Him? Perhaps in the rat?...in that window?...in the stones on the ground? For in me, He no longer existed! In me, He was no longer to be seen!

Then the revenge of the weak suddenly occurred to me: so this was what it was like? Very well, I shall break my silence and reveal everything. I know that it is ignoble to enter into someone's confidence and then reveal their secret, but I am going to speak. Say nothing, for love's sake, say nothing! Keep His shameful secrets to yourself! – but I am determined to speak...to explain what has happened to me. This time I shall not be silenced, I shall reveal what He has done to me. I shall destroy His reputation.

...Who knows...perhaps it was because the world is also a rat and I had thought myself prepared...because I imagined myself to be stronger, and converted love into a mathematical calculation which happened to be wrong. I foolishly believed that, by adding up points of understanding, I was expressing my love. I failed to recognize that it is only by adding up misunderstandings that one comes to love. Just because I felt affection, I thought love would be easy. I felt no desire for solemn love, failing to understand that solemnity makes a ritual of misunderstanding and transforms it into an offering. But I have always been difficult by nature and have always put up a fight. I have always tried to go my own way and still have not learned to give in. And because deep down I want to love what I would choose to love rather than what is there to love. For I am still not myself and my punishment is loving a world which is not itself. Also because I am easily offended. Perhaps I need to be told these things bluntly for I am very stubborn. I am also extremely possessive, which may explain why I was asked with some irony whether I also wanted the rat for myself. For I shall only be able to be the mother of things when I can pick up a dead rat in my hand. Yet I know that I shall never be able to pick up that dead rat without dying my worst death. So let me intone the *Magnificat* which blindly exalts what it can neither know nor see. Let me adopt the formalities which distance me, because formalities have not wounded my simplicity but rather my pride. For it is my pride at having been born that makes me feel so intimate with the world – this world which still draws a muffled cry from my heart. The rat exists just as I exist, but perhaps neither I nor the rat is capable of being seen by ourselves, for distance makes us equal. Perhaps I must first accept this nature of mine which seeks a rat's death. Perhaps I consider myself much too delicate simply because I did not commit any crimes. Having suppressed them, I believe my love to be innocent. Perhaps I shall never be able to face the rat until I am able to look into this unruly soul of mine without turning pale. Perhaps I should call the world this habit of mine of being a little of everything. How can I love the world's grandeur if I am unable to love the dimensions of my own nature? So long as I imagine that God is good simply because I am evil, I shall find myself loving nothing: it will simply be my way of accusing myself. Without even having examined all of myself, I have chosen to love my opposite, whom I wish to call God. I, who shall never got used to myself, have asked the world to spare me any distress. Having succeeded only in forcing myself to submit to myself (for I am so much more inexorable than myself), I hoped to compensate myself with an Earth less violent than myself.

For as long as I love God only because I do not love myself, I shall be a marked dice, and the game of my greater life will not be played. As long as I go on inventing God, He will never exist.

SUNDAY

Such perfume! It is Sunday morning. The terrace has been swept. So he switches on the radio. A late lunch gives one thoughts. He smiles, and gives those thoughts form. There is water on the table but no one is thirsty on a Sunday. And he begins sipping wine without much enthusiasm. At four o'clock they will hoist the flag on the pavilion. (But what he really fears are those tranquil Sunday evenings.)

POSTERITY WILL JUDGE US

When a cure is found to ward off influenza, future generations will no longer be able to understand us. Influenza, while it lasts,

159

is one of the most incurable of organic disorders. Having influenza is to know many things which, if not known, would never need to be known. It is to experience a useless catastrophe, a catastrophe without tragedy. It is a cowardly lament which only another person suffering from influenza can understand. How will future generations ever be able to understand that for us, having influenza was a human condition? We are flu-stricken creatures who will be subjected to censure or ridicule by future generations.

YOUR SECRET

Poisoned flowers in a vase. Red, blue, pink, they carpet the air. How they transform a hospital ward. I have never seen such beautiful and dangerous flowers. So this is your secret. Your secret resembles you so closely that it tells me nothing beyond what I already know. And I know so little, as if I were your enigma. Just as you are mine.

TEN YEARS OLD

— Tomorrow I shall be ten years old. I intend to make the most of this last day of my ninth year.
There is a pause. Sadness.
— Mummy, my soul is not yet ten years old.
— How old then?
— I guess about eight years old.
— Don't worry, that's how it should be.
— But I think we should count our years by our soul. People would then say: that chap died at twenty. And the chap had died, but with a seventy-year-old body.
Later he began to sing, then stopped and said:
— I am singing Happy Birthday to myself. But, Mummy, I haven't really made much of my ten years.
— Yes, you have.
— No, no, I don't mean *much* in the sense of doing this and

that. What I mean is that I have not really been very happy. What's wrong? Why are you looking so sad?

– I'm not sad. Come here and let me give you a kiss.

– Didn't I tell you? Didn't I say you're looking sad? You can't stop kissing me and when you give somebody all those kisses it's because you're feeling sad.

THE LITTLE MONSTER

He is the brightest boy in his class. He never plays games. (His secret is a snail.) His hair is cropped, his eyes are gentle and attentive. His delicate skin at nine years of age is still transparent. He is polite by nature. He handles things without breaking them, lends books to his school-mates, helps them with their lessons, does not lose his patience with the square and the rule, and never misbehaves, like all the other unruly boys.

His secret is a snail. Which he does not forget for a single moment. His secret is a snail, which he treats with dispassionate and agonizing care. He keeps it safely in a shoe-box. With solicitude he pierces the box every day with a needle and string. With the utmost care he postpones its death. His secret is a snail, nurtured with insomnia and precision.

FLYING THE FLAG

– Today at school I wrote an essay about Flag Day which was so beautiful, but ever so beautiful – for I even used words without really knowing what they meant.

SPRING IN SWITZERLAND

That spring was really dry, the radio crackled, picking up atmospheric interference; my clothing bristled as it released the body's electricity, and my comb lifted magnetized hairs; it was

161

an ominous spring. And so very empty. From wherever one happened to be, the impression was the same: the journey ahead seemed long, the road endless. There was little conversation: the body was as heavy as its sleep; eyes were big and expressionless. On the terrace, the goldfish gyrated in its tank; we sipped our drinks looking at the countryside. The wind carried the daydreams of goats from the fields. By the other table on the terrace, a solitary faun. Charged with static, we stared dreamily into the glasses in our hands. 'What were you saying?' 'I didn't say a thing.' The days went by. But one moment of harmony was enough to capture once more that barbed static of spring: the rash dreams of goats, the hollow fish, a sudden urge to steal apples, the crowned faun taking solitary leaps. 'What?' 'Nothing. I didn't say anything.'

But I could hear the stirring of a murmur, like a heart beating underneath the earth. Quietly, I put my ear to the ground and could hear summer breaking through, and my heart beating underneath the earth – nothing, I said nothing – and I could sense the persistent violence with which the closed earth was opening up inside as it prepared to give birth, and knew with what burden of sweetness the summer would ripen a hundred thousand oranges, and I knew that those oranges were mine, simply because I wanted it so.

ONLY AN INSECT

It took me some time to make out what I was seeing, it was so unexpected and subtle. I was seeing a pale green insect with long legs, which was resting. It was a grasshopper, which people were always assuring me is an omen of good fortune. Then the grasshopper began to move very gently across the counterpane. It was a transparent green, with legs supporting its body on a higher and freer plane, a plane as fragile as the grasshopper's own legs, which seemed to consist only of the colour of their outer shell. There was nothing inside those threadlike legs: the inside layer was so thin that it was indistinguishable from the outer layer. The grasshopper looked like a transparency which had come off the paper and was crawling about in green. But

162

however somnambulant, it moved with determination. Somnambulant: the tiniest leaf of a tree which had achieved the solitary independence of those who pursue the blurred traces of a destiny. And it crawled with the determination of someone tracing a line which was simply invisible to the naked eye. It crawled without a tremor. Its inner mechanism was not tremulous, but it had the regular oscillation of the most delicate clock. What could love be like between two grasshoppers? Green and green, and then the same green, which, suddenly, because of a vibration of greens, turns green. Love predestined by its own semi-aerial mechanism. But where were the glands of its destiny and the adrenalines of its parched, green entrails? For it was a hollow creature, a splintered grafting, a simple attraction of green lines. Like me? Me. Us? Us. In that slender grasshopper with its tall legs, which are capable of crawling over a woman's bosom without arousing the rest of her body; in that grasshopper which cannot be hollow because a hollow line does not exist; in that grasshopper, atomic energy is conducted in silence without any drama. Us? Us.

TAKING WHAT WAS MINE

I can recall that spring. I know I ate the pear and threw away half of it. I never feel compassion in the spring. Later we drank water at the fountain and I did not dry my lips. We walked defiantly in silence. As for the swimming-pool, I know that I stayed in the pool for hours. Look at the pool! That was how I saw the pool, contemplating it with tranquil eyes. Calmly taking without compassion what was mine.

ONE FINAL CLARIFICATION

From time to time I receive letters asking me if I am Russian or Brazilian and people invent all sorts of myths about me.

Let me clarify this matter once and for all: I am sorry to have to tell you that there are no mysteries and these myths are untrue.

My story is as follows: I was born in the Ukraine, the homeland of my parents. I was born in a village called Tchechelnik, which is too small and insignificant to appear on any map. When my mother was expecting me, my parents were already planning to emigrate either to the United States or to Brazil. They waited on in Tchechelnik until I was born and then set out on their long journey. I was *two months old* when I arrived in Brazil.

I am a naturalized Brazilian and, had my parents set out a few months earlier, I should have been born in Brazil. It was the Portuguese language which influenced my spiritual life and innermost thoughts, and this was the language I used to utter words of love. I began to write short stories as soon as I could read and write and, needless to say, I wrote them in Portuguese. I spent my childhood in Recife and I firmly believe that living in the Northern or North-eastern provinces of Brazil brings one into closer contact with Brazilian life at its most authentic, because there the country is remote from outside influences. My beliefs were nurtured in Pernambuco, the food I enjoy most is from Pernambuco. And from our housemaids I absorbed the rich folklore of those regions. I was already in my teens when we moved to Rio, this vast metropolis I soon began to think of as *Brazilian carioca*.

As for the way in which I roll my r's, as if I were speaking French or some other foreign language, this is simply because of a speech defect. A defect which I have never succeeded in correcting. A defect which my good friend Dr Pedro Bloch tells me can be overcome. He has offered to help me but I am lazy and I know perfectly well I would never do the exercises once I was on my own. And besides my rolled r's are not doing anyone any harm. So that should clear up yet another mystery.

Much more difficult to explain, however, is the path my life has taken. If my family had emigrated to the United States, would I still have become a novelist, that is to say, a novelist writing in English? In all probability I would have married an American and had American children. And my life would have been completely different. I wonder what I might have written about? Which political party I would have supported? What sort of friends I would have cultivated? There is a real mystery.

It could scarcely be called singing, in so far as singing means using one's voice musically. It was scarcely vocal, in so far as the voice tends to utter words. Flamenco singing precedes utterance, it is human breathing. Sometimes, the odd word escaped, revealing how that mute singing was achieved. It was all about life, love and death. Those three unspoken words were interrupted by laments and modulations. Modulations of breath, that initial vocal phase which captures the suffering in that opening lament and also the joy in that first outcry of sorrow. And pain. And then another piercing cry, this time of happiness at the outburst of that sorrow. The audience sit huddled round the dancers, looking swarthy and unwashed. After a lengthy modulation which dies away with a sigh, the audience, sounding as exhausted as the singer, murmurs an olé, an amen, a dying ember.

But there is also that impatient song which the voice alone does not express: then the nervous, insistent tapping of feet intervenes, the olé which continually interrupts the song is no longer a response; it is incitement, it is the black bull. The singer, almost clenching his teeth, gives voice to the fanaticism of his race, but the audience demands more and more, until that final spasm is achieved: this is Spain.

I could also hear the song that was absent. It consists of silence interrupted by cries from the audience. Within that circle of silence, a short, gaunt, swarthy little man, with inner fire, hands on hips and head thrown back, hammers out the incessant rhythm of that absent song with the heels of his shoes. This is not music. Not even dance. Zapateado* predates the choreography of dancing – it is the body manifesting itself and manifesting us, feet communicating to a pitch of fury in a language which Spain understands.

The audience intensifies its wrath within its very silence. From time to time, you could hear the hoarse taunts of a gypsy, all charcoal and red tatters, in whom hunger has turned to passion and cruelty. It was not a spectacle, for there were no spectators: everyone present played as important a role as the dancer who

* Zapateado: the tap-dancing peculiar to Spanish flamenco.

was tapping his feet in silence. Becoming more and more exhausted, they can communicate for hours through this language which, were it ever to have possessed words, must have gradually lost them throughout the centuries – until the oral tradition came to be transmitted from father to son like the impetus of blood.

I watched two flamenco dancers partner each other. I have never witnessed any other dance in which the rivalry between a man and a woman becomes so naked. The conflict between them is so open that their wiles are of no importance: at certain moments the woman becomes almost masculine, and the man looks at her in amazement. If the Moor on Spanish soil is Moorish, his female counterpart has lost any languor she ever possessed when confronted with Basque severity. The Moorish woman in Spain is as proud as a peacock until love transforms her into a *maja*.*

Conquest is arduous in flamenco dancing. While the male dancer speaks with insistent feet, his partner pursues the aura of her own body with her hands outspread like two fans: in this way she magnetizes herself, and prepares to become tangible and at the same time intangible. But just when you least expect it, she puts forward one foot and taps out three beats with her heel. The male dancer shudders before this crude gesture, he recoils and freezes. There is the silence of dance. Little by little, the man raises his arms once more, and cautiously – out of fear rather than modesty – attempts with splayed hands to shadow his partner's proud head. He circles her several times and at certain moments almost turns his back to her, thus exposing himself to the danger of being stabbed. And if he has avoided being stabbed, he owes his escape to his partner's unexpected recognition of his bravado: this then is her man. She stamps her feet, her head held high, with the first cry of love: at last she has found her companion and enemy. The two withdraw bristling with pride. They have acknowledged each other. They are in love.

The dance itself now begins. The man is dark-skinned, lithe and defiant. She is severe and dangerous. Her hair has been drawn back, she is proud of her severity. This dance is so vital

* *maja*: low-class woman (especially in Madrid).

that it is hard to believe life will continue once the dance has ended: this man and woman must die. Other dances express nostalgia for their courage. But this dance *is* courage. Other dances are joyful. But the joy of this dance is solemn. Or missing. What matters here is the mortal triumph of living. The two dancers neither smile nor forgive. But do they understand each other? They have never thought of understanding each other. They have each brought themselves as their banner. And whoever is vanquished – in this dance both are vanquished – will not weaken in submission. Those Spanish eyes will remain dry with love and wrath. Whoever is vanquished – and both of them will be vanquished – will serve wine to the other like a slave. Even though that wine may prove fatal once jealous passion finally explodes. The partner who survives will feel revenged. But condemned to eternal solitude. For this woman alone was his enemy, this man alone was her enemy, and they chose each other for the dance.

BECAUSE THEY WERE NOT DISTRACTED

They felt slightly inebriated as they walked together. They felt that happiness which comes when your throat is dry and you discover to your surprise that you have your mouth open. They inhaled the air ahead of them and just to have this thirst was almost satisfying. They walked through street after street, conversing and laughing; they conversed and laughed to give substance and weight to this lightheadedness which was the happiness of their thirst. Because of the traffic and crowds, they sometimes touched, and as they touched – thirst is grace, but those waters a secret beauty – as they touched the brilliance of those waters shone, their throats becoming even drier with wonder. How they marvelled at being together!

Until everything transformed itself into denial. Everything transformed itself into denial when they craved their own happiness. Then the great dance of errors commenced. The ritual of mistaken words. He searched without seeing; she failed to see that he had not seen, she who was nevertheless present. He who was nevertheless present. Everything went wrong, and there was dust everywhere on the streets, and the more they wandered, the more bitterly they pursued their goal, unsmiling. All this simply because they had been attentive, simply because they were no longer sufficiently distracted. Simply because they had suddenly become demanding and stubborn, and wanted to possess what was already theirs. All this because they wanted to give something a name; because they wanted to exist, they who already existed. They were then to learn that unless one is distracted, the telephone does not ring; that it is necessary to be out for that letter to arrive, and that when the telephone finally does ring, the wasteland of waiting has already disconnected the wires. All this, all this, because they were no longer distracted.

WORDS PURELY PHYSICAL

In Italy, *il miracolo* is night fishing. Mortally wounded by the harpoon, the fish releases its crimson blood into the sea. The fisherman unloads his catch before sunrise, his face pale and intent in the knowledge that he is hauling the enormous load of miraculous fish over the sands: the miracle of love.

Milagre is the tear falling on the leaf. It trembles, escapes and falls: behold thousands of miraculous tears glistening on the grass.

The *miracle* has the sharp points of stars and much splintered silver.

Le miracle is a glass octagon which can be turned slowly in the palm of the hand. It remains in the hand, but only to be gazed at. It can be seen from all angles, very slowly, and on each side we see a glass octagon. Until suddenly, sensing danger and turning quite pale with emotion, we understand: in the palm of our hand we no longer hold an octagon but *le miracle*. From this moment onwards, we no longer see anything. We possess it.

To pass from the physical word to its meaning is to reduce it first to splinters, just as the firework remains a dull object until it is fated to become a brilliant flare in the sky and achieves its own death. (In its passage from being simply body to something maddened by love, the bee arrives at the supreme moment: it dies.)

Sometimes I tremble all over when I come into physical contact with animals or even so much as look at them. I seem to have a certain fear and horror of that living creature which is not human yet has the same instincts, although in the animal those instincts are freer and indomitable. An animal never substitutes one thing for another, is never forced to sublimate things as we are. And that living thing moves! It moves independently because of this nameless thing which is Life.

I once drew a friend's attention to the fact that animals do not laugh, and she informed me that Bergson makes the same observation in his essay about laughter. And although I am convinced that dogs sometimes laugh, they smile with their eyes which suddenly turn brighter, with their gaping mouths as they pant and wag their tails. But cats never laugh, although they can be playful. I have had plenty of experience with cats. As a little girl I owned a rather common tabby-cat with stripes in various shades of grey. Cunning as could be, she had that feline instinct which made her suspicious and aggressive. My tabby-cat was forever having kittens and always with the same tragic outcome: I would insist I wanted to keep all the kittens at home, while unbeknown to me they were given away to who knows whom. And I kicked up such a fuss that one day I returned from school to find that my tabby-cat had disappeared. She, too, had been given away. The shock was so great that I took to my bed with fever. My family tried to console me by giving me a cat made of felt which I thought ridiculous. How could that dead, limp thing ever replace the supple energy of a live tabby?

Speaking of live tabbies, a friend of mine has decided to have nothing more to do with cats. He finally lost his patience with his tabby-cat who would get into such a frenzy when she was on heat that she would miaow day and night and keep all the neighbours awake. Then, without any warning, she would become almost hysterical and throw herself from the roof on to the ground below, causing herself serious injury. When I told my maid this sad story, she exclaimed 'Holy Mother of God' and made the sign of the Cross.

I have little or nothing to say about the sluggish turtle with that rock-hard shell on his back, covered in dust. This dinosaur which dates from the Tertiary Period is of no interest to me. The turtle is extremely stupid and relates to nothing, not even to itself. Sexual contact between two turtles has neither warmth nor life. And although I am no scientist, I can confidently predict that the species will disappear within the next few thousand years.

As for chickens and how they relate to themselves and to humans and, above all, to the egg they conceive, I have already said all there is to say. And I have also written at some length about monkeys.

I was already married and living in Naples when I bought a mongrel from a beggar-woman in a busy thoroughfare. I felt at once that he had been born for me and he must have felt the same, for I could tell that he was overjoyed and, without so much as giving a backward glance at his former owners, he came trotting after me, wagging his tail and licking my legs. It would take forever to narrate my adventures with this dog, who reminded me of a Brazilian mulatto urchin, despite the fact that my mongrel had been born in Naples. I christened him Dilermando, a rather grand name which aptly described the wise expression and knowing ways which made him so endearing. I could tell you so much about my beloved Dilermando. There was such a strong bond between us and such a natural affinity that he could sense my every thought and emotion. Whenever I was typing, he would sit at my feet looking just like a drowsing sphinx. And if I interrupted my typing to think about something, or because I had come up against a problem, he would open his eyes at once, raise his head and gaze at me with one ear cocked...waiting. And the moment I solved the problem and returned to my typing, he would settle down again, close his eyes and go back to dreaming: because dogs – believe me – can dream. No human being ever showed me as much love and wholehearted devotion as this mongrel.

When my sons were no longer babies, we presented them with a lovely big dog who patiently allowed the younger boy to ride on his back. And without being asked, this dog decided to guard the house and the entire street with fierce barking which kept the neighbours up all night. I once gave my sons some little yellow chicks who followed us everywhere, and got under our feet as if we were the mother-hen, for those tiny little creatures

170

were as much in need of a mother as any human. The relationship between humans and animals is unique and cannot be compared to any other. Looking after animals is something everyone should experience. People who have never owned a pet animal lack a certain intuition of the living world. People who refuse to have anything to do with animals are afraid of themselves.

Yet sometimes I tremble all over when I look at animals. On occasion I can even sense that primeval cry buried inside me when I am with them. It is almost as if I no longer know who is more animal, me or the animal. I become totally confused, as if I were afraid of confronting my own suppressed instincts, which I am obliged to assume in the presence of animals, demanding as they are. And what else can we poor humans do? I once knew a woman who humanized animals, chatting to them and transmitting her own traits of character. But I do not humanize animals for I should find that offensive – one must respect nature – and it is I who *animalize* myself. Far from being difficult, this adjustment comes naturally. It is simply a question of surrendering, without putting up a struggle.

But after much thought, I have come to the conclusion that there is nothing more difficult in this world than to surrender completely. This is one of man's greatest sorrows.

To imprison a tiny bird in the palm of one's hand is horrifying. The poor little bird puts up a frantic struggle, flapping its wings in desperation. You can feel hundreds of little fluttering feathers until the feeling becomes so unbearable that you open your hand quickly and either free the bird or return it to its owner so that it might be restored to the greater freedom, relatively speaking, of its cage. Frankly, I prefer to see birds in the trees or flying through the air and well out of my reach. Perhaps one day, after rather more prolonged contact with the birds of Augusto Rodrigues in the Largo do Boticário, I shall get to know them intimately and be able to rejoice in their ethereal presence. ('To rejoice in their ethereal presence' gives me the feeling of having said in a nutshell precisely what I mean. It is a strange feeling, and who knows, I could be deceiving myself, but that is another matter.)

It would never occur to me to keep an owl. But a little friend of mine found a baby owl grounded in the woods at Santa Teresa, all alone and missing its mother. She took it home, made it comfortable, fed it, consoled it and eventually discovered that it liked raw meat. When the baby owl became stronger she expected it to fly off at once, but the owl hovered nearby, before setting off in pursuit of its own destiny and being reunited with its own species. This strange bird had obviously become attached to my little friend and was reluctant to abandon her. It would fly off a little way and then come back almost immediately. Until finally, with one great effort, as if struggling with itself, the owl made a bid for freedom and went flying off to the ends of the earth.

ANIMALS (II)

The rabbit's silence, its habit of nibbling carrots ever so quickly – its uninhibited copulation at frequent intervals and with the utmost haste – who knows why I should find the sexual habits of rabbits so futile and, to all appearances, so very superficial? Rabbits make no impression on me whatsoever; we are simply worlds apart, entirely different, our species mutually alien. Strange how the rabbit can be imprisoned and seem almost resigned yet cannot be domesticated: its resignation is merely apparent. In fact, however futile and nervous it might be, the rabbit is free and this is somehow at odds with its superficiality.

As for horses, I have written at length about horses roaming the prairie in *A Cidade sitiada* [The Besieged City] where the white horse, the king of nature, neighs triumphantly at dusk into the remote horizon. And I have experienced a close rapport with horses. I can recall in my youth standing proud and erect in imitation of the horse, as I stroked his glossy, velvety coat and ran my fingers through his wild mane. And what a perfect picture we made: 'The maiden and the horse'.

Fish in an aquarium never stop swimming for a second. This disturbs me. Besides, I find fish in an aquarium insipid, shallow creatures. But perhaps I am wrong, for not only do they gobble up food but they even manage to procreate: so they must be living matter if they can do these things. What intrigues me is that, at least in the case of fish in an aquarium, they have no instinct: they eat until they are ready to burst, do not know when

172

to stop and, all of a sudden, what you see are dead fish. They are nervous creatures when they are small, dangerous once they grow big. And furthermore they belong to an unknown world and that, too, disturbs me.

I must tell you an interesting little story. A Spanish friend of mine, Jaime Vilaseca, lived for some time with relatives in a tiny village lost amongst the snow-covered slopes of the Pyrenees. Winter invariably brought the starving wolves down into the village in search of food. Whereupon all the inhabitants moved indoors, taking their sheep, horses, dogs and goats with them. And there they remained, humans and animals snuggling up against each other in one room and listening to those ravenous wolves clawing at locked doors...

And I know a story about a rose, strange though it may seem to mention a rose when I am talking about animals. But this rose behaved in such a manner that it brings to mind the mysteries of instinct and intuition associated with animals. A medical acquaintance, Dr Azulay, is a psychoanalyst and the author of *Um deus esquecido* [A Forgotten God]. He was in the habit of taking a rose with him every other day to his consulting-rooms, where he would put it into one of those tall, narrow vases specially designed for a single rose. Every other day the flower would start to wither only to be replaced by a fresh rose. But there was one particular Rose. It was bright pink, the work of nature rather than artifice. The sheer beauty of that rose filled one's heart with joy. Proudly displaying its opulent bloom, its thick, velvety petals, that rose gave the impression of standing upright in all its splendour and beauty. Well, perhaps not altogether upright, for with infinite grace it leaned ever so slightly forward on its tall, slender stem. An intimate relationship soon developed between Dr Azulay and that rose: he was full of admiration and the rose sensed his appreciation. The rose went on being glorious under his loving gaze and as the days passed she showed no sign of withering. The rose remained there in full bloom and as fresh as ever. And so she remained for a whole week. Eventually, the rose began to show signs of fatigue and finally died. With some reluctance my friend put another rose in her place. But he never forgot that rose. And some weeks later, one of his patients unexpectedly asked: 'What became of that rose?' Dr Azulay knew at once which rose the patient was referring to. That rose which had gone on living out of love had made an impression. His patient had observed how Dr Azulay used to gaze at that flower and nourish it with his own vital energy. The patient had unwittingly perceived that there was something going on between him and the rose. That rose – which I am almost tempted to call *'joie de vivre'* – had so much natural instinct that both man and flower had experienced that deep rapport one only finds between man and beast.

Suddenly I feel unbearable pangs of nostalgia for my beloved Dilermando, the same nostalgia he must have felt when he was adopted by another family when I had to go and live in Switzerland. Alas, I was misinformed when someone assured me that the hotels where we were obliged to stay for several months would not accept animals. I cannot help smiling to this day when I remember how I once left Dilermando with a friend in Italy while I returned briefly to Brazil. Upon my return, I rushed to my friend's house to collect Dilermando. We were already in the middle of winter and I was wearing a fur coat. The dog stood there staring at me, rooted to the spot. He then approached and caught a whiff of the fur which seemed to worry him as if he sensed the presence of some threatening animal. And to add to his confusion, he could also smell my perfume. The poor dog got into a terrible state and began chasing his own tail. Without moving, I waited for him to settle down and finally recognize me. Fussing over him would only have made matters worse. After a while I began to feel hot in the warm room and removing my coat I threw it onto a sofa some distance away. Whereupon Dilermando caught my scent and jumped straight on to my lap with one mighty leap, beside himself with excitement and licking and scratching my face and arms. I laughed with joy and shrugged off those superficial bites he tried to inflict. They were hardly the real thing. Nor did they harm me, for they were love bites.

Not to have been born an animal seems to be one of my secret regrets. Their call comes to me from some remote past and I can only respond with profound disquiet. Their call summons me.

FAMILY OUTING

On Sunday evenings, the entire family would go to the pier to watch the ships. They would lean over the parapet and, if Father were alive today, perhaps he would still be watching those oily waters which he used to examine so intently. His daughters would become vaguely uneasy, they would summon him to come and look at something more interesting: look at the ships, Daddy! they would point out to him impatiently. As darkness fell, the illuminated city turned into a great metropolis with high revolving stools in every café. The youngest daughter insisted upon sitting on one of those high stools and Father found this amusing. This was great fun. Then she would try to be even more entertaining just to please him, and that was not so amusing. She chose something to drink which was not expensive, although the revolving stool increased the price of everything. The rest of the family stood around, watching this ritual of pleasure. A child's timid but voracious pursuit of happiness. This was when she discovered the Ovaltine they served in cafés. Never before had she experienced such luxury whipped up in a tall glass, made all the taller because of the froth on top, the stool high and wobbly, as she sat *on top of the world*. Everyone was watching. The first mouthfuls almost made her sick, but she forced herself to empty the glass. The disturbing responsibility of an unfortunate choice; forcing herself to enjoy what must be enjoyed, and thus adding the indecisiveness of a rabbit to her other weaknesses. There was also the terrifying suspicion that *Ovaltine* is good: it is I who am no good. She fibbed, insisting that her drink was delicious because the others were standing there watching her enjoy the luxury of happiness which cost money. Did it depend on her whether they believed or not in a better world? But she was extricated from this problem by her father, and she felt safe within this intimate circle, where to stroll holding hands constituted the family. On the way home, her father remarked: Without really doing anything, we have spent so much money.

Before falling asleep, lying in bed in the dark. Through the window, on the white wall: the huge, swaying shadows of the branches, looking as if they belonged to some enormous tree which did not actually exist in the patio. All that grew there was a straggly shrub: or perhaps it was the moon's shadow. Sunday was always that immense, contemplative night which gave existence to all future Sundays and produced cargo ships and oily waters and produced a milky drink with froth and the moon and the gigantic shadow of a tiny fragile tree. Just like me.

MOTHER'S DAY. A PIOUS INVENTION

Location – Refuge for Abandoned Children; an old building in colonial style; innumerable pavilions with spacious rooms; high ceilings; barred windows.

Number of Children – Six hundred.

Age of Children – Varied.

History – Founded around 1778.

Founder – A Portuguese millionaire who owned the mansion and felt something must be done to rescue abandoned children.

Aims of the Refuge – To house, educate and bring up orphans or children abandoned by their parents.

Director – Sister Isabel, a nun of the Order of St Vincent: white habit; medium height; plump, smiling, imaginative, energetic and loquacious; an expressive face which becomes solemn when she is worried; she moves briskly and with remarkable agility in her white habit, which is always immaculate; a born leader; in no sense conventional; a lively creature who finds a ready solution to every problem. To all appearances oblivious of her own intelligence, she is open and spontaneous: she believes nothing is impossible and once she has made up her mind she acts without a moment's hesitation. She never shrinks from hard work.

The Facts – Sister Isabel has just been appointed Sister Superior of the Refuge for Abandoned Children, in other words, the Director. She is gradually finding her way around the Refuge. There are six hundred files to be read, one for each child. She notices that in the majority of cases, the parents of the children are unknown. An average file reads: João de Deus, born the tenth of December, 1965. Place of birth: State of Guanabara. Colour: black. Parentage: none. There is a blank space. She is gradually getting to know the children, one by one. Most of them ask her:

Who is my mummy? To conceal her embarrassment, Sister Isabel changes the subject. But the children are insistent: Who is my mummy? Sister Isabel thinks hard. Much distressed, she searches for some impossible solution. For hours she stands lost in thought before that enormous filing cabinet, biting her lips.

Result – She reaches a decision. She goes through the cards one by one, undeterred by the fact that there are six hundred of them to be read. And wherever there is an empty space after the word *Parentage* she invents a mother for every parentless child. She writes in over and over again names like Maria, Ana, Virginia, Helena, Maddalena, Sofia, etc.

Conclusion – She sends for each child without parents and informs them: Your mummy's name is Maria, or Ana, or Sofia, etc. The children are overjoyed: now they all have a mother and they are so happy that they do not even mind if she never comes to see them. Sister Isabel always finds some excuse to explain why their mother cannot be with them. A pure invention, those mothers are a fiction and non-existent. They only exist on paper yet they are somehow alive, caring and affectionate.

Finale – Here my story ends and there is nothing more to tell you.

WORDS FROM THE TYPEWRITER

I feel I have almost achieved my freedom. To the point of no longer needing to write. If I could, I would leave my space on this page blank: filled with the greatest silence. And readers, on seeing this blank space, would fill it with their own desires.

To be frank, this can scarcely be called a column. It is simply what it is. It does not correspond to any genre. Genre no longer interests me. What interests me is mystery. Is there some ritual attached to mystery? I believe there is. In order to adhere to the certainty of things. Meanwhile, I somehow already adhere to the earth. I am a daughter of nature: I want to hold things, feel them, touch them, I want to exist. And all this is part of a totality, of a mystery. I am but one being. Before there was a difference between the writer and me (or am I wrong? I cannot be certain). But no longer. I am but one being. And I leave you to be yourself.

Does that frighten you? I believe it does. But it is worthwhile. Even if it hurts. For the pain soon passes.

And now I want to tell you about certain realities which leave me astonished. These refer to animals.

An acquaintance once told me that when you catch a crab by a claw, the claw comes away so that its body can escape. And a new claw soon grows to replace the one which has been discarded.

Another acquaintance was once staying with friends and she opened the fridge to get some iced water.

She saw something strange inside.

It was something white, stark white. Headless but breathing. Like a lung. Moving up and down, up and down. My friend got the fright of her life and slammed the door shut. And she stood there, paralysed, her heart pounding.

Then she discovered what it was. Her host was an experienced deep-sea diver. And he had caught a turtle. After removing its shell, he had cut the head off and put the turtle in the fridge, with the intention of cooking and eating it next day.

But until it was cooked, that headless, denuded turtle was in there wheezing away like bellows.

I have already written about turtles. I wrote the following: 'I have little or nothing to say about the sluggish turtle with that rock-hard shell on its back, covered in dust. This dinosaur which dates from the Tertiary Period is of no interest to me (when I called it a dinosaur, I did not know that I was right. I was merely guessing). I find the turtle exceedingly stupid. It does not relate to anything, not even to itself. It is an abstraction. Sexual contact between two turtles must be devoid of any warmth or life. And while I am no scientist, I can confidently predict that the species will disappear within the next few thousand years.'

I forgot to add that I find the turtle completely immoral.

An acquaintance of mine, suspecting that my lack of interest in turtles was insincere, loaned me a little book about them which was written in English. Here is an extract I have copied out:

'The turtle is any land or marine chelonian which is descended from a rare and ancient species of reptile. Its ancestors appeared for the first time two hundred thousand years ago, long before dinosaurs. While these large animals became extinct a long time ago, the turtle with its strange and ugly appearance, managed to survive and has remained relatively unchanged for at least the last one hundred and fifty thousand years.'

Without its shell, headless, and panting up and down. Alive.

How can one comprehend a turtle? How can one comprehend God?

The point of departure must surely be: 'I do not know'. Which means total surrender.

My typewriter carries on typing. It types out the following: Anyone who achieves a high level of abstraction has reached the frontiers of madness. Perhaps those great mathematicians and physicians might be able to confirm this. I know a great man who is very abstract but acts as if he were just like everyone else: he eats, drinks, sleeps with his wife and has children. In this way he prevents himself from turning into an X or a square root. When I recall that as a girl I used to give private tuition in Mathematics and Portuguese to other children, I can scarcely believe it. Because now I could not work out a square root to save myself. As for Portuguese, I used to get terribly bored explaining rules of grammar. Fortunately for me, I eventually

A RIDE ON A CAMEL, THE SPHINX AND A BELLY-DANCER

On one of my trips to Europe, the plane, for some reason never explained, had to make a detour. And quite unexpectedly, I found myself spending three days in Egypt. I first saw the Pyramids by night. I went there by car and the sky was pitch black. As I got out of the car I asked: But where are the Pyramids? They were only two metres away. An overwhelming apparition. By day, they seem less threatening. I also saw the Sahara desert in the daylight. The sands are not so much white as light yellow. There was a camel hirer on hand and for a pittance tourists could ride a camel. I sat between its two humps. It is the strangest creature and never stops chewing its food. I believe the camel has two stomachs or am I imagining things? I also saw the

Sphinx. I could not decipher her meaning, nor could she decipher mine. We confronted each other as equals. She accepted me and I accepted her. Each with her own mystery.

In Morocco, I was invited to go and see the famous *belly-dance*. I could scarcely believe my eyes. Or my ears. The dancer was shaking her belly to the tune of: '*Mamá, yo quiero, mamá yo quiero mamar!*' ['Mummy I want, Mummy I want to suckle.']*

LOVE

A long time ago I met Ivan Lessa in some queue or other, and we were deep in conversation when Ivan, sounding startled, said to me: look at that odd sight. I looked behind me and saw a man coming round the corner, with his placid little dog on a lead.

Except that it was not a dog. The animal behaved like a dog, and the man behaved like a man walking his dog. But this was no dog. It had the elongated snout of an animal capable of drinking from a tall glass, and a long, hard tail. Admittedly, it could have been simply an unusual crossbreed. Ivan suggested that it might be a raccoon. But I thought the animal was too much like a dog in the way it trotted to be a raccoon. Unless it was the most domesticated and abnormal raccoon I had ever seen. Meanwhile the man was calmly approaching. Well, perhaps not calmly: there was a certain tenseness about him. It was the calm of some-one who has accepted a challenge: he had the look of a born fighter. There was nothing eccentric about his behaviour; it was an act of courage that he should appear in public walking his pet. Ivan suggested it could be some other species, but the name had momentarily escaped him. I was not convinced. Only later did I understand my embarrassment; it was not exactly mine, but stemmed from the fact that the animal no longer knew what it was, and was unable, therefore, to project any clear image of itself.

Until the man passed us. Unsmiling, his shoulders drawn back, proudly appearing in public. No, it has never been easy, being judged by people standing in a queue and demanding more of us. The man pretended to have no need of admiration

* An old Carnival song associated with the late Carmen Miranda.

or pity; but we can all recognize the martyrdom of someone who is cherishing a dream.

– What animal is that? I asked the man, intuitively adopting a gentle tone of voice rather than offend him with my curiosity. I asked him what animal it was, but my question also implied: 'Why are you doing this? What has driven you to invent a dog? Why not a real dog? for dogs do exist! Or had you no other means of capturing the grace of this creature except with a collar? Don't you realize that you destroy a rose if you crush it in your hand?' I know that tone is a unity which cannot be divided by words, but to splinter silence into words is one of my clumsy ways of loving silence. And by shattering silence I have so often killed what I understand. Although – glory be to God – I am more familiar with silence than with words.

Without stopping, the man replied briefly but without being curt. It was a raccoon. We kept on staring. Neither Ivan nor I smiled. There was an atmosphere of tension and intuition. We just stood there staring.

It was a raccoon which believed itself to be a dog. At times, with dog-like gestures, it would pause to sniff at things, which caused the lead to tighten and delayed its master in that familiar synchronization between man and dog. I stood there watching the raccoon which did not know what it was. I thought to myself: if the man is taking it to play in the park, there will come a moment when the raccoon will start to feel uneasy: 'Why for heaven's sake are dogs staring and barking at me so ferociously?' I also imagined that the raccoon, after having spent such a perfect day as a dog, might sadly be thinking to itself, as it looked up at the stars: 'What have I achieved in the end? What is missing in my life? I am as contented as any dog, so why this sense of emptiness, this longing? What is this anxiety, as if I were only capable of loving what I do not know?' And the man, the only person capable of ridding the raccoon of its uncertainty, that man will never answer those questions, for fear of losing the raccoon forever.

I also thought about the threatening hatred which existed in the raccoon. It felt love and gratitude for the man. But deep down, there was no way of avoiding the truth; only the raccoon did not perceive that it hated the man because it was essentially confused.

Suppose the mystery of its true nature had suddenly been

revealed to the raccoon? I tremble to think of the fatal chance which might have brought that raccoon to an unexpected confrontation with another raccoon, and therefore to self-recognition. I tremble to think of that moment when the raccoon would have experienced the most blissful shame which is given to us... to me... to us... I know full well that the raccoon would have every right, on discovering the truth, to savage the man with all the hatred that one creature can inflict upon another – to defile the other's essence in order to exploit him. I sympathize with the animal, I side with the victims of perverted love. But I beseech the raccoon to pardon the man and to pardon the man with infinite love. Before abandoning him.

TO REMEMBER WHAT NEVER EXISTED

To write often means remembering what never existed. So how can I know what has never existed? Like this: as if I were remembering. By an effort of memory, as if I had never been born. I was never born. I have never lived. But I remember, and remembering is like an open wound.

ONE OF THE CHOSEN

Even as a boy he was someone who insisted on choosing. Among the thousand things which he might have been, he exercised the right to choose. Putting on his spectacles, he would set to work, trying to see whatever he could and probing with sweaty hands the things he could not see. He was trying to choose and indirectly chose himself. Little by little, he forged his own personality. He went on and on selecting the essentials. In relative freedom, if one discounted the furtive determinism which quietly operated without giving itself a name. Discounting this furtive determinism, he was free to choose himself. He separated the so-called wheat from the chaff and ate only the best. Sometimes he ate the worst: and that was his most difficult choice. He separated perils from the great peril, and found to his dismay that what he was left with was the great peril itself. To his horror, he found himself determining the weight of things. He pushed aside the lesser truths which he ended up ignoring. The truths he craved were the most difficult to bear.

But after ignoring the lesser truths, he began to resemble other beings, as if enshrouded in mystery. His ignorance transformed him into a mysterious being. He had also become a mixture of what others thought of him and what he really was: a wise ignoramus; an ingenuous sage; oblivious, yet well aware of other things; an honest rogue; an unconscious thinker; a man full of nostalgia for the things he once knew, and full of regret for the things he had irretrievably lost after making a definite choice; a courageous human being because it was now too late and he had already chosen. Paradoxically, this gave him the discreet and wholesome contentment of the peasant who only has to cope with simple things. This gave him that unintentional austerity which all essential labour confers. When it came to choosing and adjusting, there was no fixed time for starting or finishing: it was the task of a lifetime.

Paradoxically, all this gradually gave him that deep happiness which one must shout and communicate to others. This presented no problem because he liked communicating with others. This was not something he had chosen or cultivated: it was truly a gift. He enjoyed the deep happiness of others, and his innate gift helped him to discover the happiness of others. The same gift also allowed him to discover the solitude of others. It also helped him to treat life as a game by transforming it into colours and forms. An inborn instinct taught him that gestures, without causing offence or scandal, could convey the liking he felt for others. Without so much as feeling that he was using this gift, he revealed himself; he gave to others without realizing that he was giving; he loved without knowing that this was what was known as love. The gift was like the shirt this contented man did not possess. Because he felt so poor and had nothing to give, he gave himself. He gave himself in silence, and gave what he had made of himself, just as one summons others to come and take a look.

Little by little he came to be surrounded by misunderstanding: the others looked at him as if he were a statue, as if he were a photograph. They failed to understand that in order to forge his personality, he had undergone a painful process of stripping away rather than embellishment. Because of a misunderstanding, he found himself being fêted. Because of a misunderstanding, he found himself being loved. But to feel oneself being loved was like recognizing oneself in the love received. And this man was loved as if he were someone else: one of the chosen. He shed the tears of the unmoving statue which weeps at night in the public square. The darkness in the square had never been so intense. Until daylight returned and that person was reborn. The earth's rhythm was so generous that dawn broke. But when night returned, darkness fell once more. The square was once more engulfed in solitude. Those who had chosen, slept in fear. Afraid because they thought they would have to dwell in the solitude of the square. They did not know that this solitary square was his place of work. That he, too, felt lonely. He had organized his entire life in order to function outside the square. It is true that once he felt prepared, anointed with oils and perfumes, he realized there was not enough time left to exist like the others: he was different, however reluctantly. Something had gone wrong for, when he saw himself in the photograph the others had taken, he was alarmed and embarrassed by what he saw there. They had turned him, no more, no less, into one of the chosen. They had robbed him of his freedom. How could he rectify their mistake? In order to make their task easy and save time, they had photographed him in only one pose. And now they no longer referred to him but simply to the photograph. All they had to do was open a drawer and take out his photograph. Besides, anyone could acquire a copy. It did not cost much.

When they told him: I love you, he felt uncomfortable and could not even express his gratitude. And me? What about me? Why only my photograph? But he did not protest because he knew that the others were not acting out of malice. Sometimes in his loneliness he tried in vain to imitate the photograph. This only served to make the false image in the photograph seem all the more authentic. At times he became quite confused: he found himself unable to copy the photograph and had even forgotten what he looked like in reality. So, like the laughing clown, he often wept beneath his painted mask of court jester.

Then he secretly tried to destroy the photograph. He did or said such contradictory things to the photograph that the corners turned up with rage as it lay there in the drawer. He hoped to become more real than his image. But what happened? It turned out that all he did was to touch up the image in the photograph.

And so it went on until all his hopes were dashed and he died of loneliness. But he finally escaped from that statue in the square after considerable effort. He had a number of falls before learning to walk by himself. And, as the saying goes, earth had never seemed more fair. He recognized that this was the land for which he had prepared himself. So he had not been mistaken, after all, and the map locating the treasure had given the right directions. As he walked, he touched everything in sight, and smiled. Even though alone, he was smiling. He had learned to smile on his own.

LONDON'S BRIDGES

Every time I think of London I can see those bridges again. I felt quite at home in London, but to think that I actually lived there for a time now makes me realize my good fortune. For me, London was mysterious and pulsating with life, yet grey. And everything grey has a strange effect on me, as if all the muted shades were being merged into one.

I saw the ugliness of the English at close quarters, which is one of the most appealing things about England. It is such a peculiar ugliness, and yet so beautiful. I am being serious. The winters were chilly and the harsh wind brought a rosy colour to cheeks and hands which made people look all too real. Women in London go shopping with baskets; the men who work in the City wear bowler-hats. And the Thames looks foul with its muddy waters. London was once stricken by plague. And a great fire razed the entire city to the ground. I could sense the presence of both plague and fire when I lived there.

Londoners drink the most horrid coffee out of large cups which give off steam. The whole island gives off steam, its blackened bridges emerging from perpetual mist. Fog emanates from the city's cobblestones and enshrouds the bridges. London's bridges make a deep impression. Some are solid and menacing. Others almost skeletal.

The English themselves are not all that intelligent. Yet England has shown herself to be one of the most intelligent nations in the world. We went around by car. There are mazes of tiny villages between one large town and the next. A fine drizzle spatters on the car windows. People on the streets are so badly dressed that they end up giving the impression of being quite stylish. And they do know how to wrap up in bad weather. I can picture a child I once saw, smothered in a heavy, dark overcoat, wearing thick woollen socks and a hood which tied under the chin. The child had a pinched little face with bright, knowing eyes and rosy cheeks. And that pure intonation peculiar to English voices, at once superior and questioning.

Only now do I appreciate just how much I loved those London winds which made my eyes water and caused my skin to look chapped.

And then there were those outings into the countryside and the English landscape which is so unlike any other. I can still see those incredibly tall trees.

The English love exploring their own island and there is a sense of restless toing and froing in all directions.

A visit to the theatre in London is a memorable experience. Watching English actors sends a shiver down the spine. The English actor is the most serious man in England. Within the space of a few hours, he makes each member of the audience aware of those essential things one tends to lose sight of in everyday life. You step out of the theatre into rain and darkness, on to wet pavements and those quaint English streets which make one long for some perilous adventure. We go to dinner. The traditional fare served in English restaurants is quite dreadful and makes one irritable. Fortunately there are plenty of ethnic restaurants in London where the food is much more appetising.

Remnants of medieval England can be seen in the city's towers. The self-assurance of certain Englishmen can be amusing. Accustomed to war, they stride rather than walk along the pavements. And were the world not such a sad place, this struggle for survival might have a certain charm.

I remember with affection English writers who are no longer alive. Especially D.H. Lawrence.

The Queen has a sweet smile. English newspapers are curiously provincial. Any English men or women with good features

186

somehow acquire an extraordinary beauty. But English children are always endearing and when they open their little mouths to speak, they become irresistible.

I am indulging in nostalgia as I try to recapture my memories of London from random notes. I am writing this in haste before they fade forever.

THE OLD LADY

She lived in a boarding-house on São Clemente Street. She was enormous and smelled like a chicken when it is brought half-cooked to the table. She had five teeth, withered lips and a dry throat. Her past reputation was no invention. She still spoke in French whenever she found an opportunity, even if the other person spoke Portuguese and would have preferred to be spared the embarrassment of listening to his or her own poor accent. The absence of saliva removed any trace of fluency, and gave the old girl an air of restraint. There was majesty in that huge body supported on tiny feet, in the strength of those five teeth, in those stray hairs which escaped from a sparse bun and trembled with the slightest breeze.

But one Monday morning instead of coming down from her room, she came in from the street. Her skin looked smooth, her neck washed, and there was no longer any smell of half-cooked chicken. She explained that she had spent Sunday at her son's house where she had stayed overnight. She was wearing a dowdy black satin dress. Instead of going up to her room to change into an old cotton dress and revert to being a lonely guest living in a boarding-house, she sat in the lounge to make the most of her Sunday and commented that the family is the pillar of society. She referred in passing to the leisurely bath which she had enjoyed in her daughter-in-law's comfortable bathroom, which explained why she looked clean and was no longer smelling. She made the other residents, who were still in their pyjamas and dressing-gowns, feel awkward as she sat there for hours on end by the tall vase of flowers in the lounge, holding a conversation intended for some invisible audience.

As the afternoon wore on, it became clear that her boots were pinching, but she continued to sit there, all dressed up, holding her large head erect as if she were a prophet. When she enthused about the sumptuous meals served at her son's house, her eyes closed with nausea. She rushed to the bathroom. They could hear her vomit but she refused any offer of assistance when they knocked at the door.

When it was time for dinner she came down to ask for a cup of tea; there were brown circles round her eyes, and she was wearing an ankle-length floral-patterned dress, and was once again without a bra. What still looked strange was the clearness of her skin. The other guests avoided looking at her in her distress. She spoke to no one: King Lear. She was silent, enormous, dishevelled, and clean. Her happiness had been short-lived.

CORRECT ASSUMPTIONS

Let us assume that the telephone system has broken down throughout the city, which happens to be true. Let us assume that I dial a number and it is engaged, which happens to be true. Let us assume that the unengaged tone suddenly starts ringing when I finally make a connection, which happens to be true. Let us assume no one answers, which happens to be true. Let us assume that, instead of getting an answer, I get a crossed line, which happens to be true. Let us assume that out of curiosity I overhear a conversation between a man and a woman, which happens to be true. Let us assume that, as they end their conversation, I distinctly hear a certain phrase, which happens to be true. Let us assume that the phrase I hear distinctly is: 'May God bless you', which happens to be true. Let us then assume that I feel myself well and truly blessed because that phrase was also intended for me. Is that not true? Yes. That phrase was intended for me. I shall make no more assumptions. But simply say *Yes* to the world.

MISTAKEN ASSUMPTIONS

Let us assume that I am a strong person, which does not happen to be true. Let us assume that when I reach a decision I then carry it through, which does not happen to be true. Let us assume that one day I shall write something which will lay bare the human soul, which does not happen to be true. Let us assume that I always have this serious expression I confront in the mirror when I wash my hands, which does not happen to be true. Let us assume that those whom I love are happy, which does not happen to be true. Let us assume that I have fewer serious defects than I have, which does not happen to be true. Let us assume that it only needs a pretty flower to uplift my spirits, which does not happen to be true. Let us assume that I am finally smiling on this day of all days which is not my day for smiling, which does not happen to be true. Let us assume that among my defects there are also many good qualities, which does not happen to be true. Let us assume that I never tell lies, which does not happen to be true. Let us suppose that one day I might turn over a new leaf and change my way of life, which does not happen to be true.

MARRIAGE IN PROGRESS

After a phase in which they exchanged words of love, words of anger, or simply words, relations between them became so strained that words and facts became obscured. They had been married for so long that their differences, mutual suspicions and a certain rivalry no longer came to the surface, although this was the level on which they understood each other. This stage virtually ruled out any offence or defence, or any explanations. They were what is normally referred to as an ordinary married couple.

This was a dream which made me sad and frightened. It began somewhere in the middle. There was a jelly which was alive. What were the jelly's feelings? Silence. Alive and silent, the jelly dragged itself with difficulty to the table, wobbling precariously without falling apart. Who touched it? No one had the courage. When I looked at it, I saw my own face mirrored there, slowly merging with the jelly's existence. Deformed in essence. Deformed without falling apart. I, too, barely alive. Plunged into horror, I wanted to escape the jelly. I went on to the terrace, prepared to throw myself from my top-floor apartment on to the street below. From my terrace I peered into the pitch-black night, and I was terrified at the thought of my approaching end: everything which is too strong by far appears to be nearing its end. But before jumping, I decided to put on some lipstick. It struck me that my lipstick was curiously soft. I then realized that my lipstick, too, was living jelly. And there I stood on the dark terrace, my lips moistened by this living substance.

My legs were already over the edge and I was just about to let go, when suddenly I saw the eyes of darkness. Not *eyes in the darkness* but the eyes of darkness. The darkness was watching me with two enormous eyes set wide apart. So the darkness, too, was alive. Where could I find death? For I knew that death was living jelly. Everything was alive. Everything is alive, primary and slow; everything is primarily immortal.

With almost insuperable difficulty, I succeeded in rousing myself, as if I were pulling myself by the hair in order to escape from that living quagmire.

I opened my eyes. The room was in darkness, but it was a familiar darkness, not the profound darkness from which I had dragged myself. I felt more peaceful. It had been nothing but a dream. Then I noticed that one of my arms was exposed. With a start, I pulled it under the sheet. No part of me should be exposed, if I still hoped to save myself. Did I want to save myself? I think so: then I switched on my bedside lamp in order to wake up properly. And I saw the room with its firm outlines. I had solidified the living jelly into a wall – I continued to feel I was dreaming – I had solidified the living jelly into a ceiling; I had killed everything that could be killed in my efforts to restore the tranquillity of death around me; fleeing from what was worse than death: pure life, living jelly. I switched off the light. Suddenly a cockerel was crowing. A cockerel in an apartment block? A hoarse cockerel. In that white-washed building, a living cockerel? Outside, a freshly-painted building, and inside that cry? thus spoke the Book. Outside death – accomplished, pure, definitive, and inside the jelly, essentially alive. This was what I learned in the dead hours of night.

IN PURSUIT OF PLEASURE

And so much suffering, sometimes even unawares, because one is in pursuit of pleasure. I do not know how one can make pleasure come of its own accord. And it is so dramatic: you need only look at others in the semi-darkness of a night club: the pursuit of pleasure which does not come alone or of its own volition. The pursuit of pleasure has brought the taste of rank water: I put my lips to the rusting tap. Two drops of lukewarm water come trickling out: the tap is dry. No, real suffering is better by far than forced pleasure.

SUMMER BALL

Fanning herself, the fat matron is lost in thought. The fan helps her to think as she sits there fanning herself rigorously. Then with a sudden click, she abruptly arrests her thoughts. Empty, smiling, rigid in her tight corset, she looks distracted. The fan reclines distracted and open on her ample bosom. 'No doubt, they'll all find a husband', she concedes like a visitor being received in a drawing-room. But suppressing her agitation, there she is fanning herself with a thousand sparrows' wings.

SHADY DEALINGS

After I discovered in myself how people think, I was no longer able to believe in the thoughts of others.

What has often saved me has been to improvise some gratuitous act. If any reasons exist for such an act, they are unknown. And if there are any consequences, they are unforeseen.

A gratuitous act is the opposite of our struggle for life. It is the opposite of our frantic pursuit of money, work, love, pleasure, taxis, buses, our daily existence in short. And there is a price to be paid for all of this.

One afternoon, not so long ago, I was typing away under a blue sky flecked with tiny clouds, white as white could be, when suddenly I felt something inside me.

A sudden weariness of this perpetual struggle.

And I realized I was thirsty. A thirst for freedom had stirred inside me. I was simply weary of living in an apartment. I was weary of extracting ideas from myself. I was weary of listening to my typewriter. And then this strange, deep thirst had appeared. I suddenly felt an urgent need to make a bid for freedom. An act which needs no justification. An act capable of showing, quite independently of me, what I was really like inside. And this called for an act which would *have to be paid for*. I do not mean *paid for in money*, but paid for in broader terms, at the high price it costs to live.

Then my own thirst guided me. It was two o'clock on a summer's afternoon. I interrupted my work, quickly changed, went downstairs and hailed a taxi. I told the taxi-driver: Drop me off at the Botanical Gardens. 'Where is that?' he asked. 'You don't understand', I explained, 'It's not a street or district. I mean *the* Botanical Gardens.' This was enough to make him peer at me for a second.

I left the taxi windows open as it gathered speed and sat back to enjoy my freedom as a sharp gust of wind blew my hair about and grazed my grateful cheeks, my eyes half-closed with happiness.

Why had I chosen the Botanical Gardens? Just to look. To see things. To feel them. Just to live.

I leapt out of the taxi and went through the wide gates. Into the welcoming shade. I stood there motionless. Green life in those gardens was so abundant. I could see no meanness there: everything gave itself completely to the wind, to the atmosphere,

192

to life, everything reached for the sky. And what is more: also surrendered its mystery.

Mystery surrounded me. I looked at the delicate shrubs which had just been planted. I gazed at a tree with its dark, gnarled trunk which was so wide my arms would never be able to embrace it. How could sap flow inside this solid wood, through those heavy roots, hard as claws? Sap, this almost intangible substance which is also life. For there is sap in everything just as there is blood in our veins.

I shall not describe what I saw there. Everyone must discover it for themselves. All I will say is that there were swaying, secret shadows. In passing, I shall touch briefly on the freedom of the birds. And on my freedom. But that is all. The rest was a moist green rising inside me through unknown roots. I walked and walked. Sometimes I would pause. I had left the main gates far behind me, and they were already out of sight as I explored a labyrinth of tree-lined avenues. I felt pleasantly apprehensive – the tiniest tremor in my soul – the nervous thrill of perhaps being lost and of never, but never more, being able to find the exit.

There was a fountain where water played incessantly. The water spouted from the mouth of a head carved in stone. I drank some water and got completely drenched. This did not worry me. Such nonchalance seemed in keeping with the abundance in those Gardens.

Here and there the ground was covered with tiny pods from the pepper-trees, those pods one found scattered on the pavements as children and instinctively trampled with the greatest satisfaction. As I trampled them again after all these years, the same sense of satisfaction came back to me: mysterious yet such a comfort.

I began to feel pleasantly tired. It was time to go home. The sun was no longer warm.

I shall return one day when there is heavy rain, just to see that dripping garden submerged.

PS: Could I ask the kind person who converts my column into Braille for the blind to omit this particular article. I have no desire to offend eyes which cannot see.

TOO GOOD TO BE TRUE

I got into a taxi but before it could drive off, a young man appeared, young but with thinning hair which was already flecked with grey. He popped his head through the window and inquired:

– Are you by any chance going my way?

I told him I was heading for Copacabana. He then asked me in a plaintive voice: Would you mind giving me a lift? I live in the same direction and at this hour it's impossible to find a taxi. I told him to get in. He sat beside the driver. Turning round in his seat, he then proceeded to bombard me with endless chatter: he was married and extremely happy; he did not mind in the least that his wife was beginning to age because he still loved her dearly, and he had sent her some roses that very morning. No, it was not her birthday or some special anniversary, simply to tell her that he loved her... Well, well – I thought to myself – here is one man who deceives his wife at the first opportunity.

All this talk about conjugal love was beginning to get on my nerves, not to mention that unctuous voice of his, as he lied through his teeth about his private life, oblivious to my lack of interest. Suddenly he announced: You can drop me off right here. The taxi came to a halt, he got out, popped his head through the window and had the affrontery to whisper in my ear:

– The lady is a perfect gentleman.

REFUGE

I have a lovely picture in my mind, which I can conjure up at will, and it invariably comes back to me in its entirety. It is the image of a forest, and in that forest I can see a green clearing, enveloped in semi-darkness and surrounded by tall trees. And in the midst of this pleasing darkness there are many butterflies, and a tawny lion is reclining, while I sit embroidering on the ground nearby. The hours pass like countless years, and the years pass in reality; the large butterflies have decorative wings and the tawny lion is speckled but the speckles are only there to show that he is tawny, and from the speckles one can see

194

what the lion would look like if he were not tawny. The nice thing about this image is the penumbra, which demands nothing beyond my powers of vision. And there I sit with butterfly and lion. My clearing has a wealth of minerals: these consist of colours. There is only one danger: the dread knowledge that outside the clearing I am lost. For it will no longer be the forest (something love has already taught me) but only an empty field (which fear has taught me): so empty that I might just as easily go in one direction as in the other, a wilderness so devoid of cover and concealment that I should never be able to find an animal there to call my own. I put my fears aside, take a deep breath to regain my composure and settle down to enjoy my intimacy with the lion and the butterflies; we do not think, we simply enjoy ourselves. In this image-cum-refuge I am not black and white. Even without being able to see myself, I know that to these creatures I am coloured; without exceeding their powers of vision for that would unsettle them and we are in no sense unsettling. I am speckled with blue and green simply to show that I am neither blue nor green. Just look at what I am not! The penumbra is dark green and moist. I know that I have mentioned this already, but I am repeating it out of happiness: I want to repeat it over and over again. Until we actually feel that we are there. And really enjoying ourselves. Truly, I have never been so contented. Why? What does it matter? Each of us is in the right place, and I am perfectly happy with mine. I cannot resist repeating myself for things are getting better all the time: the tame lion, and the butterflies flitting quietly as I sit on the ground embroidering. We are thoroughly enjoying our clearing in the forest. We are contented.

A FLOWER BEWITCHED AND TOO BRIGHT BY FAR

I swear, believe me – the drawing-room was in darkness – but the music summoned me to the centre of the room – there was something lurking there – the entire room grew dark within the darkness – I was in darkness – yet I felt that, however dark, the room was bright – I took refuge in my own fear – just as I had already taken refuge from you in you yourself – what did I find?

– nothing except that the dark room lit up with the brightness of a smile – and that it was inherent in the flower – I was trembling in the centre of this awkward light – believe me, even though I cannot explain – it was as if I had never seen a flower – it was something perfect and full of grace which seemed superhuman, but was life – and I nervously pretended that the flower was the soul of someone who had just died – I invented this because I did not have the strength to look directly at the life of a flower – and I looked at that bright centre whose energy was so light that it appeared to stir and become dislocated – and the flower was as vibrant as if a menacing bee were hovering overhead – a bee frozen by fear? – no – it would be more accurate to say that the excited bee and flower were meeting – one life up against another, one life on behalf of another – or frozen by fear before the suffocating grace of this flickering candle which was the flower – I was the bee – and the flower trembled before the dangerous sweetness of the bee – believe me, even if I myself cannot explain it – some fatal rite was being accomplished – the room was filled with that penetrating smile – yet it was nothing more than the whitening of shadows – there was no remaining proof of what I had experienced – I can swear to nothing – I am the only proof of myself – and by giving myself I can explain what I alone witnessed – I cannot understand how anyone could be afraid of a rose – for that flower was a rose – I have had the same experience with violets which were extremely delicate – but I was afraid – they smelled of the grave – and the flowers and bee already summon me – alas I cannot refuse – I am being summoned – and at heart I truly want to go – this rash encounter with a flower is my encounter with my destiny.

WITHOUT ANY WARNING

There were so many things which I did not know at the time. No one had told me, for example, about this fierce sun at three o'clock in the afternoon. Nor had anyone told me about this dry rhythm of living, this relentless dust. They had vaguely warned me it might be painful. But I had no idea that what would bring me hope from afar would spread over me like an eagle's wing.

I had no idea what it meant to be protected by great outspread, menacing wings, an eagle's beak lowered towards me and smiling. In adolescence, when I triumphantly wrote in my diary that I did not believe in love, that was precisely when I loved most of all. I had no idea how harmful lies could be. I began to lie as a precaution, and because no one warned me about the danger of being wary, I was no longer able to rid myself of the habit of lying. And I told so many lies that I began to lie even to my very lies. And this – I was amazed to discover – was the same as telling the truth. Until I became so degenerate that I would tell the most shameless lies: I was telling the naked truth.

FEAR OF THE UNKNOWN (EXTRACT)

So this was happiness. To begin with she felt empty. Then her eyes became moist: this was happiness, but since I am mortal, this love for the world transcends me. Love for this mortal life was gently killing her little by little. And what does one do when one is happy? What do I make of happiness? What am I to make of this strange, penetrating tranquillity which is already beginning to cause me anguish like some great silence? To whom shall I give this happiness of mine which is beginning to frighten me and tear me apart? No, she did not want to be happy. For fear of entering some unknown territory. She preferred the humdrum life she knew. Afterwards she tried to laugh in order to mask her awesome and fatal choice. And pretending to be amused, she thought: To be happy? God offers nuts to those without teeth. But she was not amused. She was sad and thoughtful. She was returning to the death of everyday existence.

THE GIFT

...Perhaps love is to give one's own solitude to others? For it is the very last thing we have to offer.

197

The food was awful, but there was one good thing: it would revive me for some better meal in the future whenever that might be.

Blanquette de Veau. We went to the restaurant with the sole intention of eating well. We were more interested in food than any conversation. When the *maître* recommended *Blanquette de Veau*, something told me I should choose something else. I brought up the same old excuse that I did not really care for anything with a white sauce. My friend, who is a great gourmand, assured me that a white sauce is not to be despised. So we decided to compromise and share any risk by ordering one *Blanquette* and one *Tournedos* cooked in a wine sauce.

When the food arrived, I set about sampling it and after the first few mouthfuls, I felt there was something wrong.

I asked my friend hesitantly: Don't you get the impression that something here has been burnt? There is a slight taste of something charred. I could not decide what it was because in my hunger I had chewed everything together. Whereupon my friend tried to reassure me: The rice has probably been *overcooked*.

As for the *Blanquette*. Certain dishes, when they are too refined, provoke nausea. Excessive refinement makes one almost feel like being sick. Besides, there should always be a touch of simplicity in good cooking.

As for the *Tournedos*, that was another mistake. Good meat should give one something to chew on! And any fillet of beef which cuts like butter is a clear warning that the waiter has not heeded my instructions.

This was enough to make me lose my appetite. And nothing could take away the sense of disappointment. I felt quite frustrated, and in a fuming rage I inwardly vowed never to eat again. For I am so immature that I cannot bear to have my pleasures spoiled. 'So much for eating well', I said bitterly to my friend. 'Be patient', she told me calmly, 'your appetite will come back'. Her own mother is such a wise and practical woman that, whenever there is illness in the family, she immediately does two important things: she administers medicine and then goes off to her room to pray. And then all is well.

But that is another story. To end the first one, my appetite did come back eventually. But as for *Blanquette de Veau* – never again. And I am not joking.

FINAL SURRENDER

It is pleasant to open one's hands and allow to flow freely that emptiness-cum-fullness which one was cruelly holding back. Then suddenly to discover to one's amazement: I have opened my hands and heart and am losing nothing! And then sudden fear. Wake up! for there is danger in having one's heart so free.

Until one perceives that in this expansiveness lies the perilous pleasure of existing. And there is a strange reassurance: always having something to squander. So hold back nothing of this emptiness-cum-fullness. Squander it.

PLAYING WITH MERCURY

It always has been and always will be a red-letter day for me when a thermometer gets broken and the silver mercury spills on to the floor, runs a little way and then becomes immobilised and impregnable. I have just broken another one and I try to retrieve the mercury with the help of a sheet of paper which I cautiously slip underneath. But it resists all my efforts. No sooner do I think I have succeeded than it disintegrates between my fingers like damp fireworks. Not unlike what apparently happens to us humans after death, when the energy escapes from our soul and merges with the atmosphere. How hopeless trying to collect that sensitive liquid. It refuses to be handled and maintains its integrity even when divided into innumerable little bubbles: each tiny bubble is a separate entity, whole and entire, even when divided. One only has to prod one of those bubbles very gently for it to be sucked in by another next to it and together they form a larger and rounder bubble. Ever since childhood I have had this same dream whenever I break a thermometer. I dream of thousands of broken thermometers and of an endless stream of dense, lunar, cold mercury spilling all over.

And there I am, serious and absorbed, as I play with the living matter of this vast expanse of silver metal. I imagine myself sinking into this pool of mercury which has escaped from the thermometers. As I sink deeper, thousands of bubbles are released, one by one, thick and impenetrable. Mercury is an impregnable substance. In what sense impregnable? I cannot explain. I refuse to explain. There is nothing to explain. Mercury is impregnable and that is that. It seems to possess a cerebral coolness which controls its reaction. I feel as if I am in love with mercury but mercury feels nothing for me. There is none of that submissiveness one expects from material things. For mercury has a life of its own. Coping with mercury is not like coping with other material things. It submits to no one. And no one is allowed to handle it. Our soul uses our body in order to avoid being contaminated by life and this tiny gleaming nucleus is the ultimate refuge of mankind. Wild beasts also possess this shining nucleus which helps to keep them completely wild and alive.

I see that I have moved on from mercury to the mystery of wild beasts. The fact is that mercury – which constitutes lunar matter – causes me to think, leads me from one truth to another, until I come to the nucleus of that purity and integrity which each of us possesses. Who? I ask. Who has not played with a broken thermometer?

THE SLOTH

They asked the sloth.
– Sloth, would you like some porridge?
The sloth replied slowly:
– Yeeeees, pleeeeease.
– Well, come and get some.
– Nooooo, thaaaaanks...I've change my miiiiind...
A rainy day makes one feel so lazy. When it rains I can never settle down to write. I am on my way to spend the weekend in Nova Friburgo. It is raining and near the main bus station I come across some sloths. It is more than I can bear and almost sends me to sleep. I stare at those soggy sloths, motionless, and dying of sloth. They give off a nice animal smell. The colour of stone,

one could almost say they have no colour.

Nova Friburgo is quite a place. And the farm where we are staying has everything: horses, chickens, jaboticaba trees, daisies, banana plants, lemons, roses. It has an open-air oven for baking bread. In other words, a real farm. And Nova Friburgo itself has an aristocratic air. I go to the main bus-station where I find a copy of the *Jornal do Brasil* [The Brazilian Times] with an article by Drummond de Andrade. I lunch on *steak au poivre*. Only instead of being served beef, my steak is pork. This is on a Saturday which is my own special day in the week. Last night I had such a vivid dream that I got up, dressed, and put on some make-up. When I realized it was all a dream, I went back to bed but not before eating something, for I suddenly felt famished. In my dream, I had become a man. I was on my way to meet someone and was anxious not to be late. I must not say any more. The details are much too personal.

On the farm I inspect the cattle and poultry. This morning I had bacon and eggs for breakfast. Nova Friburgo is delightful. The houses are painted pink and blue. Nature seems so peaceful when it rains! I can still see those sloths rooted to the same spot and soaking wet. Never stirring. The same could be said of me. This is my day for sloth. But I do not want to sleep: I want to take advantage of being on a farm with lots of animals. Time seems to have stopped still in Nova Friburgo. How I wish that oven were still in good working order and I could watch bread being baked. I see a coffee tree and this is enough to make me feel like drinking coffee. Scanning the pages of the *Jornal do Brasil*, I have come to the conclusion that the world is MAD. I missed the Charity Fair in Rio because of this trip to Nova Friburgo. I forgot to mention that there is a dog on the farm. A cross between a greyhound and a mongrel: a really friendly and playful dog. I must have another cup of coffee. I won't be long.

I am back again. My transistor radio is tuned in to Mozart. Such a light-hearted piece of music. On the farm I have also seen a white horse which is completely naked. The rain has stopped. Time to get down to some work. But I have nothing to say. What am I going to say, for heaven's sake? I shall say I picked a daisy and put it in the buttonhole of my black leather jacket where it looked so pretty. I must take another look at the sloths and inhale their damp odour. It is October, a neutral month. September,

201

like May, is a happy month. The horse only comes back to sleep, and me too. I have decided to have a rest after lunch. A siesta does one good. I shall lunch at midday and read *Portnoy's Complaint* while I am eating. A truly courageous book. I fall asleep halfway through it.

After my siesta I shall go back into town. I should like to visit the Faculty of Letters. But it seems unlikely. I have a special affection for this Faculty and for Marly de Oliveira: a great poet and one of the most cultured women I know. I want to go into town but I feel drowsy. I must drink some Coca-Cola to wake me up. It was João Henrique who taught me that Coca-Cola with coffee helps to keep you awake. He assured me that long-distance lorry drivers drink this concoction. João Henrique taught me many things. I am eternally grateful to him. I now seem to remember that Míriam Bloch told me the same thing.

I finally went into town. Crowds had gathered on the streets. I inquired what was happening. They told me the police were looking for a rapist who had stabbed six women before escaping into the bush. I was horrified. I am afraid of dying. Death is so awful.

For some strange reason I found myself heading for the Faculty of Letters. I was not interested in visiting the library. I am not cultured. The nun in charge was unable to give me any information. There was a lecture that evening on the History of Art. I felt no inclination to attend. I have heard quite enough about art even though I am something of an artist myself. It makes me feel almost ashamed to be a writer. Such a meaningless word. And it gives the impression of something much more intellectual than intuitive.

It is beautiful when the sun goes down in Nova Friburgo. I can also hear loud singing coming from the general store where they sell alcohol, which keeps the men cheerful. Here everything is cheerful, except for those attacks on women. I wonder if the police have caught the rapist yet? Let us hope so.

Nature is so indolent. The horses go on grazing. Now they are neighing. I can also hear crickets. Someone is playing the flute. Music by Bach or perhaps Vivaldi. It is four o'clock in the morning and all is silent. Only now can I hear the toads croaking. I have already drunk my coffee. Now I am smoking a cigarette. There are no pictures on the walls in this house. Unlike the place where I stayed in Cabo Frio which had some excellent paintings by Scliar, João Henrique and José de Dome. Scliar has a weakness for ochre. João Henrique likes green while José de Dome prefers a paler yellow. But there is a very attractive soup tureen on the dresser. What I miss most of all is my typewriter. I have two at home: an Olivetti and an Olympia. I prefer the Olivetti which is stronger and can withstand the constant pressure of tapping fingers. Everyone is asleep. Everyone, that is, except me. There is a horseshoe hanging on the wall to bring good fortune. The little birds outside are chirping with hunger. Everything here seems too good to be true. I am reading a thriller by Simenon. I adore his books. They read much better in French than in any translation. Let me give you a brief quotation: 'Falling across the room, a broad beam of light revealed fine particles of dust. It was as if that light were suddenly exposing the intimate life of the atmosphere.' Don't you find that splendid?

BUYING A PIG IN A POKE

– Have you ever mistaken cat for sucking pig? I was once asked in a moment of distraction.

I replied:

– I'm forever mistaking cat for sucking-pig. Out of foolishness, distraction, ignorance. And sometimes even out of courtesy. People offer me cat and I thank them for the sucking-pig and when the cat starts miaowing, I pretend not to hear. Because I know the deception was intended to please me. But I am not quite so forgiving when I know the offer was made in bad faith.

The variations on this theme could fill an encyclopaedia. Such as, for example, when the cat imagines itself to be a sucking-pig. And because one is dealing with a cat which is obviously unhappy with its condition, then I indulge its fantasy. After all, a cat has every right to want to be a sucking-pig.

And there are even instances where the cat genuinely wants to be a cat but *cochon de lait oblige*, and then things really do get difficult.

Some people even refuse to admit that they enjoy eating cat meat and try to persuade us they are eating sucking-pig. And we keep up the pretence just to keep them happy.

In a treatise on the subject, an expert on melancholia would claim to have passed off many an alley cat as sucking-pig. An expert in irascibility would say something unprintable.

I feel really ashamed when I refuse sucking-pig because I suspect it might be cat. (There is a proverb which says: Better to be cheated by a friend than to mistrust him.) This is the price of mistrust.

But truly, when I mistake a cat for a sucking-pig, the one who comes off worst is the person who offered it to me. The only mistake on my part was to have been gullible.

I am enjoying writing this. A number of sucking-pigs have been miaowing on the nearby roof-tops and now I have had my chance to miaow back. For cats, too, can be rabid.

WHAT IS ANGUISH?

A teenager asked me this difficult question. Much depends on the person suffering from anguish. Some people use this word freely, as if anguish somehow improved their status: that in itself is yet another form of anguish.

Anguish can also be having no hope in hope. Or conforming without resignation. Or refusing to confess even to oneself. Or never being oneself, should one ever know oneself. Anguish can be the misery of being alive. It can also be not having the courage to suffer anguish – and escape is yet another form of anguish. But anguish is part of life: all that lives, simply by being alive tends to recoil.

This same teenager asked me: Don't you find there is a frightening emptiness in everything? Yes, there is. Meanwhile one waits for the heart to understand.

THE OBEDIENT (I)

What follows is straightforward, something to be related and forgotten.

But I have been imprudent enough to pause for a moment longer than I should have done and now find myself compromised. From the moment that I, too, put myself at risk – for I have identified myself with the couple I am about to speak of – from that moment it is no longer simply a fact to be related and for this reason words begin to fail me. By now I feel at quite a loss. The fact ceases to be a simple fact and its widening repercussions have become much more important.

Those repercussions have been delayed and suppressed far too long and it was almost inevitable they should eventually explode.

And now they have finally exploded on this Sunday afternoon, when there has been no rain for weeks and the dessicated beauty of flowers and fruits persists, arid and shining and empty. In the presence of this disquieting beauty I become solemn, as if standing before a tomb. But what has happened to the initial fact? It has merged with this aggressive Sunday. Unable to cope with this afternoon, I hesitate before also becoming aggressive or retreating slightly wounded. The initial fact is suspended in the sun-drenched dust of this scorching Sunday filled with solitude. Until, finally summoned to the telephone, I go rushing off gratefully to lick the hand of this person who loves me and frees me.

Chronologically, the situation was as follows: a man and a woman had been married for twenty-five years without any children.

The moment I discovered this I was intrigued. I was obliged to think, however irksome. And even if I were to say nothing more and end the story with this discovery, I should have already compromised myself with my most impenetrable thoughts. As if I had seen a pen-drawing against a white background, a man and a woman tied to each other. And my eyes are glued to this white background and find much to observe there, for every word has its shadow.

This man and this woman, who were extremely taciturn and had a mute, impassive expression, began – perhaps driven by that urge even experienced by people who look as if they are half-dead – began trying to live with greater intensity. In search of what? That destiny which precedes us? And to which we are fatally driven? But what destiny?

This attempt to live with greater intensity led them to weigh up what was or was not important. They did this in their own way: with a lack of know-how and experience and modesty. They were feeling their way about. Now that they had discovered this vice much too late in life, they tried independently to distinguish between the essential and the non-essential, not that they would ever have used the word *essential*, nor did they try to understand what was happening to them because such things had no meaning in their social milieu. It was as if they wanted to discover what was essential in order to live their lives accordingly. But nothing came of the vague, almost self-conscious effort they were making: the very plot of life forever escaped them. And it was only by summing up the day's events that they could get any feeling of having lived, of somehow having lived despite themselves. But by then it was already night and they were putting on their slippers.

None of this really created a situation for the couple. That is to say, something that each of them might recount to themselves as they turned their backs on each other in bed, their eyes momentarily open and almost startled before they finally fell asleep. People so badly need to be able to tell themselves their own story. But they had nothing to tell. With a sigh of false comfort, they closed their eyes and fell into a troubled sleep. And when they weighed up their lives, they could not even include this attempt to live with greater intensity, or discount it as when dealing with one's income tax. A weighing-up which they gradually began to engage in more and more frequently, without even the technical equipment of a terminology to match their thoughts. If this represented a situation, it was not exactly a situation with which one could ostensibly live.

But it did not simply happen like this. They were able to keep calm because 'not to lead', 'not to invent', 'not to err', was for them really much more than just a habit, it was a question of honour to which they were tacitly pledged. It would never have occurred to them to break that pledge. And offend God. Offend society? What society? Which God did they serve?

Their proud conviction stemmed from a noble awareness that they were two individual human beings amongst thousands like themselves. 'To be an equal' was the role they had been given, the task with which they had been entrusted. Both of them had been singled out for their respect for obedience and they solemnly responded with civic gratitude to the confidence that their equals had placed in them. They belonged to a caste. The role they fulfilled with pride and decorum was that of anonymous persons, of children of God, of members of a community.

Yet, perhaps because of the relentless passage of time, all this had started to become dull, dull, dull. Sometimes claustrophobic. (The man as well as the woman had already reached the critical age.) They would open the windows and comment that it was extremely hot. Without exactly living a life of boredom, it was as if no one ever sent them any news. Besides, boredom was part of this obedience to a life of honest sentiments.

THE OBEDIENT (II)

But since all of this was beyond their understanding, and they found so many things above their heads which, even if expressed in words, they would have failed to understand, all this began to look like irremediable life. A life to which they submitted in silence and with that somewhat wounded expression which is common amongst men of good will. It resembled that irremediable life for which God destined us. Or did He? Doubts began to creep in.

Life irremediable, but not concrete. In fact, it was an unattainable life of dreams. Sometimes, when they were speaking about someone who was eccentric, they would say, with the condescension one class shows towards another: 'Ah, he takes life seriously, he leads the life of a poet.' One could say, judging from the few words I heard the couple say, that they both led, leaving aside any extravagance, the life of a second-rate poet: a life which consisted only of dreams.

No, no, that is not true. It was not a life of dreams, for that would never have enriched them. But one of unreality. Although there were moments when suddenly, for one reason or another, they would plunge into reality. And then they had the impression of touching depths no one could hope to transcend.

As, for example, when the husband came back earlier than usual to find his wife was not at home. The husband felt as if a chain had been broken. Feeling put out, he sat down to read the newspaper in a silence so hushed that even a corpse at his side would have broken the spell. He sat there, pretending in all honesty to be completely wrapped up in his newspaper, his senses on the alert. This was the moment when he touched the bottom with startled feet. He could not remain for long like this without the risk of drowning, for touching the bottom was the same as having water above one's head. These were the more concrete thoughts in his subconscious. Which caused him, level-headed and sensible as he was, to extricate himself at once. He extricated himself at once, yet somehow reluctantly, for his wife's absence held out such a promise of forbidden pleasure that he experienced what might be called disobedience. He extricated himself reluctantly but without discussion, conforming to what was expected of him. Who expected it of him? He could not be sure. He was no deserter, capable of betraying the trust of others. But if this were reality, there was no way he could live with it.

As for his wife, she touched on reality rather more frequently, for she had more leisure and fewer worries to contend with, such as colleagues at work, overcrowded buses, and all those administrative chores. She would sit down to do some mending, and little by little would find herself confronting reality. The mere act of sitting down to do some mending was intolerable while it lasted. The sudden way the dot falls neatly on the i, that sensation of being so much a part of existence, and everything being so clearly itself, was unbearable. But when the feeling passed, it was as if the wife had drunk from some possible future. Little by little, this woman's future started to become something which she brought into the present, something contemplative and secret.

It was surprising how the two of them remained indifferent, for example, to politics, to the change of government, to developments in general, although, like everyone else, they too discussed these things from time to time. Truly, they were so reserved these two that, were anyone to tell them so to their face, they would have been surprised and flattered. It would never have occurred to them to think of themselves as being reserved. Perhaps they would have understood if someone had said to them: 'You two are the very symbol of military and patriotic reserve.' Some acquaintances said of them after the event: they were decent people. And there was nothing more to be said, for they were decent people.

There was nothing more to be said. They lacked the burden of any grave error, which is often precisely what one needs to open a safety exit. They had once taken something very seriously. They were obedient.

Not simply out of craven submission, but as in a sonnet. It was obedience out of their love for symmetry. For them, symmetry was the only possible art.

Strange that each of them should have reached the same conclusion that, alone, the one could live longer than the other. It would be a long road of rehabilitation and of useless effort, because from different angles many had reached the same conclusion.

The wife, under the continuous spell of fantasy, not only arrived at this bold conclusion, but found her life transformed into something broader and more disturbing, into something richer and even superstitious. Each thing became the cipher of something else, everything was symbolic and even vaguely spiritualistic, within the limits permitted by Roman Catholicism. Not only did she come to this rash conclusion but – provoked solely by the fact that she was a woman – she began to think some other man would save her. The idea was not all that absurd. She knew it was not. To be half-right confused her and plunged her into meditation.

Her husband, influenced by the anguished masculinity of his new environment, and by his own waning masculinity, which was timid but real, started to believe that endless love affairs would bring new life.

Dreamers, they began practising tolerance: it was heroic to be tolerant. They silenced any suspicions, disagreeing about the most convenient hour to dine and arguing freely, the one making a sacrifice for the other, because love is sacrifice. What love?

Until the day arrived when the woman was finally roused from her dream when she bit into an apple and felt one of her front teeth breaking. With the apple still in her hand, she examined herself closely in the bathroom mirror – and thus losing all perspective – she saw the pale face of a middle-aged woman with a broken tooth which made her look pathetic, and her own dark, mysterious eyes... At rock-bottom and the water already up to her neck, in her fifties, and with no message to leave behind. Instead of going to the dentist, she threw herself from her apartment window, a person for whom one could feel so grateful, so deeply grateful, because she was the pillar of our disobedience.

As for her husband, once the river-bed was dry and without any water in which he might drown, he walked over the bottom without looking at the ground, as nimbly as if he were using a cane. The river-bed had suddenly become dry. Bewildered, he walked over the river-bed with the false confidence of someone who is about to fall flat on his face at any moment.

WHAT LOVE CAN LEAD TO

— (I love you)
— (Is that what I am then?)
— (You are the love which I have for you)
— (I feel that I am about to see myself...I can almost see...I am almost there)
— (I love you)
— (Ah, that's better. Now I can see myself. So this is me. Portrayed in full.)

ENLISTMENT

The footsteps are growing louder. They are getting nearer. Now they sound quite close. Closer still. Really close. Still approaching. Now they are not simply close, they are inside me. Will they overtake me and carry on? I hope so. It would mean my salvation. I am no longer sure with which sense I measure distance. For those footsteps are no longer simply close and heavy. They are no longer simply inside me. I am marching with them. I have enlisted.

SUBMISSION TO THE PROCESS

The process of living consists of errors – most of them essential – of courage and indolence, the despair and hope of inert awareness, of constant feeling (not thought) which leads nowhere, leads absolutely nowhere, and suddenly what you thought was *nothingness* turns out to be your own terrifying contact with the fabric of life. And that moment of recognition (akin to revelation) must be accepted with the greatest innocence, with the same innocence with which one is born. The process is difficult? But that is like saying that the extremely capricious and natural manner in which a flower is made is difficult. (Mummy, said the little boy, the sea is beautiful, green and blue, and with waves! It's all naturalized! Nobody made it!) The nagging impatience (standing beside a plant to watch it grow yet without seeing anything) is not in relation to the thing itself, but to this monstrous patience (the plant grows at night). As if one were to say: 'I cannot bear to be patient for another second', 'the patience of the watchmaker puts my nerves on edge', etc.: it is an impatient patience. But the greatest burden of all is torpid patience: an ox pulling the plough.

MORE THAN SIMPLE WORD-PLAY

What I feel, I do not put into action. What I put into action, I do not think. What I think, I do not feel. I am unaware of what I know. I am not unaware of what I feel. I do not understand myself yet behave as if I had no difficulty in doing so.

A MERE SPECK OF DUST

And all of a sudden that terrible pain in my left eye, tears streaming down my face, and the world becoming sinister. And distorted; for on closing one eye the other automatically half-closes. No fewer than four times during the past year some strange object has got into my left eye: on two occasions a speck

211

of dust, once a grain of sand, and on the last occasion an eyelash. All four times I was obliged to consult an optician. On my last visit I asked this man who is entrusted, as it were, with our vision of the world, why it should always be the left eye. A mere coincidence?

The answer was in the negative. He explained that, however normal a person's eyesight, one eye sees better than the other and is therefore more sensitive. He referred to it as the guiding-eye. And because the latter is more sensitive, it picks up any foreign body in the atmosphere and there it remains.

In other words, our best eye is at the same time more powerful and more delicate: it creates problems which are not imaginary but all too real. As in the case of this unbearable pain when a speck of dust is grazing and irritating one of the most delicate organs of our body. I remained pensive.

Does this only happen to our eyes? Could it be that those who see things more clearly are also those who feel and suffer most? And those who are afflicted with pain as real as that caused by a speck of dust? I remained pensive.

Suddenly I have remembered that a New Year is about to begin. Let us hope that nineteen seventy-four will turn out to be a happy year for all of us.